Louis J. Kruger, PsyD
David Shriberg, PhD
Editors

High Stakes Testing: New Challenges and Opportunities for School Psychology

High Stakes Testing: New Challenges and Opportunities for School Psychology has been co-published simultaneously as *Journal of Applied School Psychology*, Volume 23, Number 2 2007.

Pre-publication REVIEWS, COMMENTARIES, EVALUATIONS . . .

"A MUCH-NEEDED RESOURCE FOR ALL EDUCATORS and should be required reading for legislators and policymakers prior to engaging in the reauthorization process for NCLB."

Diane Smallwood, PsyD
Associate Professor
Philadelphia College
of Osteopathic Medicine

More pre-publication
REVIEWS, COMMENTARIES, EVALUATIONS . . .

"AT LONG LAST, THERE IS A SERIOUS REVIEW of the many issues related to NCLB high-stakes testing that is relevant to school psychologists... PARTICULARLY VALUABLE was the manner in which the authors show how school psychologists have a role in helping schools to manage the effects of high-stake testing at the school, classroom, and individual student levels. . . . SCHOOL PSYCHOLOGISTS SHOULD READ THIS BOOK and consider how they can minimize the unintended negative consequences of high-stakes testing through consultation and direct service, while continuing to support school- and classroom-level efforts to implement evidence-supported instructional practices."

Michael J. Furlong, PhD
*University of California
Santa Barbara;
Chair
Department of Counseling,
Clinical, and School Psychology*

The Haworth Press, Inc.

High Stakes Testing:
New Challenges
and Opportunities
for School Psychology

High Stakes Testing: New Challenges and Opportunities for School Psychology has been co-published simultaneously as *Journal of Applied School Psychology*, Volume 23, Number 2 2007.

> **Monographic Separates from the *Journal of Applied School Psychology*™**
>
> For additional information on these and other Haworth Press titles, including descriptions, tables of contents, reviews, and prices, use the QuickSearch catalog at http://www.HaworthPress.com.

The *Journal of Applied School Psychology*™ is the successor title to *Special Services in the Schools*, which changed title after Vol.19, No. 2, 2002.

High Stakes Testing: New Challenges and Opportunities for School Psychology, edited by Louis J. Kruger, PsyD, and David Shriberg, PhD (Vol. 23, No. 2, 2007). *Examination of up-to-date practical strategies for school psychologists in the practice of high stakes testing, including interpreting test results, prevention, stress management, decision making, academic intervention, and leadership.*

Multicultural Issues in School Psychology, edited by Bonnie K. Nastasi, PhD (Vol. 22, No. 2, 2006). *Theoretical and empirical models that address cross-cultural concerns and introduce culturally specific services in school psychology practice.*

School Sport Psychology: Perspectives, Programs, and Procedures, edited by Charles A. Maher, PsyD (Vol. 21, No. 2, 2005). *"WELL-ORGANIZED AND REFERENCED. . . . THE AUTHORITATIVE SOURCE of literature review in this area . . . Serves as a useful tool for professionals in medicine, psychology, school administration, athletic directorship, coaching, and substance abuse. As a physician engaged in creating programs for school health and safety, including childhood obesity, this book has already proven to be AN INVALUABLE SOURCE OF REFERENCE MATERIAL AND PRACTICAL INFORMATION." (Robert Gillio, MD, Adjunct Assistant Professor, Hershey Medical Center, Pennsylvania State University, Chairman and Chief Medical Officer, Project Breathe and Project Fitness, InnerLink)*

Single-Subject Designs for School Psychologists, edited by Christopher H. Skinner, PhD (Vol. 20, No. 2, 2004). *"This book is exactly what is needed to promote evidence-based practice. IN THIS AGE OF ACCOUNTABILITY, IT SHOULD BE ON THE DESK OF EVERY SCHOOL PSYCHOLOGIST. The book splendidly achieves its goal—to illustrate how school psychologists can evaluate their interventions in a rigorous, scientific manner and yet do so in a way that is both feasible and practical for applied settings. Single-subject designs are ideally suited to the work of school psychologists and the topics covered in this book reflect the real-life problems confronting them. Excellently conceived and rigorously evaluated interventions are described for increasing reading and arithmetic fluency, reducing anxiety, increasing on-task behavior, and reducing transition time." (Jeff Sigafoos, PhD, Professor, Department of Special Education, The University of Texas at Austin)*

Computers in the Delivery of Special Education and Related Services: Developing Collaborative and Individualized Learning Environments, *edited by Louis J. Kruger, PsyD (Vol. 17, No. 1/2, 2002). "An excellent compendium. . . . The topics selected cover a broad conceptual spectrum, yet provide specific and useful information for the practitioner. A valuable resource for professionals at all levels. I highly recommend it." (David G. Gotthelf, PhD, Director of Student Services, Lincoln-Sudbury Regional School District, Massachusetts)*

Inclusion Practices with Special Needs Students: Theory, Research, and Application, *edited by Steven I. Pfeiffer, PhD, ABPP, and Linda A. Reddy, PhD (Vol. 15, No. 1/2, 1999). Provides a much needed and balanced perspective of the issues faced by educators committed to understanding how to best serve children with disabilities in schools.*

Emerging School-Based Approaches for Children with Emotional and Behavioral Problems: Research and Practice in Service Integration, *edited by Robert J. Illback, PsyD, and C. Michael Nelson, EdD (Vol. 10, No. 2, and Vol. 11, No. 1/2, 1996). "A stimulating and valuable contribution to the topic." (Donald K. Routh, PhD, Professor of Psychology, University of Miami)*

Educational Outcomes for Students with Disabilities, *edited by James E. Ysseldyke, PhD, and Martha L. Thurlow (Vol. 9, No. 2, 1995). *"Clearly directed at teaching staff, psychologists, and other educationists but has relevance to all who work with children and young people with disabilities in schools of further education. . . . A useful book."* (Physiotherapy)

Promoting Student Success Through Group Interventions, *edited by Joseph E. Zins, EdD, and Maurice J. Elias, PhD (Vol. 8, No. 1, 1994). *"Contains clear, concise, and practical descriptions of a variety of group interventions designed to promote students' success in school and life."* (Social Work with Groups Newsletter)

Promoting Success with At-Risk Students: Emerging Perspectives and Practical Approaches, *edited by Louis J. Kruger, PsyD (Vol. 5, No. 3/4, 1990). *"Essential to professionals interested in new developments in the education of at-risk students, guidelines for implementation of approaches, and the prevention of student crises and discipline problems."* (Virginia Child Protection Newsletter)

Leadership and Supervision in Special Services: Promising Ideas and Practices, *edited by Leonard C. Burrello, EdD, and David E. Greenburg, EdD (Vol. 4, No. 1/2, 1988). *A rich source of ideas for administrative personnel involved in the delivery of special educational programs and services to children with handicapping conditions.*

School-Based Affective and Social Interventions, *edited by Susan G. Forman, PhD (Vol. 3, No. 3/4, 1988). *"Provides a valuable starting point for the psychologist, counselor, or other special service provider, special educator, regular classroom teacher, nurse, vice-principal, or other administrator who is willing to get involved in the struggle to help children and adolescents feel good about themselves and get along better in this world."* (Journal of Pediatric Nursing)

Facilitating Cognitive Development: International Perspectives, Programs, and Practices, *edited by Milton S. Schwebel and Charles A. Maher, PsyD (Vol. 3, No. 1/2, 1986). *Experts discuss the vital aspects of programs and services that will facilitate cognitive development in children and adolescents.*

Emerging Perspectives on Assessment of Exceptional Children, *edited by Randy Elliot Bennett, EdD, and Charles A. Maher, PsyD (Vol. 2, No. 2/3, 1986). *"Contains a number of innovative and promising approaches to the topic of assessment. It is an important addition to the rapidly changing field of special education and should be read by any individual who is interested in the assessment of exceptional children."* (Journal of Psychological Assessment)

Health Promotion in the Schools: Innovative Approaches to Facilitating Physical and Emotional Well-Being, *edited by Joseph E. Zins, Donald I. Wagner, and Charles A. Maher, PsyD (Vol. 1, No. 3, 1985). *"Examines new approaches to promoting physical and emotional well-being in the schools. . . . A good introduction to new-style health education."* (Curriculum Review)

Microcomputers and Exceptional Children, *edited by Randy Elliot Bennett, EdD, and Charles A. Maher, PsyD (Vol. 1, No. 1, 1984). *"This volume provides both the experienced and novice micro buff with a solid overview of the potential and real uses of the technology with exceptional students."* (Alex Thomas, PhD, Port Clinton, Ohio)

ALL HAWORTH BOOKS AND JOURNALS
ARE PRINTED ON CERTIFIED
ACID-FREE PAPER

High Stakes Testing: New Challenges and Opportunities for School Psychology

Louis J. Kruger, PsyD
David Shriberg, PhD
Editors

High Stakes Testing: New Challenges and Opportunities for School Psychology has been co-published simultaneously as *Journal of Applied School Psychology*, Volume 23, Number 2 2007.

The Haworth Press, Inc.
www.HaworthPress.com

High Stakes Testing: New Challenges and Opportunities for School Psychology has been co-published simultaneously as *Journal of Applied School Psychology*™, Volume 23, Number 2 2007.

© 2007 by The Haworth Press, Inc. All rights reserved. No part of this work may be reproduced or utilized in any form or by any means, electronic or mechanical, including photocopying, microfilm and recording, or by any information storage and retrieval system, without permission in writing from the publisher. Printed in the United States of America.

The development, preparation, and publication of this work has been undertaken with great care. However, the publisher, employees, editors, and agents of The Haworth Press and all imprints of The Haworth Press, Inc., including The Haworth Medical Press® and Pharmaceutical Products Press®, are not responsible for any errors contained herein or for consequences that may ensue from use of materials or information contained in this work. With regard to case studies, identities and circumstances of individuals discussed herein have been changed to protect confidentiality. Any resemblance to actual persons, living or dead, is entirely coincidental.

The Haworth Press is committed to the dissemination of ideas and information according to the highest standards of intellectual freedom and the free exchange of ideas. Statements made and opinions expressed in this publication do not necessarily reflect the views of the Publisher, Directors, management, or staff of The Haworth Press, Inc., or an endorsement by them.

Library of Congress Cataloging-in-Publication Data

High stakes testing : new challenges and opportunities for school psychology / Louis J. Kruger, David Shriberg.
      p. cm.
    "Co-published simultaneously ad Journal of Applied School Psychology, Volume 23, Number 2, 2007."
    Includes bibliographical references and index.
    ISBN-13: 978-0-7890-3521-9 (hard cover : alk. paper)
    ISBN-13: 978-0-7890-3539-4 (soft cover : alk. paper)
    1. School psychology–United States. 2. Educational tests and measurements–United States. I. Kruger, Louis J. II. Shriberg, David.
LB1027.55.H54 2007
350.15--dc22

2007031778

The HAWORTH PRESS Inc.
Abstracting, Indexing & Outward Linking
PRINT and ELECTRONIC BOOKS & JOURNALS

This section provides you with a list of major indexing & abstracting services and other tools for bibliographic access. That is to say, each service began covering this periodical during the the year noted in the right column. Most Websites which are listed below have indicated that they will either post, disseminate, compile, archive, cite or alert their own Website users with research-based content from this work. (This list is as current as the copyright date of this publication.)

Abstracting, Website/Indexing Coverage . . . . Year When Coverage Began

- *(IBR) International Bibliography of Book Reviews on the Humanities and Social Sciences (Thomson)* <http://www.saur.de> 2006
- *(IBZ) International Bibliography of Periodical Literature on the Humanities and Social Sciences (Thomson)* <http://www.saur.de> 2001
- ***Academic Search Premier (EBSCO)*** <http://search.ebscohost.com> 2006
- ***LISA: Library and Information Science Abstracts (ProQuest CSA)*** <http://www.csa.com/factsheets/list-set-c.php> 1992
- ***MasterFILE Premier (EBSCO)*** <http://search.ebscohost.com> 2006
- *Academic Source Premier (EBSCO)* <http://search.ebscohost.com> 2007
- *Advanced Polymers Abstracts (ProQuest CSA)* <http://www.csa.com/factsheets/ema-polymers-set-c.php> 2006
- *Aluminium Industry Abstracts (ProQuest CSA)* <http://www.csa.com/factsheets/aia-set-c.php> 2006
- *British Library Inside (The British Library)* <http://www.bl.uk/services/current/inside.html> 2006

(continued)

- Cabell's Directory of Publishing Opportunities in Educational Technology & Library Science <http://www.cabells.com> 2006
- Cambridge Scientific Abstracts (now ProQuest CSA) <http://www.csa.com> 2006
- Ceramic Abstracts (ProQuest CSA) <http://www.csa.com/factsheets/wca-set-c.php> 2006
- Composites Industry Abstracts (ProQuest CSA) <http://www.csa.com/factsheets/ema-composites-set-c.php> ... 2006
- Computer and Information Systems Abstracts (ProQuest CSA) <http://www.csa.com/factsheets/computer-set-c.php> 2004
- Corrosion Abstracts (ProQuest CSA) <http://www.csa.com/factsheets/corrosion-set-c.php> 2006
- CSA Engineering Research Database (ProQuest CSA) <http://www.csa.com/factsheets/engineering-set-c.php> 2006
- CSA High Technology Research Database With Aerospace (ProQuest CSA) <http://www.csa.com/factsheets/hightech-set-c.php> 2006
- CSA Technology Research Database (ProQuest CSA) <http://www.csa.com/factsheets/techresearch-set-c.php>...... 2006
- CSA/ASCE Civil Engineering Abstracts (ProQuest CSA) <http://www.csa.com/factsheets/civil-set-c.php> 2006
- Current Abstracts (EBSCO) <http://search.ebscohost.com> 2007
- Current Citations Express (EBSCO) <http://search.ebscohost.com> 2007
- EBSCOhost Electronic Journals Service (EJS) <http://search.ebscohost.com> 2001
- Electronic Collections Online (OCLC) <http://www.oclc.org/electroniccollections/> 2006
- Electronics and Communications Abstracts (ProQuest CSA) <http://www.csa.com/factsheets/electronics-set-c.php> 2006
- Elsevier Eflow -D <http://www.elsevier.com> 2006
- Elsevier Scopus <http://www.info.scopus.com> 2005
- Engineered Materials Abstracts (ProQuest CSA) <http://www.csa.com/factsheets/emaclust-set-c.php> 2006
- Google <http://www.google.com> 2004
- Google Scholar <http://scholar.google.com> 2004

(continued)

- *Haworth Document Delivery Center*
  <http://www.HaworthPress.com/journals/dds.asp> 1979
- *Index Guide to College Journals* 1999
- *Index to Periodical Articles Related to Law*
  <http://www.law.utexas.edu> 1992
- *Informed Librarian, The* <http://www.informedlibrarian.com> ... 1993
- *INIST-CNRS* <http://www.inist.fr> 2000
- *Internationale Bibliographie der geistes- und sozialwissen-
  schaftlichen Zeitschriftenliteratur ... See IBZ ...*
  <http://www.saur.de> 2001
- *Journal of Academic Librarianship: Guide to Professional
  Literature, The* 2006
- *JournalSeek* <http://www.journalseek.net> 2006
- *Konyvtari Figyelo (Library Review)*
  <http://www.oszk.hu/index_en.htm> 1997
- *Library Literature & Information Science Index / Full Text
  (H.W. Wilson)* <http://www.hwwilson.com> 1984
- *Library, Information Science & Technology Abstracts
  (EBSCO)* <http://search.ebscohost.com> 2006
- *Library, Information Science & Technology Abstracts
  with Full Text (EBSCO)* <http://search.ebscohost.com> 2007
- *Links@Ovid (via CrossRef targeted DOI links)*
  <http://www.ovid.com> 2005
- *Materials Business File (ProQuest CSA)*
  <http://www.csa.com/factsheets/mbf-set-c.php> 2006
- *Materials Research Database with METADEX (ProQuest CSA)*
  <http://www.csa.com/factsheets/materials-set-c.php> 2006
- *Mechanical & Transportation Engineering Abstracts
  (ProQuest CSA)* <http://www.csa.com/factsheets/
  mechtrans-set-c.php> 2006
- *METADEX (ProQuest CSA)*
  <http://www.csa.com/factsheets/metadex-set-c.php> 2006
- *NewJour (Electronic Journals & Newsletters)*
  <http://gort.ucsd.edu/newjour/> 2006
- *OCLC ArticleFirst* <http://www.oclc.org/services/databases/> 2007
- *Ovid Linksolver (OpenURL link resolver via CrossRef targeted
  DOI links)* <http://www.linksolver.com> 2005

(continued)

- *Scopus (See instead Elsevier Scopus)*
  <http://www.info.scopus.com>........................... 2005
- *Solid State and Superconductivity Abstracts (ProQuest CSA)*
  <http://www.csa.com/factsheets/solid-state-set-c.php>......... 2006
- *SwetsWise* <http://www.swets.com>......................... 2000
- *TOC Premier (EBSCO)* <http://search.ebscohost.com>......... 2007
- *WilsonWeb* <http://vnweb.hwwilsonweb.com/hww/Journals/>.... 2005
- *zetoc (The British Library)* <http://www.bl.uk>................ 2004

Bibliographic Access

- **Cabell's Directory of Publishing Opportunities in Educational Psychology and Administration** <http://www.cabells.com>

- **MediaFinder** <http://www.mediafinder.com/>

- **Ulrich's Periodicals Directory: The Global Source for Periodicals Information Since 1932** <http://www.Bowkerlink.com>

Special Bibliographic Notes related to special journal issues (separates) and indexing/abstracting:

- indexing/abstracting services in this list will also cover material in any "separate" that is co-published simultaneously with Haworth's special thematic journal issue or DocuSerial. Indexing/abstracting usually covers material at the article/chapter level.
- monographic co-editions are intended for either non-subscribers or libraries which intend to purchase a second copy for their circulating collections.
- monographic co-editions are reported to all jobbers/wholesalers/approval plans. The source journal is listed as the "series" to assist the prevention of duplicate purchasing in the same manner utilized for books-in-series.
- to facilitate user/access services all indexing/abstracting services are encouraged to utilize the co-indexing entry note indicated at the bottom of the first page of each article/chapter/contribution.
- this is intended to assist a library user of any reference tool (whether print, electronic, online, or CD-ROM) to locate the monographic version if the library has purchased this version but not a subscription to the source journal.
- individual articles/chapters in any Haworth publication are also available through the Haworth Document Delivery Service (HDDS).

As part of Haworth's continuing commitment to better serve our library patrons, we are proud to be working with the following electronic services:

AGGREGATOR SERVICES

EBSCOhost

Ingenta

J-Gate

Minerva

OCLC FirstSearch

Oxmill

SwetsWise

LINK RESOLVER SERVICES

1Cate (Openly Informatics)

ChemPort (American Chemical Society)

CrossRef

Gold Rush (Coalliance)

LinkOut (PubMed)

LINKplus (Atypon)

LinkSolver (Ovid)

LinkSource with A-to-Z (EBSCO)

Resource Linker (Ulrich)

SerialsSolutions (ProQuest)

SFX (Ex Libris)

Sirsi Resolver (SirsiDynix)

Tour (TDnet)

Vlink (Extensity, formerly Geac)

WebBridge (Innovative Interfaces)

High Stakes Testing:
New Challenges and Opportunities for School Psychology

CONTENTS

About the Contributors   xvii

Introduction and Overview: High Stakes Testing   1
    David Shriberg
    Louis J. Kruger

SECTION 1: THE CHALLENGES, PROBLEMS, AND DILEMMAS ASSOCIATED WITH HIGH STAKES TESTING

Large-Scale Assessment, Rationality, and Scientific Management:
    The Case of *No Child Left Behind*   7
    Andrew T. Roach
    Jennifer L. Frank

Measurement Issues in High Stakes Testing:
    Validity and Reliability   27
    Emanuel J. Mason

High-Stakes Testing: Does It Increase Achievement?   47
    Sharon L. Nichols

The Unintended Outcomes of High-Stakes Testing   65
    Brett D. Jones

SECTION 2: NEW ROLES FOR SCHOOL PSYCHOLOGISTS

Providing Academic Support for Teachers and Students
    in High Stakes Learning Environments   87
    Judy Elliott

Coping with the Stress of High Stakes Testing   109
   Louis J. Kruger
   Caroline Wandle
   Joan Struzziero

Using Data from High-Stakes Testing in Program Planning
and Evaluation   129
   Jeffery P. Braden

The School Psychologist as Leader and Change Agent
in a High-Stakes Era   151
   David Shriberg

Index   167

ABOUT THE EDITORS

Louis J. Kruger PsyD, is Associate Professor in the Department of Counseling and Applied Educational Psychology. He is Director of the School Psychology Program at Northeastern University, where he also serves on the faculty of the early intervention program and the combined PhD Program in the School of Counseling Psychology. A former Associate Editor of the *Journal of Applied School Psychology*, he presently serves on the journal's editorial board. He has published extensively on organizational psychology issues related to schools and school psychology. Dr. Kruger has consulted with many school systems on organizational issues, including strategic planning. He has conducted research on teamwork and computer-mediated communication. His current research interest focuses on stress and high stakes testing of adolescents. He is also currently working on a documentary film about high stakes testing in Massachusetts. He has been on the board of directors of the Massachusetts School Psychologists Association for almost 20 years. He is a member of the National Association of School Psychologists and the American Psychology Association. He has received multiple awards, including Massachusetts School Psychology Trainer of the Year.

David Shriberg, PhD, is Assistant Professor in the School Psychology Program at Loyola University Chicago. His dissertation focused on high-stakes testing in Massachusetts and its relation to students' opportunities to learn. Dr. Shriberg is the co-editor of *Practicing Leadership: Principles and Applications*, which is published by Wiley and is now in its third edition. He currently serves as a member of the editorial review board of the *Journal of Applied School Psychology*, the *Trainer's Forum*, and as an ad-hoc reviewer for *School Psychology Review*. Dr. Shriberg has published and presented extensively in the areas of leadership, high-stakes testing, and cultural diversity/social justice and maintains active research programs in these areas. He is a member of several professional organizations, including the National Association of School Psychologists, the American Psychological Association, the International School Psychology Association, the American Educational Research Association, and the Illinois School Psychology Association. Dr. Shriberg has worked as a school psychologist in a variety of settings, including urban, rural, and suburban school districts.

About the Contributors

Jeffery P. Braden, PhD, is Professor in the Department of Psychology at North Carolina State University.

Judy Elliott, PhD, is Assistant Superintendent of School Support Services in the Long Beach (CA) Unified School District.

Jennifer L. Frank, MS, is Research Coordinator in the Center for Assessment and Intervention Research, Peabody College of Education and Human Development Learning Sciences Institute at Vanderbilt University.

Brett D. Jones, PhD, is Assistant Professor of Assessment and Evaluation, in the School of Education of Virginia Tech University.

Louis J. Kruger, PsyD, is Associate Professor in the Department of Counseling and Applied Educational Psychology at Northeastern University.

Emanuel J. Mason, PhD, is Professor in the Department of Counseling and Applied Educational Psychology at Northeastern University.

Sharon L. Nichols, PhD, is Assistant Professor in the Department of Counseling, Educational Psychology, and Adult Higher Education, at the University of Texas at San Antonio.

Andrew T. Roach, PhD, is Assistant Professor in the Department of Counseling and Psychological Services at Georgia State University.

David Shriberg, PhD, is Assistant Professor in the School Psychology Program at Loyola University Chicago.

Joan Struzziero, PhD, is a School Psychologist in the Scituate (MA) Public Schools.

Caroline Wandle, PhD, is Director of the School Psychology Program at Tufts University.

Introduction and Overview: High Stakes Testing

David Shriberg

Loyola University Chicago

Louis J. Kruger

Northeastern University

SUMMARY. This overview article addresses the different meanings of high takes testing, which takes into consideration accountability at different levels, such as teacher, school, and state. In this regard, "high-stakes" may mean different things in different states or countries. We will advance an argument for why school psychologists should (a) be actively involved with implementation of high stakes assessment programs, (b) work to prevent the potential negative consequences of high stakes testing, and (c) advocate for the appropriate use of these assessments. Finally, we will offer a preview of each article. Collectively, the articles provide an overview of why high stakes testing is relevant to the profession of school psychology and how high stakes testing has created new opportunities for the practice of school psychology. doi:10.1300/J370v23n02_01 *[Article copies available for a fee from The Haworth Document Delivery Service: 1-800-HAWORTH. E-mail address: <docdelivery@haworthpress.com> Website:*

Address correspondence to: David Shriberg, PhD, School Psychology Program, 820 North Michigan Avenue, Lewis Towers #1147, Loyola University Chicago, Chicago, IL 60611 (E-mail: dshribe@luc.edu).

[Haworth co-indexing entry note]: "Introduction and Overview: High Stakes Testing." Shriberg, David, and Louis J. Kruger. Co-published simultaneously in *Journal of Applied School Psychology* (The Haworth Press, Inc.) Vol. 23, No. 2, 2007, pp. 1-6; and: *High Stakes Testing: New Challenges and Opportunities for School Psychology* (ed: Louis J. Kruger, and David Shriberg) The Haworth Press, Inc., 2007, pp. 1-6. Single or multiple copies of this article are available for a fee from The Haworth Document Delivery Service [1-800-HAWORTH, 9:00 a.m. - 5:00 p.m. (EST). E-mail address: docdelivery@haworthpress.com].

Available online at http://japps.haworthpress.com
© 2007 by The Haworth Press, Inc. All rights reserved.
doi:10.1300/J370v23n02_01

<http://www.HaworthPress.com> © 2007 by The Haworth Press, Inc. All rights reserved.]

KEYWORDS. High stakes testing, school psychology, accountability, school psychologists, assessment

Historically, school psychologists have been more closely involved with students with special needs than the entirety of the student population, and more closely involved with individualized assessments than with group assessments of students. It is time for things to change. The stakes in public education have risen dramatically. The federal No Child Left Behind Act of 2001 (NCLB) is one of the landmark events in the history of public education in the United States. The field of school psychology cannot purport to be preventative, systems oriented, culturally sensitive, and concerned about promoting healthy learning environments, while paying scant attention to the central mandate of NCLB. At the heart of NCLB are the requirements for states to assess the academic progress of all students in third through eighth grades and for schools to meet stringent annual yearly progress criteria in order to receive federal funds. This assessment mandate has had and will continue to have a wide-ranging impact on the education of all children, including those with special needs.

The widespread use of achievement testing in U.S. public schools is far from a new phenomenon (Linn, 2001). Nearly everyone who has attended public schools in the U.S. likely has experienced taking one or more standardized achievement tests and then much later receiving a printout filled with scores, percentiles, stanines, and the like. Thus, while the NCLB Act provides a new mechanism for evaluating students' achievement performance, the fact that student achievement data are being sought is not what makes this part of the law so controversial and so salient to current educational practice. Rather, it is the "high stakes" component of the current law that attracts the most attention and, depending on one's vantage point, possibly concern. In many states, for example, those high stakes include the requirement of passing a test in high school before receiving a diploma. In some states, teachers or other school personnel experience rewards (e.g., increased salaries) or penalties based on student test scores.

The stated goal of NCLB is for all students to achieve 100 percent proficiency in language arts and mathematics by 2014. What "proficient" means is determined at the state level, and all students in grades three through eight take proficiency tests in these subject areas every spring. The results are tabulated and summarized by demographic subgroups for each school. Every state sets its own benchmarks and all schools that receive Title I funds are required to demonstrate "adequate yearly progress" (AYP) in test score performance for every subgroup of students, such as students with disabilities. If a school does not demonstrate AYP (again defined at the state level) in its test scores for all grades and demographic groups, the school is subject to accountability measures that begin with public warnings and ultimately can escalate to school restructuring and removal of administrators.

In an era when school test scores are published and made widely available, and in an era when parents and politicians scrutinize these scores in the same way that devoted sports fans follow the performance of their favorite teams, schools are under tremendous pressure to raise their scores every year. Thus, student test score performance and the extent to which a school or district's test scores either improve or decline across grades and demographic categories can affect the well-being of students, families, school personnel, the school district, and even the community in which the school district resides. This makes these exams very high stakes endeavors and it is in this context that the term "high stakes" is employed in this volume.

THE RELATION OF HIGH-STAKES TESTING TO SCHOOL PSYCHOLOGY PRACTICE

School psychologists, because of their expertise in assessment, intervention, prevention, consultation and program planning and evaluation, can be a positive influence on how students, teachers, parents, schools and communities cope with the challenges and opportunities associated with high stakes testing. Yet, to date, despite geometric increases in articles on high stakes testing appearing in leading education journals during the last five years, this research has been largely absent from the school psychology literature. For example, as of September 2006, if one typed in the keywords "high stakes testing," which by itself would yield 423 references, and then added the modifier "school psychology" into the ERIC database, it would yield exactly two references. If one used the keywords "high stakes testing and school psychologist," it would yield no references. Thus, in both practice and scholarship, school psychology has neglected the implications of high stakes testing. The following collection is intended to provide a beginning to redress this oversight. Our hope is that practitioners will find the information both timely and groundbreaking.

PURPOSE, STRUCTURE, AND CONTENT OF THIS VOLUME

The purpose of this volume is to disseminate useful and thought-provoking information about high stakes testing and its implication for the practice of school psychology. The articles are connected by the central themes of what school psychologists need to know in order to meet the challenges of high stakes testing and what new roles can be created for school psychologists as a result of high stakes testing. The first section, entitled, "The Challenges, Problems, and Dilemmas Associated with High-Stakes Testing," provides important background information about high stakes testing, including the legal, historical, and political context of high stakes testing, pertinent psychometric issues, and a review of research on academic and non-academic outcomes as it relates to high stakes testing. In the first article, "Large-Scale Assessment, Rationality, and Scientific Management: The Case of *No Child Left Behind*," Andrew Roach and Jennifer Frank take a systems and historical perspective on high stakes testing. In particular, they point out that organizations are pursuing ever-increasing efficiency and performance, and NCLB has provided the impetus to pursue these two goals by means of quantifying student achievement. The authors discuss the strengths and weaknesses of this approach, and conclude with ideas of how school psychologists can advocate for the appropriate use of state-wide assessments.

In the second article of this section, "Measurement Issues in High Stakes Testing: Validity and Reliability," Emanuel Mason discusses to what extent high stakes tests meet widely accepted psychometric standards of measurement. He addresses the influence of item response theory (IRT) on the development of high stakes tests, and how IRT alters traditional assumptions about reliability and validity. He points out the implications of these altered assumptions for the interpretation of high stakes tests. Finally, he considers the practical implications of the interpretations, including how they might affect the lives of students. In the third article, "High-Stakes Testing: Does It Increase Achievement?," Sharon Nichols tackles the important question of whether the accountability system of NCLB is producing the desired results, namely, an increase in academic proficiency among students. She discusses the concept of pressure, and to what extent higher levels of pressure result in higher levels of achievement. Her authoritative review of the relevant research yields some interesting conclusions, including that the there is little evidence of a positive relationship between high stakes testing and academic achievement. In the fourth and final article of this first section, Brett Jones, in a paper entitled, "The Unintended Outcomes of High Stakes Testing," examines several intriguing issues including the effects of high stakes tests on classroom instruction and student motivation. Jones concludes that, in sum, the unintended outcomes of high stakes testing have been more negative than positive, and he offers suggestions for ways in which school psychologists can educate others about the limitations of current procedures and to advocate for assessment practices that are more likely to produce positive outcomes.

The second section, entitled, "New Roles for School Psychologists," builds upon the information presented in the first section and identifies possible roles for school psychologists with respect to high stakes testing. The first article of this section, "Providing Academic Support for Teachers and Students in High Stakes Learning Environments," is by Judy Elliott and focuses on practical and empirically supported strategies for helping students succeed on high stakes tests. Particular attention is given to providing academic support to English language learners and students with disabilities, two groups who are particular risk for failing high stakes tests. Elliott points out how these support activities dovetail with the emerging roles of the school psychologist in prevention and instruction. The next article, authored by Louis Kruger, Caroline Wandle, and Joan Struzziero, is entitled "Coping with the Stress of High Stakes Testing." They review the research about stress in regard to schools, teachers, and students, and relate this research to high stakes testing. They highlight the types of resources that schools, teachers, and students can use to cope with the stress associated with high stakes testing. They conclude with a discussion of how the stress associated with high stakes testing might provide new service delivery opportunities for school psychologists. The third article in this section, "Using Data from High-Stakes Testing in Program Planning and Evaluation," written by Jeffery Braden, focuses on how school psychologists can appropriately use data from high stakes tests to evaluate and improve instructional programs. He discusses the advantages and disadvantages of the status, improvement, and growth models for evaluating a school's academic progress. Braden emphasizes the judicious use of such data within recognized standards of practice and guided by a systematic decision-making process. This process takes into consideration contextual realities and resource constraints. The section concludes with an article by David Shriberg entitled "The School Psychologist as Leader and Change Agent in a High-Stakes Era." Although school psychologists have been encouraged to assume leadership roles in the schools (e.g., Branden-Muller & Elias, 1991) the leadership literature is not well known in school psychology. In this article, Shriberg provides a review of major leadership theories most relevant to the practice of school psychology. He challenges school psychologists to be leaders in their school and districts' high stakes efforts and offers suggestions on how to accomplish this. Shriberg also provides two case studies of practicing school psychologists who have assumed such leadership roles.

CONCLUSION

The NCLB Act of 2001 has had a profound impact on educational practices in the United States and likely will continue to have a strong impact for many years to come. School psychologists are not immune from this impact, yet, to date, there has been surprisingly little scholarship in school psychology that speaks directly to high stakes testing. It is in this spirit that this volume has been conceptualized and written. It is our hope and belief that the articles contained in this volume will serve as a useful guide for practitioners seeking information on how they can help students in this high-stakes era.

REFERENCES

Branden-Muller, L., & Elias, M. (1991). Catalyzing the primary prevention revolution in the schools: The role of school psychologists. *Educational and Psychological Consultation, 2* (1), 73-88.

Linn, R.L. (2001). A century of standardized testing: Controversies and pendulum-swings. *Educational Assessment, 71*, 29-38.

doi:10.1300/J370v23n02_02

SECTION 1:
THE CHALLENGES, PROBLEMS, AND DILEMMAS ASSOCIATED WITH HIGH STAKES TESTING

Large-Scale Assessment, Rationality, and Scientific Management: The Case of *No Child Left Behind*

Andrew T. Roach

Georgia State University

Jennifer L. Frank

Vanderbilt University

Address correspondence to: Andrew T. Roach, Department of Counseling and Psychological Services, College of Education, Georgia State University, P.O. Box 3980, Atlanta, GA 30302 (E-mail: aroach@gsu.edu).

[Haworth co-indexing entry note]: "Large-Scale Assessment, Rationality, and Scientific Management: The Case of *No Child Left Behind*." Roach, Andrew T., and Jennifer L. Frank. Co-published simultaneously in *Journal of Applied School Psychology* (The Haworth Press, Inc.) Vol. 23, No. 2, 2007, pp. 7-25; and: *High Stakes Testing: New Challenges and Opportunities for School Psychology* (ed: Louis J. Kruger, and David Shriberg) The Haworth Press, Inc., 2007, pp. 7-25. Single or multiple copies of this article are available for a fee from The Haworth Document Delivery Service [1-800-HAWORTH, 9:00 a.m. - 5:00 p.m. (EST). E-mail address: docdelivery@haworthpress.com].

Available online at http://japps.haworthpress.com
© 2007 by The Haworth Press, Inc. All rights reserved.

SUMMARY. This article examines the ways in which NCLB and the movement towards large-scale assessment systems are based on Weber's concept of formal rationality and tradition of scientific management. Building on these ideas, the authors use Ritzer's McDonaldization thesis to examine some of the core features of large-scale assessment and accountability systems. According to Ritzer, McDonaldized systems and routines are characterized by four central features: (a) a pursuit of efficiency; (b) emphasis on calculability or quantification of outcomes; (c) predictability and uniformity; and (d) control through nonhuman technologies. Strengths and shortcomings of each of these features for schools and educators are discussed. The article concludes with ideas and strategies for school psychologists interested in maximizing the benefits and minimizing the negative outcomes of large-scale assessment and accountability systems. doi:10.1300/J370v23n02_02 *[Article copies available for a fee from The Haworth Document Delivery Service: 1-800-HAWORTH. E-mail address: <docdelivery@haworthpress.com> Website: <http://www.HaworthPress.com> © 2007 by The Haworth Press, Inc. All rights reserved.]*

KEYWORDS. Large scale assessment systems, No Child Left Behind, accountability, scientific management, rationality

Henry Ford created a world-class company, a leader in its industry. More important, Ford would not have survived the competition had it not been for an emphasis on results. We must view education the same way. Good schools do operate like a business. They care about outcomes, routinely assess quality, and measure the needs of the children they serve.

–*U.S. Secretary of Education Rod Paige, October 2003*

Although the No Child Left Behind Act of 2001 (NCLB) did not introduce the concept of large-scale assessment systems to the nation's schools, teachers, and students, it has highlighted the centrality of assessment systems as a policy tool in state and federal educational reform efforts. The current legislative embrace of large-scale assessment systems is based on a theory of action that assumes increased information about student achievement coupled with salient incentives for increased performance, and corresponding punishments for lack of improvement, will motivate educators and produce improved student outcomes (Baker & Linn, 2002). Researchers have dubbed this the "new accountability" and have outlined the following additional characteristics of these systems: (a) the use of student achievement data as an indicator of system and educator functioning; (b) public reporting of student performance data; and (c) utilization of the school as the unit of analysis for change efforts (Elmore, Abelman, & Fuhrman, 1996; O'Day, 2002). Large-scale assessment and accountability systems assume the existence of hierarchical, linear relationships between parts of the educational system (e.g., the US Department of Education, state and local educational agencies, and school-based practitioners). From this structural policy design and traditional educational planning perspective, large-scale assessment programs have a direct influence on the educational system and its agents (e.g., school administrators, teachers, and students).

In many ways, the foundations for NCLB and accompanying large-scale assessment systems can be found in the work of Max Weber and Frederick Taylor. Weber (1864-1920) was a German economist and sociologist whose work dealt with *formal rationality* and its effect on society, organizations, and individuals. He suggested the movement towards formal rationality results in the development of practices and interactions intended to facilitate efficiency or calculation rather than to promote tradition, morality, or aesthetics (Lippman & Aldrich, 2003). Moreover, Weber conceptualized bureaucracy as the organizational form that maximized the influence of rationality on individual and group behaviors (Bolman & Deal, 1997). With its emphasis on structure and delegation, rules and regulations, and hierarchical power relations, Weber believed bureaucracy allowed organizations to complete a large number of tasks in a highly efficient and predictable manner. In addition, Weber indicated bureaucratic organizations generally embrace quantification of tasks because it allows for easier operationalization and measurement of success and productivity (Ritzer, 2000, p. 23).

A contemporary of Weber's, Frederick Winslow Taylor (1856-1915) was an American engineer who undertook a series of time-and-motion studies to determine the "one best way" of completing various manufacturing tasks. Taylor is associated with the concept of scientific management, which aims to increase performance and results by making work more rational and workers more efficient (Evans, 1996). As conceptualized by Taylor, scientific management emphasized (a) discovering efficient and effective ways of working via the use of scientific methods; (b) identifying and recruiting the best, most skillful workers to complete tasks; (c) providing training and professional development to improve the efficiency of these workers; and (d) closely monitoring workers' attainment of clearly identified goals and standards (Evans, 1996; Morgan, 1986; Ritzer, 2000).

NCLB is not the first attempt to apply Weber and Taylor's work to education. At the beginning of the twentieth century, administrative progressives (including Ellwood Cubberley and Edward Thorndike) posited that there were "scientific" solutions that could rectify the inefficiencies in the American educational system. Using Taylor's principles of scientific management, these educational leaders reorganized schools to place students in classes by age and ability, hired professional administrators to oversee the work of teachers and schools, constructed tests to monitor student mastery of academic and vocational skills, and used the resulting test scores to compare schools and districts to one another (Cuban, 2004).

In his work *The McDonaldization of Society,* Ritzer (2000) indicated we have entered an era in which the majority of the organizations and systems have embraced and enacted the basic tenets of rationality and scientific management. He identifies a familiar modern organization–McDonald's–whose structures and practices illustrate and exemplify Weber and Taylor's ideas in action. Ritzer suggests that McDonald's (and the "McDonaldization" of other modern organizations) is not a new or novel phenomenon, but the product of rationalization processes that have been occurring throughout the last century (influencing educational, governmental, and commercial organizations). McDonaldized organizations have four common features or purposes:

- *Calculability,* or an emphasis on the quantitative aspects of products and services offered;
- *Efficiency,* or the optimum method of getting from one point to another;
- *Predictability,* the assurance that products and services will be the same over time in all locales; and
- *Control* over people who enter the organizations through non-human technology (Lippmann & Altman, 2003).

Because most readers are undoubtedly familiar with McDonald's and other McDonaldized organizations, this article will use Ritzer's four components of McDonaldizaton as a framework for considering the influence of formal rationality and scientific management in the development of NCLB and large-scale assessment systems.

THE NO CHILD LEFT BEHIND ACT OF 2001

NCLB is a revision and expansion of the Elementary and Secondary Education Act (ESEA). This act is the largest federal education funding program in U.S. history, and has provided a new array of requirements, incentives, resources, and challenges for states. In enacting NCLB, the federal government took on a broader and stronger role in education than ever before. The Act builds on earlier school reform legislation and the standards-based education movement by establishing challenging academic standards, but it is far more than a simple revision of existing law. NCLB marks a significant change in federal and state responsibilities in education. The objectives of NCLB are far reaching and ambitious: to ensure that all children become "proficient" in reading, mathematics, and science and to close the achievement gap.

In May 2006, four years after NCLB was signed into law by President Bush, the US Department of Education released a document entitled *No Child Left Behind Is Working* that reviewed student performance on standardized test programs and indicated that "because of NCLB's accountability provisions, schools and parents are getting the information and help they need to focus attention and resources on the children who need it most–and it's working" (USDOE, 2006). Using Ritzer's McDonaldization concept as a framework for considering NCLB and some of its provisions may provide us with (a) an understanding of the ways in which NCLB "works" and (b) insights into how school psychologists can practice within the constraints of this policy to facilitate improved outcomes for *all* children.

CALCULABILITY: NCLB'S EMBRACE OF LARGE-SCALE ASSESSMENT

Ritzer suggests that calculability–the emphasis on quantitative aspects of work undertaken and products completed–is the linchpin that supports all the other aspects of McDonaldization. For example, a quantitative index of production or results makes it easier to monitor and evaluate the efficiency of workers (or educators and students). Moreover, when quantity becomes a substitute or proxy for quality, highly predictable and uniform modes of work are more likely to be promoted and embraced, resulting in greater predictability and increased control of worker behavior (Ritzer, 2000).

Under NCLB, the results of states' large-scale assessment systems are used to provide a quantitative index of educational outcomes or productivity. Although previous versions of ESEA required states to test students in at least one elementary, middle school or junior high school, and high school grade annually (e.g., grades 4, 8, and 10); NCLB is more expansive, and explicit, in defining assessment and accountability than previous legislation. Among the most important changes is the mandate for annual testing in reading and mathematics of every student in grades 3-8 and at least one high school grade. In addition, annual science assessment in at least one grade in elementary, middle school, and high school is to be initiated by the 2007-2008 school year.

NCLB also requires states to identify schools not making Adequate Yearly Progress (AYP), and specifies a series of consequences for schools failing to meet AYP for two or more consecutive years. AYP is defined as progress toward meeting the goal of 100% of all children in a state meeting state proficiency standards by 2014. At a most basic level, NCLB requires states to develop assessments closely aligned with state content standards. Although local school or districts may use non-standardized testing components to address NCLB requirements, these forms of assessment may not meet NCLB's technical quality and comparability requirements. Currently, NCLB requires state assessments to be constructed in such a way that results can be reported in terms of percentages of students in at least three performance categories, and that results are able to be disaggregated by subgroups based on gender, race/ethnicity, poverty level, English-language proficiency, and disability status.

Other indicators (e.g., attendance) may also be used to track progress, but achievement as measured by standardized tests is considered the most salient outcome.

In addition, schools are required to track (and attain) AYP for identifiable subgroups, including groups defined by race/ethnicity, poverty, gender, disability, and English proficiency. States also must ensure that their assessment program achieves at least 95% participation for the students in each of these subgroups.

The Promise of Calculability

Ritzer (2000) suggests the emphasis on calculability brings with it many advantages, especially the ability to obtain data on a large number of individuals and services at relatively little cost. This cost-effectiveness is one of the central appeals of standardized testing programs. In comparison to more personalized classroom-based methods of assessment (e.g., portfolio, observation, performance assessments), the multiple-choice and constructed-response standardized tests used in most states' assessment programs provide a wealth of information on student performance with relatively small financial outlays needed to support implementation, scoring, and reporting. Moreover, although many educators and other stakeholders assert that testing programs take an inordinate amount of instructional time, students tested annually spend less than 1% of their school time taking tests (Elliott, Braden, & White, 2000). Although the time dedicated to test preparation is likely to vary across states, schools, and teachers, the actual instructional time lost to mandated assessment requirements is arguably quite small.

In addition, NCLB's emphasis on annual assessment coupled with the inclusion of students with disabilities and English language learners in assessment systems means that there is more available information on overall student achievement than at any point in our nation's history. Historically, there has been low participation rates for students with disabilities and English language learners in statewide assessments. Excluding these students from state and district-wide assessment resulted in: (a) unrepresentative mean scores and norm distributions, (b) reinforcing beliefs that students with disabilities and English language learners cannot do challenging work, and (c) undermining inclusion efforts for many students who can benefit from–and have the right to–the same instruction as their peers (Elliott, Braden, & White, 2000). However, as Thurlow, Quenemoen, Thompson, and Lehr (2001) indicate, "There has been remarkable progress during the past decade in moving toward more inclusive assessment systems. Starting from the point when the Education Summit of 1989 set an agenda for education reform that called for higher expectations, rigorous educational standards, and assessments of progress for all students (later reinforced by Goals 2000, ESEA Title I, and IDEA 97), the changes have been remarkable" (p. 3). The results of inclusive accountability systems may be serving as important policy levers, providing both information and motivation to support improved educational experiences and outcomes for *all* students.

The Perils of Calculability

Although NCLB's emphasis on large-scale assessments and inclusive accountability systems clearly has produced a wealth of quantitative information about the performance of students, the legislation's embrace of calculability also presents a number of dilemmas. Ritzer (2000) outlines aspects of calculability that may be viewed as shortcomings in the implementation of NCLB, including (a) an emphasis on quantity over quality and (b) reducing products and services (in this case education) to numbers. These aspects are particularly troubling when applied to schools and students. As Ritzer suggests, "In education ... the focus seems to be on how many students (the "products") can be herded through the system and what grades (or test scores) they earn rather than the quality of what they have learned and of the educational experience" (2000, p. 66).

According to Ritzer (2000), McDonaldized systems often use quantification and statistics to produce the "illusion of quality." In the context of NCLB, this can be observed in the arbitrary nature with which states can set proficiency standards on the state assessments. Although the legislation mandates that each state must "develop a set of challenging academic achievement standards for every grade and content area assessed," how each state defines and operationalizes "proficient" achievement varies considerably. Research by Linn (2003) demonstrates the considerable variability in what "proficient" means across states. As Table 1 illustrates, states identified as employing the most *lenient* proficiency standards (i.e., Colorado and North Carolina) report nearly 10 times the number of students being identified as achieving proficiency compared to states using the most *stringent* proficiency standards (i.e., Missouri and Arizona).

These differences are unlikely to reflect the actual differences in mathematics skills and understanding for students in these states. "Instead, the huge differences ... reflect the radically different definitions of proficient achievement in different states. It is clear that valid inferences cannot be made about the relative proficiency of students in states based on comparisons of percentage proficient statistics" (Linn, 2005, p. 25). In light of this, educators and other stakeholders might question the meaning of NCLB's stated goal of 100% of the each state's overall

TABLE 1. Variability in Mathematics Proficiency for 4th Grade Students

	Most Lenient Standard	Most Stringent Standard
4th Grade	Colorado–79.5% proficient or above	Missouri–8.3% proficient or above
8th Grade	North Carolina–74.6% proficient or above	Arizona–7% proficient or above

student population attaining proficient performance in core academic areas by 2014.

Some prominent educational researchers (Kohn, 2000; Nichols, Glass & Berliner, 2005) have questioned whether scores on large-scale assessments are the most appropriate and meaningful index of educational outcomes (see also Nichols, this volume). Cuban (2004) suggests the skills measured on standardized achievement tests may not be the skills students need to succeed in the information-based global economy. "It is thus simply rash to suggest that students who are pressed by centralized, standards-based reforms to . . . do well on standardized achievement tests will succeed in entry-level jobs or in college" (p. 237). As Popham (2001) points out, a number of features of standardized large-scale assessments make them inappropriate as indices of student, educator, and school functioning:

1. On many standardized tests, there is a mismatch (or lack of alignment) between what is tested and the skills and concepts that are supposed to be taught as part of the curriculum.
2. Standardized tests are designed to include items that create the widest distribution of scores (i.e., items with low p-values) and typically eliminate items that represent the skills and concepts most likely to be taught by teachers and mastered by students (i.e., items with high p-value).
3. Students' ability to answer some standardized tests questions is influenced by factors (e.g., socioeconomic standing, cultural background, and inherent aptitude) other than the adequacy of their instructional experiences.

The factors identified by Popham severely limit the utility of standardized tests and the validity of inferences regarding (a) students' mastery of important knowledge and skills, and (b) the effectiveness of teachers and schools.

EFFICIENCY: THE PURSUIT OF SCIENTIFICALLY BASED RESEARCH

Efficiency refers to "choosing the optimum means to a given end" (Ritzer, 2000, p. 40). As expressed in the previous section on calculability, large-scale assessment systems are an incredibly efficient method for gathering a lot of information about the achievement of a large number of students in a cost-effective manner. In addition to the use of large-scale assessment as indices of student and school performance, NCLB embraces the concept of *scientifically-based research* (SBR) as a guide to efficient and effective educational practices. SBR is referenced over 100 times in the NCLB Act, and schools and districts using federal funds are now required to implement instructional programs and materials, assessments, and professional development programs that have been proven to be effective through scientifically based research.

In addition, NCLB has provided nearly one billion dollars of funding for the *Reading First* program, which is intended to encourage states and school districts to select, implement, and provide professional development for teachers using scientifically based reading programs. *Reading First* also aims to ensure accountability through ongoing, valid and reliable screening, diagnostic, and classroom-based assessment. The *Early Reading First* program embraces a similar tactic to increase the reading readiness of preschool age children.

The pursuit of efficiency also is intertwined with calculability because improved performance on standardized measures of academic achievement often becomes the criterion for demonstrating program effectiveness in SBR. In *A Consumer's Guide to Evaluating a Core Reading Program Grades K-3: A Critical Elements Analysis,* Simmons and Kame'enui (2003) state "A key assumption of a core program is that it will (a) address all grade-level standards and (b) ensure that high priority standards are taught in sufficient depth, breadth, and quality that all learners will achieve or exceed expected levels of proficiency" (p. 4). In addition, this document suggests that educators should select early reading programs that have sufficient evidence of efficacy established through experimental studies using standardized tests of reading achievement as one of the key outcome measures.

The underlying logic of NCLB's mandate to use methods based on SBR is that "school personnel (will) focus on the outcomes they are trying to improve, examine indicators of the extent which they are achieving their goals, and alter the components of the education system to enable all students to meet high standards of excellence" (Towne, 2005, pp. 47-48). Upon identifying and implementing scientifically based programs to address students' needs, educators would then conduct evaluations of these new practices to determine if they were effective in producing the desired changes in student performance (i.e., increased proficiency as measured by standardized tests).

PREDICTABILITY: CONTENT STANDARDS AND ALIGNMENT

Predictability involves the pursuit of uniformity of services across settings and times. To use the McDonald's metaphor, people want to know that the Big Mac they order will be the same whether they are in Albuquerque or Atlanta. For educational policymakers and other stakeholders, emphasizing standards-based assessments and accountability systems is expected to result in relative consistency in the curricular content and instructional approaches employed across classrooms, schools, and communities. In fact, many early advocates of standards-based reform and accountability believed it would serve as the critical lever for enhancing equity and equal opportunity in the educational system (Resnick, Rothman, Slattery, & Vranek, 2003).

Research on the effectiveness of these efforts suggests that standards do have the potential to drive educational change and improvement, but only if states and districts are committed to establishing alignment among elements of the educational system. Alignment may be defined as the extent "to which expectations and assessments are in agreement and serve in conjunction with one another to guide the system toward students learning what they are expected to know and do" (Webb, 2002, p. 1). The concept of alignment is prominent in NCLB; in fact–like SBR–this term appears more than 100 times in the legislation (Resnick, Rothman, Slattery, & Vranek, 2003). NCLB requires schools, districts, and states have a system of K-12 standards that are "aligned" with the large-scale assessments used in their accountability systems. Moreover, schools, districts, and states are not considered to be in compliance with NCLB until they have demonstrated that the assessment tools used in their state accountability system have appropriate technical adequacy, *and* are aligned with standards.

Based on the assumptions of standards-based reform, NCLB views coordination of various policy components–curriculum, instruction, and assessments–as necessary for creating of effective educational programs. Understanding the overlap or links among these components can provide us with an index of the "power" of educational programs to produce changes in student achievement. When classroom curriculum and instruction are well-aligned with desired outcomes (as measured by a large-scale assessment), the majority of students might reasonably be expected to make "adequate yearly progress." When these components are poorly aligned with expectations, students will be less likely to demonstrate their proficiency on outcomes-focused assessments (Roach, Niebling, & Kurz, 2006).

Serious questions have been raised, however, about the influence of large-scale assessments on teachers' decision making about curriculum and instruction. Because of the high stakes attached to large-scale assessment results, teachers may feel pressure to "teach to the test" rather than attend to the breadth of skills and concepts in the state content standards. If large-scale assessments (rather than content standards) become teachers' instructional targets, narrowing of the curriculum and de-emphasis of other important educational experiences (e.g., music, art, athletics, and community services) may be an unintended consequence of NCLB (Baker & Linn, 2002). In this volume, Jones provides a detailed account of this and other potential unintended consequences of NCLB.

CONTROL:
ADEQUATE YEARLY PROGRESS
AND "HIGHLY QUALIFIED" TEACHER

McDonaldized systems also pursue increased control of workers via non-human technologies. "Direct, personal control is difficult, costly, and likely to engender personal hostility....Control through a technology is easier, less costly in the long run, and less likely to engender hostility toward supervisors" (Ritzer, 2000, p. 105). Under NCLB, monitoring and reporting the results of large-scale assessments provide a technology for shaping and controlling educators' behavior from the top down. For example, NCLB requires that concrete steps be taken if a school fails to make adequate yearly progress (AYP) on large-scale assessments. Schools that fail to meet AYP targets for 3 or more consecutive years must offer students from low-income backgrounds supplemental educational services that may include academic tutoring, remediation, or other types of educational interventions. Supplemental student services must be research-based, focused on increasing academic achievement, and provided outside of the regular school day. If a school fails to meet AYP targets for 4 consecutive years, the district must implement concrete corrective actions. These actions may vary, but might include implementing a new curriculum or replacing staff. If a school fails to achieve AYP targets for 5 consecutive years, it must develop a plan to restructure and then implement alternative governance actions. These alternative actions can include conversion to a charter school, contracting with a private management firm, state takeover of the school, or staff restructuring.

Beyond mandating particular responses based on the results of large-scale assessments, NCLB requires states to implement testing and assessments of teacher knowledge and skills. Schools and districts receiving Title 1, Part A funds must take measures to ensure that teachers of core academic subjects be "highly qualified" no later than the end of the 2005-2006. To be considered "highly qualified," elementary teachers must be fully licensed and pass a state competency test demonstrating mastery of subject knowledge, and knowledge of instruction in reading, writing, math, and other areas of the elementary school curriculum. Middle and high school teachers must also be fully licensed or certified, and demonstrate competence in the subject matter of the courses they teach. Middle and high school teachers can demonstrate competence by: (a) passing a state sponsored competency test, (b) meeting the requirements of a state evaluation standard used to judge competence, or (c) completing an academic major or coursework equivalent to a major, a graduate degree or advanced certification. Close consideration of these regulations suggest many teachers may be able to meet these competency criteria without truly being "highly qualified." Developing and certifying a "highly qualified" teaching workforce may require states to develop a more individualized and intense assessment and evaluation system beyond what most currently have in place. Ensuring the availability of "highly qualified" teachers is also likely to require a substantial investment on the part of states to address critical shortages in well-trained and experienced teachers (especially in districts and schools serving lower socio-economic communities).

RESPONSES TO NCLB AND LARGE-SCALE ASSESSMENT

Because of the innate appeal of its stated goal of increasing the proficiency for *all* students, the NCLB legislation and accompanying large-scale assessment systems are unlikely to disappear in the near future. Moreover, as outlined above, NCLB conforms to the ideas of formal rationality and scientific management that are evident in many organizations and routines of modern life.

Educators and school psychologists, however, can take steps to ensure NCLB and large-scale assessments do more good than harm. Although there are certainly roles for legislators, administrators, and other organizational leaders to influence policies, we focus our recommendations on individual practitioners and their schools. Most steps we suggest are driven by the assumption that "knowledge is power." Educational stakeholders are often uninformed, or misinformed, about large-scale assessment programs, results, and consequences. Because of their lack of knowledge, they may fail to realize the intended consequences of tests, and instead succumb to tests' unintended consequences. The following suggestions may help educational stakeholders make better decisions about how to respond to large-scale assessments and NCLB's accountability provisions.

Promote Assessment Literacy

Research conducted at the National Center for Research on Evaluation, Standards, and Student Testing (CRESST) suggests that the difficulties with understanding and meaningfully applying assessment data is pandemic at all levels of the educational system–from the statehouse to the schoolhouse (Baker & Linn, 2002; Baker, Bewley, Herman, Lee, & Mitchell, 2001). This is unfortunate because NCLB places an unprecedented emphasis on student achievement in conjunction with increased levels of accountability for the professionals that work with students in our public schools. Educators need more knowledge about the use and interpretation of standardized group achievement tests with ALL students because of the increased consequences associated with such tests in statewide assessment programs. To prepare educators to meet these demands, NCLB includes a mandate for high quality professional development that extends beyond content knowledge and instructional strategies to include support for inclusive instruction and assessment practices. Specifically, NCLB requires state and local educational agencies to provide professional development that focuses on instruction for children with special needs and the use of assessment data to inform classroom practice [Title IX, Section 9101(34)]. This requirement mirrors national trends towards enhancing the assessment literacy of teachers evident in state licensure requirements (Stiggins, 1999) and professional standards of practice (Wise, 1996). School psychologists can take the lead in helping other educators, parents, and students accurately interpret the results of large-scale assessments. Increasing educational stakeholders' assessment literacy can increase good decision making, and decrease misguided and potentially harmful responses to test results.

Use Results to Get Results

Although test scores often arrive too late in the year to help plan instruction for individual students, scores can provide valuable insights for instructional planning. Identifying which instructional objectives are more or less likely to be mastered in a given grade may lead to educators to analyze and reflect on their educational practices for the following year's student cohort. Such annual planning can include strategic decisions related to instructional practices and support materials, sequencing instruction within and across grades (e.g., curriculum mapping), and other decisions to increase student learning. Professionals who understand how to provide and interpret data from large-scale assessments can help teachers use test results to transform and improve student learning.

Additional research needs to be conducted to determine the instructional utility and effects of large-scale assessments. In the meantime, school psychologists can take the lead in identifying more meaningful reporting mechanisms and implementing additional classroom-based assessments that can provide students, parents, and educators with information that can support instructional improvement. Shinn and Bamanto's (1998) discussion of the "three big ideas" underlying the development of curriculum-based measurement (CBM) can be adapted to provide a useful framework for discussing the characteristics of assessments that can support and inform educational change. Shinn and Bamonto's "three big ideas" suggest:

1. Educational assessments should be "dynamic indicators" of important skills and knowledge.
2. Educational assessments should provide meaningful information for formative evaluation.
3. Educational assessments should be acceptable and user-friendly for making instructional decisions.

Shinn and Bamonto (1998) define "dynamic" measures as instruments sensitive to differences among and changes within individuals. The use of time-efficient indicator measures of academic progress (e.g., CBM, DIBELS) can give test users information about possible performance on a broader number of tasks in the same domain (e.g., large-scale assessments) and provide information for guiding instruction and intervention.

Hang Out in the "Skunk Works"

Ritzer (2000) describes how some high-tech organizations have encouraged the development of "'skunk works,' where people can be insulated from routine organizational demands and do their work as they see fit. Skunk works emphasize creativity and innovation, not conformity" (p. 225). School psychologists may need to search out the "skunk works" within NCLB and large-scale assessment systems. One possibility is to become involved in alternate assessment for students with disabilities and English language learners. With their emphasis on idiographic, classroom-based assessment, alternate assessments provide an opportunity for innovative responses to NCLB, accountability, and standards-based reform. School psychologists' skills in assessment and behavioral observation make them natural choices to participate in the design and development of alternate assessment programs. Another option is for school psychologists to take the lead in the development of NCLB-mandated supplemental services for students in schools that fail to meet AYP targets, which must be implemented beyond the scope of the existing instructional program.

Closing the Gap and Moral Purpose

One of the stated objectives of the NCLB legislation is to close the gaps between (a) actual levels of performance and expected achievement; and (b) the performance of the lowest achieving students (or classrooms or schools) and the general level of achievement for the entire population. Fullan (2003) suggests that focusing on reducing these gaps can provide educational systems with a moral purpose that can drive the process of creating educational change. Indeed this is the logic embraced by many within the inclusion community, who believe that efforts to include and ensure the success of students with disabilities in general education environments can provide the impetus for improved services to all students (Capper, Frattura, & Keyes, 2000; O'Brien & O'Brien, 1995). Moreover, when our gap-closing efforts take place in natural settings, we maximize the probability of "spillover effects" from these efforts that can create improvement in other individuals or parts of the system (Kendall, 2000).

A recent study of student performance in 32 nations illustrates the importance of these efforts (OECD, 2000). The countries that had the largest gaps in students' achievement demonstrated equally troubling trends in other social indicators (e.g., indices of mental and physical health, competence and coping skills, and workers' skill-level and employability). These results suggest reducing the gap in educational performance is essential, not only for educational success, but also as a strategy for promoting social and economic development at the community, state, and national level.

CONCLUSION

In the conclusion to his book, Ritzer (2000) provides a number of additional ideas for coping with, resisting, or escaping the McDonaldized systems and routines of modern society. Since formal rationality and scientific management are likely to play increasing larger roles in social organizations and public institutions (e.g., schools and districts), Ritzer's recommendations for school psychologists might include the following:

1. School psychologists should try to mitigate the worst aspects of large-scale assessments and NCLB. This may mean emphasizing that large-scale assessments are only one index of student and school performance. Moreover, there may be more appropriate and useful data that could be collected to demonstrate the effectiveness of schools' programs; school psychologists should take the lead in collecting this data.
2. School psychologists should encourage and support innovative practices and programs in their schools. "One size fits all" programming is unlikely to result in improved performance for all students. In addition, rigid standardization and manualization of instruction runs counter to the individualized accommodations and modifications that we know many students need to be successful.
3. School psychologists should be willing to "speak truth to power." NCLB and large-scale assessment programs support centralized (i.e., federal) power and decision making. Although this centralization may result in greater equity across states, districts, and schools, it also limits local creativity and responsiveness to community needs.

Finally, Ritzer (2000) suggests expressing individual or collective concern and skepticism about the influence and scope of policies like large-scale assessments and accountability systems may build feelings of efficacy and influence. Certainly, advocacy for and support of "best practice" in the area of large-scale assessment is our professional duty as school psychologists.

REFERENCES

Baker, E.L., Bewley, W.L., Herman, J.L., Lee, J.J., & Mitchell, D.S. (2001). *Upgrading America's use of information to improve student performance* (Proposal to the U.S. Secretary of Education). Los Angeles: University of California, National Center for Research on Evaluation, Standards, and Student Testing.

Baker, E.L., & Linn, R.L. (2002). *Validity issues for accountability systems*. Los Angeles, CA: University of California, National Center for Research on Evaluation, Standards, and Student Testing.

Bolman, L. G., & Deal, T. E. (1997). *Reframing organizations: Artistry, choice, and leadership* (2nd ed.) San Francisco, CA: Jossey-Bass.

Capper, C. A., Frattura, E., & Keyes, M. W. (2000). *Meeting the needs of students of all abilities: How leaders go beyond inclusion*. Thousand Oaks, CA: Corwin Press.

Cuban, L. (2004). *The blackboard and the bottom line: Why schools can't be businesses*. Cambridge, MA: Harvard University Press.

Elliott, S. N., Braden, J. P., & White, J. (2000). *Assessing one and all: Educational accountability for students with disabilities*. Arlington, VA: CEC.

Elmore, R.F., Abelman, C.H., & Fuhrman, S.H. (1996). The new accountability in state education reform: From process to performance. In H.F. Ladd (Ed.), *Holding schools accountable: Performance-based reform in education* (pp. 65-98). Washington, DC: Brookings Institute.

Evans, R. (1996). The human side of school change: Reform, resistance, and the real-life problems of innovation. San Francisco, CA: Jossey-Bass.

Fullan, M. (2003). *Change forces with a vengeance*. New York: Rutledge Falmer.

Jones, B. (2007). The unintended outcomes of high stakes testing. *Journal of Applied School Psychology, 23* (2), 65-86.

Kendall, P.C. (Ed.) (2000). *Child and adolescent therapy: Cognitive-behavioral procedures* (2nd ed.). New York: Guilford Press.

Kohn, A. (2000). *The case against standardized tests: Raising the scores, ruining the schools*. Portsmouth, NH: Heinemann, 2000.

Linn, R. L. (2005). Scientific evidence and inference in educational policy and practice: Implications for evaluating adequate yearly progress. In C.A. Dwyer (Ed.), *Measurement and research in the accountability era* (pp. 21-30). Mahwah, NJ: Lawrence Erlbaum Associates.

Linn, R. L. (2003). Accountability: Responsibility and reasonable expectations. *Educational Researcher, 32*(7), 3-13.

Lippman, S, & Aldrich, H. (2003). The rationalization of everything? Using Ritzer's McDonaldization thesis to teach Weber. *Teaching Sociology, 31,* 134-145.

Morgan, G. (1986). *Images of Organization*. Newbury Park, CA: Sage.

Nichols, S.L. (2007). High stakes testing: Does it increase achievement? *Journal of Applied School Psychology, 23* (2), 47-64.
Nichols, S. L., Glass, G. V, & Berliner, D. C. (2006). High-stakes testing and student achievement: Does accountability pressure increase student learning? *Education Policy Analysis Archives, 14*(1). Retrieved from http://epaa.asu.edu/epaa/v14n1/.
OECD (2000). *Knowledge and skills for life: First results from PISA 2000.* Paris: Organization for Economic Cooperation and Development.
O'Brien, J., & O'Brien, C. L. (1995). *Inclusion as a force for school renewal.* Syracuse, NY: Center on Human Policy.
O'Day, J.A. (2002). Complexity, accountability, and school improvement. *Harvard Educational Review, 72*(3), 293-329.
Paige, R. (2003, October 6). Letter to the editor. *New Yorker*, p.12.
Popham, W. J. (2001). *The truth about testing: An educator's call to action.* Alexandria, VA: Association for Supervision and Curriculum Development.
Resnick, L. B., Rothman, R., Slattery, J. B., & Vranek, J. L. (2003). Benchmarking and alignment of standards and testing. *Educational Assessment, 9* (1&2), 1-27.
Ritzer, G. (2000). *The McDonaldization of society: New century edition.* Thousand Oaks, CA: Pine Forge Press.
Shinn, M. R., & Bamonto, S. (1998). Advanced applications of curriculum-based measurement: "Big ideas" and avoiding confusion. In M. R. Shinn (Ed.), *Advanced applications of curriculum-based measurement* (pp. 1-31). New York, NY: Guilford Press.
Simmons, D.C., & Kame'enui, E. J. (2003). *A Consumer's Guide to Evaluating a Core Reading Program Grades K-3: A Critical Elements Analysis.* Eugene, OR: Institute for the Development of Educational Achievement.
Stiggins, R. J. (1999). Evaluating classroom assessment training in teacher education programs. *Educational Measurement: Issues and Practice, 18*, 23-27.
Thurlow, M., Quenemoen, R., Thompson, S., & Lehr, C. (2001). *Principles and characteristics of inclusive assessment and accountability systems* (Synthesis Report 40). Minneapolis, MN: University of Minnesota, National Center on Educational Outcomes.
Towne, L. (2005). Scientific evidence and inference in educational policy and practice: Defining and implementing "scientifically based research." In C.A. Dwyer (Ed.), *Measurement and research in the accountability era* (pp. 41-56). Mahwah, NJ: Lawrence Erlbaum Associates.
United States Department of Education (2006, May). *No Child Left Behind is Working.* Retrieved from: http://www.ed.gov/nclb/overview/importance/nclbworking.pdf.
Webb, N. L. (2002, April). *An analysis of the alignment between mathematics standards and assessments for three states.* Paper presented at the annual meeting of the American Educational Research Association, New Orleans, LA.
Wise, A. (1996). Building a system of quality assurance for the teaching profession: Moving into the 21st Century. *Phi Delta Kappan, 78,* 191-192.

doi:10.1300/J370v23n02_02

Measurement Issues in High Stakes Testing: Validity and Reliability

Emanuel J. Mason

Northeastern University

SUMMARY. Validity and reliability of the new high stakes testing systems initiated in school systems across the United States in recent years in response to the accountability features mandated in the No Child Left Behind Legislation largely depend on item response theory and new rules of measurement. Reliability and validity in item response theory and classical test theory are reviewed. Additionally, practices in the states are considered. The conclusion of the paper is that the new test technology is theoretically better suited to assess achievement than classical test theory, but has not been shown to be valid and reliable enough for use as the sole criterion for determination of what was learned in school. Further, there is no evidence that they will ever be found to be valid and reliable enough for that purpose. Areas of additional needed research are considered. doi:10.1300/J370v23n02_03 *[Article copies available for a fee from The Haworth Document Delivery Service: 1-800-HAWORTH. E-mail address: <docdelivery@haworthpress.com> Website: <http://www.HaworthPress.com> © 2007 by The Haworth Press, Inc. All rights reserved.]*

Address correspondence to: Emanuel J. Mason, Department of Counseling and Applied Educational Psychology, 203 Lake Hall, Northeastern University, Boston, MA 02115 (E-mail: e.mason@neu.edu).

[Haworth co-indexing entry note]: "Measurement Issues in High Stakes Testing: Validity and Reliability." Mason, Emanuel J. Co-published simultaneously in *Journal of Applied School Psychology* (The Haworth Press, Inc.) Vol. 23, No. 2, 2007, pp. 27-46; and: *High Stakes Testing: New Challenges and Opportunities for School Psychology* (ed: Louis J. Kruger, and David Shriberg) The Haworth Press, Inc., 2007, pp. 27-46. Single or multiple copies of this article are available for a fee from The Haworth Document Delivery Service [1-800-HAWORTH, 9:00 a.m. - 5:00 p.m. (EST). E-mail address: docdelivery@haworthpress.com].

Available online at http://japps.haworthpress.com
© 2007 by The Haworth Press, Inc. All rights reserved.
doi:10.1300/J370v23n02_03

KEYWORDS. High-stakes tests, validity, reliability, testing

A key feature of the No Child Left Behind (NCLB) Act, signed into law by President Bush on January 8, 2002, is the emphasis on accountability in the schools through a system of assessment procedures. This law mandates a system of accountability requiring assessment for students, teachers, schools, school systems, and districts. Important decisions that may have long-term and wide-ranging consequences are made based on the results of these tests. For example, promotion to the next grade level and high school graduation for students, job continuation or salary elevation for teachers and administrators, and the determination of whether a school board will continue control of its schools or be required to transfer this responsibility to the state may be based on the interpretations of performance on these "high stakes" tests.

The theory underlying the development of traditional normative assessments (classical test theory) differs from the theory underlying the new kinds of tests based on Rasch and item response testing models (Clark & Watson, 1995; Croker & Algina, 1986; Embretson, 1999; Embretson & Reise, 2000; Lord & Novick, 1968; MacDonald, 1999). Classical tests are based on individual differences and a normative interpretation in which a person's test scores are represented in terms of how others performed on the test. Scores might be expressed as standard scores which are based on distances from the mean of the normative group. The newer kinds of tests are based on latent trait theory (also known as item response theory). This approach represents a different perspective on scores and their interpretation than classical testing. Rather than comparing tests results to the performance of a normative group, scores are interpreted in terms of a continuum of the trait being assessed (Embretson & Reise, 2000).

The present paper explores the validity and reliability of high stakes tests for supporting the kinds of decisions for which they are currently being used. Our principal focus will be on the validity and reliability of these tests. First, the standard definitions and methods of establishing reliability and validity in traditional testing will be reviewed. Then the newer methods of designing and scaling achievement tests common in high stakes testing programs will be considered. This will be followed by a review of how high stakes testing is being implemented across the United States. The relationship between reliability and validity, and topics such as test bias, alternative assessment for groups of students with disabilities, school climate, teaching to the test and other issues will be explored. Finally, the issue of validity of using a single test score as the sole evidence of the quality of effects of several years of a child's education will be addressed.

RELIABILITY AND VALIDITY IN CLASSICAL TEST THEORY

Classical test theory (CTT) began to be developed in the early 1900s but was more formally established mid century with works like those of Gulliksen (1950) and Magnussen (1966). Test reliability and validity are required of all tests according to the *Standards for Educational and Psychological Testing* (1999) published jointly by the American Psychological Association (APA), the American Educational Research Association (AERA), and the National Council on Measurement in Education (NCME). These standards are widely accepted by professional groups that use educational and psychological assessments. Reliability and validity, characteristics familiar to most test users, take on a somewhat different meaning in high stakes testing than in CTT.

Reliability in Classical Tests

Methods for establishing reliability and validity in CTT have been fairly well established. Their estimation depends on assumptions about individual variability originally proposed by Spearman (1907, 1913), and developed further by Gulliksen (1950) and Magnussen (1967). CTT is based on a model of an observed score (X_o) that is equal to an actual underlying and unobservable true score (X_t) and random error (e) so that

$$X_o = X_t + e \qquad (1)$$

Reliability may be defined as the degree of reproducibility or consistency of the score on the test. When the above equation reflects a high portion of error for everyone who takes the test, the test-retest correlations will be lower because of the greater influence of random variation. This consistency of the test is usually investigated by correlating test scores between repeated administrations of the same test (stability) or parallel forms of the test, or a combination of test-retest and parallel forms. In this approach, the higher the correlation, the more reliable the test is said to be. Practical reasons, many of them obvious, make stability and parallel forms reliability difficult to ascertain (Nunnally &

Bernstein, 1994). Another approach, called internal consistency, seeks to explore the degree to which random variation in test scores can be due to the consistency within the items. For example, internal consistency procedures may be based how half of the test correlates with the other equivalent half, or how items of the test correlate with each other.

The reliability (r_{xt}) formula shown below permits estimation of the standard error of measurement (s_{em}), a term that is useful for estimating the limits of the range of a confidence interval containing the true score (s_x represents the standard deviation of the test scores).

$$\sigma_{em} = \sigma_x \sqrt{1 - r_{xt}} \qquad (2)$$

As can readily be seen from the equation, the lower the reliability, the larger the standard error of measurement up to the value of the standard deviation of the test scores (s_x). Thus, a test with low reliability has a large standard error of measurement and must be interpreted with a large range of possible true scores.

Validity in Traditional Testing

Test validity can be defined as the degree to which the test measures what it was designed to measure, and further the degree to which inferences based on the scores can be interpreted meaningfully and usefully (Croker & Algina, 1986; Magnussen, 1966; *Standards for Educational and Psychological Testing,* 1999). Validation of tests has been greatly influenced by the 1955 article by Cronbach and Meehl which identified four kinds of validity studies: *predictive, concurrent, content,* and *construct*. The first two were merged into the single category of *criterion-related*.

Criterion-related validity can be investigated by correlation methods. Specifically, one can correlate the scores on the test to the functional behaviors one is using the test to measure. For example, one can correlate score on a music ability test to a student's performance in learning music. Within the criterion-related category, a predictive validity study will correlate past or current scores with future ones, and a concurrent validity study will involve correlation of current scores.

Content validity is a matter of showing that the content of the test is a representative sample of the domain or universe of items. For example, a test in American history from 1865 to 1900 would contain items about reconstruction after the Civil War, the assassination of President Lincoln, civil rights decisions such as Plessy vs. Ferguson, the development of the railroad, and the changing of the economy from relatively rural to more urban and manufacturing-based. The exact proportion of the items from the topics within the domain would be indicated based on the views of a panel of experts (e.g., of historians and history teachers) convened to reflect the curriculum being tested.

Construct validity is more difficult to summarize. In the view of Cronbach and Meehl (1955), construct validity "is involved whenever a test is to be interpreted as a measure of some attribute or quality that is not 'operationally defined'" (p. 282). Many of the variables of interest in psychological tests are constructs in the sense that they represent an idea but are not precisely defined (e.g., intelligence tests, tests of depression, or spatial ability). In construct validity, various methodologies may be utilized to provide evidence that the test is a valid measure of the construct of interest. The test developer should provide evidence that the test results correspond to behavior, traits, or performance that would have been expected by the theory behind the construct. For example, one would expect that intelligence tests are valid for assessment of the construct of intelligence. One index of construct validity would be the relationship between school performance and the test scores with higher scores obtained by students who are better performers in school. Another approach would be to compute correlations with assessments that measure similar traits and behavior, and assessments that represent less similar characteristics to the instrument of interest. Confirmatory factor analysis might be utilized to show that relations among parts of the test are consistent with theory (Hair, Anderson, Tatum & Black, 1998; MacDonald, 1999; Maruyama, 1998).

The kind of validity demonstrated should be based on the claims for the test. For example, a music ability test should emphasize predictive validity and be likely to show that high scores on the test predict successful attainment of music skills. An academic achievement test should show content validity by having a high degree of correspondence between the items on the test and the domains being assessed as defined by the school curriculum. Construct validity should be evident in tests that are based on scientifically defined constructs such as intelligence, and personality or emotional state.

VALIDITY AND RELIABILITY IN THE NEW ASSESSMENT MODELS

It is not the purpose of the present paper to go into the details of item response testing (IRT). The interested reader is directed to works by Embretson and Reise (2000), MacDonald (1999), and Hambleton,

Swaminathan, and Rogers (1991) as examples of resources that provide more complete treatment of the subject. However, because high stakes testing tends to rely heavily on this approach to test design and development, some discussion and explanation is appropriate to clarify the issues related validity and reliability of IRT-based assessments.

In classical test theory, a person's score is represented by a summation of the items. For example, a classroom mathematics test of ten items will have a maximum score of ten items correct. The assumption is that the ten items represent the knowledge a person has of the domain. However, no differentiation is made between the person who gets a score of 3 on the test by correctly answering the first three items and another who gets the same score by answering the last three items. In IRT, the primary concern is not just on the total score, but the responses to individual items. It is assumed that underlying the test instrument is a trait or ability that the test measures. Each person's score on the test places them on a scale that represents a continuum of the ability or trait, often represented by the Greek letter theta (θ). Each item in the scale each has a certain probability that a person with that ability will pass the item. Easier items, those with a high probably of being answered correctly, will be passed by a large number of respondents. More difficult items with a lower probability of correct response will be answered correctly by a smaller number of respondents. If the probability of responding correctly was plotted for each item along the ability scale, the resulting graph would display the results for each item as an S-shaped curve as shown in Figure 1 where the characteristic curves of two test items, an easy one and a more difficult one are diagrammed.

In the figure, there is an arbitrary score scale from -3 to $+3$ shown on the horizontal axis, and the probability of being correct on that item at each score level shown on the vertical axis. Thus, a person who is at the $+1$ ability level has approximately a .8 probability of answering the easy item correctly but only a .1 probability of responding correctly on the more difficult item. The S-shaped curve is known as the item-characteristic curve. This curve has certain properties that must be mentioned. First, item difficulty determines where the item functions along the scale of ability. Second, the slope of the curve determines how well it differentiates between people who are at higher and lower levels of θ. Items with steep slopes differentiate most effectively. While the two items in Figure 1 have similar slopes, they are clearly in different places along the scale of θ because of their different levels of difficulty. Therefore these two items can be said to be about equally effective in discrim-

FIGURE 1. Item Characteristic Curves (ICCs) for Two Items, One Difficult and One Easy

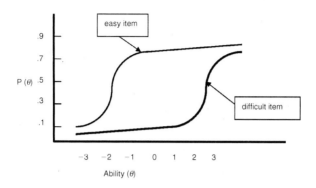

inating among individuals with different abilities even though their difficulty levels are different. Compare these two item curves to the ones depicted in Figure 2. The two items in Figure 2 are very different in how they differentiate between individuals of higher and lower ability. Item a shows a fairly abrupt demarcation suggesting that respondents who answered the item correctly tended to be close to or above the 0.0 level on the scale. On the other hand, item b does not differentiate between scores at different ability levels. For example, it would be difficult knowing where to place someone who answers this item correctly along the ability scale. Item difficulty and item discrimination are two parameters that are often used in high stakes implementations in state testing programs. A third, based on the probability of guessing, is less often used.

Reliability and validity are no less important in IRT then they are in CTT. However, the different scaling methods used in IRT have implications for reliability and validity. In the last century, reliability and validity of classical tests has been developed extensively. Despite this extensive development, many inadequacies have been recognized. For example, two inadequacies are the implausibility of the existence of parallel forms of tests that meet all the stringent theoretical criteria for test equivalence, and the recognized difficulties with specifying the underlying construct in construct validity (Cronbach & Meehl, 1955; MacDonald, 1999). Measurement based on the Rasch principles and IRT can offer some solutions. Susan Embretson, who has done research and written extensively on item response theory, has taken the position

FIGURE 2. ICCs for Two Items, One a Good Discriminator (a), and One Not as Good a Discriminator (b).

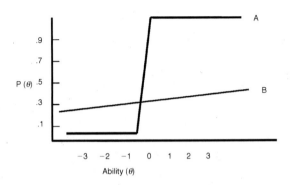

that the differences between CTT and IRT measurement theory and methodology is great enough to be considered a true paradigm shift resulting in new rules of measurement (Embretson, 1983; Embretson, 1996; Embretson & Reise, 2000). Embretson and Reise (2000) provide a discussion of the differences between IRT and CTT.

Reliability in IRT

Reliability in IRT as in CTT refers to the ability of the test to provide accurate and consistent interpretation of scores. However, the nature of IRT tests and the way they are constructed challenges some of the ways in which reliability is applied in IRT compared to classical testing. In this section, the issues of interpretation, standard error, parallel forms, effects of test length, and related issues are addressed.

Interpretation of scores is a major issue to anyone who uses tests or takes them. In CTT, the usual procedure in discussing reliability is to take the total scores on a set of items, and establish a scale based on the distance from the mean in standardized units (e.g., z-scores). In IRT, on the other hand, items are ordered in terms of difficulty so that the person who gives a correct answer for a moderately difficult item will be more likely to have passed the items below it. Thus, focus of interpretation is on the items, not on the normative scale.

In classical tests, the standard error of measurement (equation 2 above) is assumed to apply to all scores within the population from which the representative sample was drawn to norm the test. However, in IRT the standard error of measurement is score-dependent but applies across populations. Thus, each score must be interpreted with respect to its unique standard error. This issue is critical to interpretation of reliability because the standard error is used to construct confidence intervals around observed scores, and this could be important in setting and interpreting cut-off scores in rendering of high stakes decisions.

Parallel forms of tests may be used in classical test theory to investigate reliability. The correlation of two perfectly parallel tests should be high indicating that a large portion of the scores are due to the common true scores underlying the observed performance. The difficulty inherent in developing perfectly parallel tests is well known (Nunnally & Bernstein, 1994). However, in IRT parallelism of test forms may be defined based on item characteristic curves (ICC) (MacDonald, 1999). Evidence for the superiority of the IRT approach for developing equivalent tests has been given by Embretson and Reise (2000).

Test length is directly related to reliability in CTT, a relationship shown mathematically in the Spearman-Brown formula (Magnussen, 1966). That is, the longer the test, the more likely that reliability will be higher. This well-known relationship is directly challenged in item response theory by data provided by Embretson and Reise (2000) in a simulation study in which shorter adaptive tests (i.e., different test given at each ability level) had universally smaller standard errors of measurement than tests with fixed content that were longer. This provocative finding needs to be more systematically addressed in some of the applications of IRT to high stakes testing. For example, research on the relationship of test length to content and criterion validity in high stakes settings would be useful to guide test development.

Unbiased estimates of item properties in CTT require representative samples from populations of potential test takers. However, item response theory does not emphasize the need for representative populations. Some data are available in support of this. For example, Embretson and Reise (2000) compared a high ability group with a group lower in ability in a simulation study and found that the item probability estimates were not linearly related in CTT (suggesting sample dependence) but the difficulties were in linear relationship in IRT (suggesting sample independence) when low ability score levels were correlated to high ability score levels.

These and other issues can affect estimations of reliability directly. While internal consistency methods (e.g., Cronbach's α) are used in both CTT and IRT applications, the interpretation and meaning of other time-honored methods of CTT reliability such as parallel forms and test-retest are less clear or inappropriate. This also appears to be the case with validity.

Validity in IRT

One of the most contentious areas with respect to validity between classical test theory and item response theory is in regard to construct validity. The issue of construct validity, including how it is defined, determined, and interpreted has long be an unsettled issue in CTT as well (Cronbach & Meehl, 1956; MacDonald, 1999; Nunnally & Bernstein, 1994). It has been argued that the construct validation in IRT is a matter of task decomposition (Embretson, 1983). In achievement testing, this approach would require analysis of the cognitive processes and knowledge specifically targeted by the measure. Thus, construct validity would require systematically demonstrating that the items specifically represent the theoretical structure of the content being assessed. One approach would be to use structural equation modeling (Maruyama, 1998) and confirmatory factor analysis (Embretson, 1983; Hair, Anderson, Tatum, & Black, 1995; MacDonald, 1999).

TEST FAIRNESS FOR ALL GROUPS

When groups of people, males and females for example, respond differently to a test item, that item is said to be biased. Test bias can occur when groups within a target population systematically respond differentially to the test. In such cases, the validity of the item can become a concern since it is assumed that the item measures the same trait or behavior in all people, and that the item and test have the same predictive value regardless of the groups (racial, ethnic, gender, etc.) to which they belong. Further, the definition of bias and identification of groups within a population for whom the test is biased can be difficult (Nunnally & Bernstein, 1994). Classical test theory provides a number of ways of detecting and dealing with item bias among them, using linear regression of test scores on some criterion for the standard group and the group that might experience bias, and studying residuals to find extraneous variables that may lead to bias (Nunnally & Bernstein, 1994).

The differential item function (DIF) is at the core of the IRT approach to test fairness. "An item shows DIF if individuals having the same ability, but from different groups, do not have the same probability of getting the item right" (Hambleton, Swaminathan, & Rogers, 1991, p. 110). One approach to DIF would be to compare the item parameters from the ICC obtained by administering the test to the groups of interest. If the item parameters are the same, the test would be considered unbiased for these groups. This approach requires putting the results of the testing of the two groups on a common scale, and comparing the parameters. When the parameters adjusted to the common scale are not different, no DIF exists and the test can be considered fair for the subgroups of interest. DIF is commonly used in high stakes achievement testing programs across the United States to investigate bias.

Generally all students in a school district are required to participate in the state and school district testing programs including the high stakes programs. This includes children with disabilities who may be receiving special education services. Also, students who have limited facility with English should be given opportunity to respond to tests that allow them to accurately demonstrate what they know. Fairness requires that alternative methods of assessment be available to accommodate these children's needs. There are few standards or methodologies such as DIF available to assist in development of equivalent testing for groups with diverse disabilities of varying severity.

HOW ARE STANDARDS FOR RELIABILITY AND VALIDITY BEING APPLIED?

The quality of application of the test standards for state high stakes assessment systems across the country is difficult to summarize. One useful way to address this issue is to consider the statements by the professional organizations that set the standards for educational and psychological assessment. These groups (e.g., American Psychological Association, 1999, 2001; American Education Research Association, 2001; National Association of School Psychologists, 2003) are fairly consistent on the following points:

1. A single test should not be the only criterion for making high-stakes decisions about the total educational experience of a student, or the complex activities and responsibilities of a school and school staff. Test scores are not infallible.

2. Test producers and those responsible for testing programs should make sure that the tests are reliable and valid for the purposes for which they are used.
3. Information about the testing programs should be made public.
4. The tests should be aligned to the curriculum (not the reverse).
5. Reliability and validity for each application for which a test is used should be assured.
6. Potential negative side effects of the testing should be recognized and made public.
7. The tests should be made fair to students with language deficits and other disabilities, limited English proficiency, and non-mainstream cultural backgrounds.
8. On-going research should be conducted to continually improve and update the assessment system.

Using these criteria, an informal review of web sites for the fifty states was done to evaluate the high-stakes testing efforts underway across the United States. It was assumed that if a state department of education wanted to comply with the recommendation for making information about the testing system available to the public, this information would be readily accessible on the Internet. The search of the Web tested this assumption. Some states provide very clear information, including technical information about reliability, validity, scaling and interpretation. Others provide less. However, even when fairly complete information was available, it was not clear that all the recommendations affecting reliability and validity were being followed.

A Single Test Should Not Be the Only Criterion for Making High-Stakes Decisions

Most states seem to be using a single assessment score to make high-stakes academic decisions. Some states (e.g., Georgia) use a variety of tests and other information to augment the high stakes tests. However, even in these states, the primary decisions for promotion, graduation and school rewards for performance (or censure for lack of it), depends alone on the high-stakes tests. Virtually no recognition is given to the fallibility of test scores or the fact that a test is an index with less than perfect reliability. Supporting the findings of an earlier study by Rhoades and Madaus (2003), the Web sites reveal a tendency to provide considerable information about the size of the standard errors, but little regarding how this information might relate to the use of a single test score to make serious decisions that may have lifelong impact on a child.

Assurance that the Tests Are Reliable and Valid for Each Application and Purpose for Which They Are Used

Most states contract to produce all facets of their testing system. Companies such as CTB McGraw-Hill, Educational Testing Service, and Harcourt Assessment, Inc. serve as contractors. The testing contractors produce professional looking materials, reports, training for teachers, and manuals for test interpretation, scoring and administration in addition to the tests. Many of these materials are thorough in explaining how reliability and validity were approached and the results of validity and reliability studies. For example, Alaska (and its contractor, Data Recognition Corporation), described how content validity was established, and that construct validity was based on Rasch Model fit and item-total correlations. The sufficiency of this evidence to support validity of the purposes of the high stakes test application was less clear. In general, information about reliability and validity in all states was incomplete; too technical for teachers or parents to understand, or complete and detailed enough to show that further study was necessary before validity could be assumed. Some referred to all types of validity and reliability but only presented Cronbach's alpha, whereas others emphasized content validity. Evidence given for content validity was often a combination of Cronbach's alpha and a description of how the tests were developed by experts working from curriculum objectives. For example, the Massachusetts Comprehensive Assessment System website provided a well-written and comprehensive report describing the development and standardization of the 2003 tests. This manual includes comparisons of IRT and classical test models, internal consistency reliability, standard errors of measurement for CTT and IRT models, DIF, but nothing on validity of the tests for the purposes for which they were being used. Presumably validity was studied, but no summary was available in this technical report released to the public.

Non-random human errors have had adverse impact on the validity and reliability of high-stakes and large-scale tests in recent years (Rhoades & Madaus, 2003). Many of these errors were also evident in the materials state education agencies place on their assessment system websites. For example, there was a widespread tendency to underplay or ignore the fallibility of tests. Tests used for high stakes decisions were portrayed as well constructed, and therefore should be considered reliable and valid and to be unquestioned evidence of a student's absolute ability to perform within the required curriculum. Tough language was often used to demonstrate the rigor and dependability of the system Often this language could be traced back to action by a state legislature. When policy makers promote or mandate tests without evidence of validity for the purposes being advocated, this is a serious error of test application. Ignoring test characteristics (e.g., standard error, type of validity required for an application) is another source of potential error. Other sources of error are ignoring inconsistencies (e.g., very large gains in a very short time span), mistakes in recording or reporting, and scoring errors.

Numerous investigations have raised questions about the validity of high stakes test scores reported in states that showed suspiciously high gain scores. Two of these instances that were extensively investigated occurred in Texas (Haney, 2000; Klein, Hamilton, McCaffery, & Stecher, 2000) and Kentucky (Koretz, & Barron, 1998). In each case, the gains were found to be invalid. Similarly, (Green, 2001) provided a glowing evaluation of the high-stakes testing in Florida after 78 public schools that had received an "F" grade in 1999 on the state assessment system, received a higher grade the following year. This concluson was contested by a re-evaluation that suggested that the apparent improvement was due to sampling selection, regression to the mean, and incorrect data aggregation (Camilli & Bulkley, 2001).

Finally, the pressure to show gains can lead teachers, administrators, and school leaders to cut corners and try to produce the best picture. This was a finding of one aspect of the investigation of the "Texas Miracle" of the decade of remarkable progress reported by the Texas educational system after implementation of high-stakes testing. Close scrutiny suggested arbitrary exclusions of students from the testing. Further, the gains were not shown in other large-scale tests, such as the National Assessment of Educational Progress (NAEP) scores for the same students. More students were taking the GED tests, probably to avoid the state assessment tests. These and other findings raised serious concerns about the validity of the system for assessing student learning across the state.

Information About the Testing Programs Should Be Made Public

While all states provided websites for the public, the nature and quality of the information varied. Some states explain the differences in classical tests and IRT models, give considerable information about reliability and validity, test construction, and interpretation. Others allude to these issues but provide very little information. Much of what was available was either too simplistic and sketchy or too technical to be useful to the typical parent or teacher seeking to learn more about the validity and reliability of the tests. A few state websites referred interested parties to the US Department of Education No Child Left Behind website. There was no effort by this writer to determine what kinds of printed materials were available to the public about the state testing programs, however, government office and email addresses were generally provided for requesting information.

The Tests Should Be Aligned to the Curriculum (Not the Reverse)

When teachers are instructed to focus their instruction on preparing for high stakes state tests, the validity of the tests is changed. Specifically the tests change from assessing the construct "What have students *learned* in across the curriculum" to "What have the children *memorized* as isolated knowledge and facts from our approved list of items to memorize." Everyone in the school is under pressure to show passing scores in a "one test decides all" high stakes setting. Teaching to the test is a way to deal with the situation. Research shows that "teaching to the test" is effective for bringing lower ability and economically disadvantaged groups of students to achieve better scores on these tests, and also that such practices produce less efficient and effective learning in higher ability and more economically advantaged schools (Firestone, Schorr, & Monfils, 2004; Lazear, 2005).

Potential Negative Side Effects of the Testing Should Be Recognized and Made Public

No states discuss the potential negative effects of their high stakes system in detail. These negative effects can include stress, depression, and other kinds of psychological distress in students (Altshuler & Schmautz, 2006). Other problems can include the harmful effects of false negatives (i.e., erroneously classifying children as having failed the test, when based on their knowledge and skills, they should have been classified as having passed the test), and the reverse effect in which students who should receive support services did not receive these services because they were classified as passing the test. A given student's test performance could be higher or lower on a given day, *even though the standard error of the IRT is score dependent,* an issue that is largely ignored on the states' websites. Further, the isolation of the test score as the sole criterion for high stakes decisions amplifies the importance that teaching to the test has on validity. Finally, personnel in the school who might be in a position to assist students with these issues (e.g., guidance counselors) are less available because they are involved in managing and monitoring the test effort for their schools (Thorn & Mulvenon, 2002).

The Tests Should Be Made Fair to Students with Language Deficits and Other Disabilities, Limited English Proficiency, and Non-Mainstream Cultural Backgrounds

State departments of education websites provide considerable information about alternative assessment procedures for students with disabilities, and those for whom English is not the first language. This emphasis is not surprising. It is required by law and encouraged by good testing practice. How states implement adjustments for cultural diversity, disability and English language difficulties varies. Most provide some disability accommodation or alternative test. Some, like Colorado, provides standard and non-standard accommodations as required by the student's needs. Connecticut has a standard list of accommodations from which a school committee can choose the appropriate situation for a given child. Research suggests that test accommodations are successful only when the accommodation is designed to help the student overcome the specific disability (Cohen, Gregg, & Meng, 2005; Fletcher et al., 2006; Johnson, 2006).

Efforts to avoid test bias for cultural groups seem to depend heavily on DIF computations. However, there seems to be some evidence that culturally diverse groups may be disadvantaged by high stakes testing (Altshuler & Schmautz, 2006; Haney, 2000). It would be unfortunate if research continues to show that despite the efforts at cultural fairness and objectivity that are built into the high-stakes testing systems, diverse groups tend to slip further in the educational system.

On-Going Research Should Be Conducted to Continually Improve and Update the Assessment System

There is considerable room for research in high-stakes testing. In the rush to implement the provisions of the NCLB Act, high-stakes testing was implemented with only limited evidence of validity. These testing systems have been designed to determine the net worth of the whole educational experience of a child and the effectiveness of teachers and school systems despite the existence of other indicators. For example, a child who wins a highly competitive state-wide science fair is seen as only as good in science as her or his state science exam score suggests. Yet the validity (and superiority over other evidence of academic success) of this score for such an all-encompassing purpose has never been satisfactorily demonstrated.

While IRT methods do not focus on individual differences, performance is determined by these differences. For example, a child who did not sleep well the evening before the exam might not perform as well as the child's potential and previous evidence would suggest. Children become ill, stressed, and rattled, causing momentary recall problems. A child who can memorize locations of all the countries on a map may not understand how the distance from the equator affects climate, economy and culture of a country, while the child who understands these things might not be able to find countries on the map as quickly. Item response theory has only been in existence a short time. Its claims are intriguing, but they should be investigated and their applications in real settings understood better. There is little widespread recognition that item response theory is based on grouped data. Research exists that supports some of the claims of item response theory, but there is little evidence that decisions based on individual performance are so valid as to justify using only the single test score and nothing else.

We need to know more about accommodations for students with disabilities, limited English skills, and cultural differences. The manner in which cultural differences can influence test performance is another area for further research. This is imperative if supporting evidence of the total of a student's educational experience is to be justifiably superseded by a single test score. This test score must be as accurate and valid as possible, not just in theory, but also in reality. Whether test technology can ever be brought to that level is debatable.

The establishment of cut-off scores for passing the test is another unsettled issue related to validity. Most states provide information about what these cut-off scores are. However, they rarely go into detail on how these scores are determined and how the standard error is used in setting and using the cut-off. More research is needed to determine how to optimize score limits for categorical decisions.

CONCLUSIONS

School psychologists, school counselors, teachers, school administrators, parents, and everyone else involved in the educational system have been affected by high stakes testing. These expensive testing systems are often used as the sole basis to make critical decisions about schools and students. Because of the importance of these decisions, these tests must be developed according to high standards of validity, reliability, and interpretability. While it is clear that great effort has gone into developing testing systems across the country, it is less clear that the tests are up to the standards set for them. Validity data beyond IRT theory is weak. It has not yet been systematically shown that these tests are better predictors of success in education or in life as has been claimed by the promoters of high stakes testing (e.g., Greene, Winters, & Forster, 2003). Nor have the questions raised by various scholars been addressed (e.g., Coleman, 1998; Haney, 2000; Klein, Hamilton, McCaffrey, & Stecher, 2000).

The central issue addressed in this paper is not whether schools should have high standards, nor is it whether there should be assessment of those standards. The issue is not even whether there should be high stakes testing or IRT models used in assessment. The issue is that the tests used to assess the standards should be valid for the purposes for which they are used. If the tests are to diagnose weak areas of the curriculum, then that should be the focus of the validity investigation. In contrast, if the purpose is to be the only source of information on which critical life-changing decisions about people who work and learn in the schools are based, then the tests must be shown to be valid for that purpose. There is still work to be done. The stakes are high!

REFERENCES

Altshuler, S. J., & Schmautz, T. (2006). No Hispanic student left behind: The consequences of high stakes testing. *Children & Schools, 28*, 5-14.

American Psychological Association, American Educational Research Association, & National Council of Measurement in Education (1999). *Standards for Educational and Psychological Testing.* Washington, D. C: Author.

American Psychological Association (2001). *Appropriate use of high stakes testing in our nation's schools.*

Baron, D., & Koretz, S. (1998). *The validity of gains in scores on the Kentucky Instructional Results Information System (KIRIS).* Santa Monica, CA: RAND.

Camilli, G., & Bulkley, K. (2001). Critique of "An evaluation of the Florida A-Plus accountability and school-choice program." *Education Policy Analysis Archives,* 9(7). Retrieved June 4, 2006 from http://epaa.asu.edu/epaa/v9n7/

Clark, L. A. & Watson, D. (1995). Constructing validity: Basic issues in objective scale development. *Psychological Assessment,* 7, 309-319.

Cohen, A. S., Gregg, N. & Meng, D. (2005). The role of extended time and item content on a high-stakes mathematics test. *Learning Disabilities Research and Practice,* 20. 225-233.

Coleman, A. L. (1998). Excellence and equity in education: High standards for high stakes tests. *Virginia Journal of Social Policy & the Law,* 6(1), 81-114.

Crocker, L., & Algina, J. (1986). *Introduction to classical & modern test theory.* New York: Holt, Rinehart and Winston.

Cronbach, L. J., & Meehl, P. (1955). Construct validity in Psychological tests. *Psychological Bulletin,* 52, 281-302.

Embretson (Whitely), S. (1983). Construct validation: Construct representation versus nomothetic span. *Psychological Bulletin,* 93, 179-197.

Embretson, S. E. (1996). The new rules of measurement. *Psychological Assessment.* 8, 431-349.

Embretson, S. E. (1999). Issues in the measurement of cognitive abilities. In S. E. Embretson, & S. L. Hershberger (Eds.), *The new rules of measurement: What every psychologist and educator should know* (p. 1-15). Mahwah, NJ: Erlbaum.

Embretson, S. E., & Reise, S. P (2000). *Item response theory for psychologists.* Mahwah, NJ: Erlbaum.

Firestone, W., Schorr, & Monfils, L. F. (2004). *The ambiguity of teaching to the test: Standards, assessment and educational reform.* Mahwah, NJ: Erlbaum.

Fletcher, J. M., Francis, D. J., Boudousquie, A., Copeland, V., Young, V., Kalinowski, S., & Vaughn, S. (2006). Effects of accommodations on high stakes testing for students with reading disabilities. *Exceptional Children,* 72, 136-150.

Green, J. P. (2001). *An evaluation of the Florida A-Plus Accountability and school choice program.* (Civic Report #32) New York: The Manhattan Institute. (ERIC Document Reproduction Service No. ED 475 488)

Greene, J. P., Winters, M. A., & Forster, G. (2003). *Testing high stakes tests: Can we believe the results of accountability tests?* (Civic Report #32) New York: The Manhattan Institute. Retrieved August 30, 2006 from http://www.manhattan-institute.org/cr_33.htm

Gulliksen, H. (1950).*Theory of mental tests.* New York: Wiley.

Hair, J. F., Anderson, R. E., Tatham, R. L., & Black, W. C. (1998). *Multivariate data analysis.* Upper Saddle River, NJ: Prentice-Hall.

Hambleton, R. K., Swaminathan, H., & Rogers, H. J. (1991). *Fundamentals of item response theory.* Newbury Park, CA: Sage.

Haney, W. (2000). The myth of the Texas miracle in education. *Education Policy Analysis Archives,* 8(4), Retrieved August 30, 2006 from http://epaa.asu.edu/epaa/v8n41/

Johnson, R. C. (2001). High stakes testing and deaf students: Some research perspectives. Research at Gallaudet, Spring/Summer 2001, 1- 6.

Klein, S., Hamilton, L. S., McCaffrey, D. F., & Stecher, B. M. (2000). What do the scores in Texas tell us? *Education Policy Analysis Archives, 8*(49), Retrieved June 5, 2006 from http://epaa.asu.edu/epaa/v8n49/

Koretz, D. M. & Barron, S. I. (1998). *The validity of gains in scores on the Kentucky Instructional Results Information System (KIRIS). (RAND report MR-1014-EDU).* Washington, DC: RAND.

Lazear, E. P. (2005). *Speeding, Tax fraud, and teaching to the test.* CSE Report 659, Center for the study of Evaluation, National Center for Research om Evaluation, Stanadrds, and Student Testing, University of California, Los Angeles. Retrieved June 5, 2006 from http://cresst96.cse.ucla.edu/reports/R659.pdf#search = 'lazear%20cresst%20speeding'

Lord, F. N., & Novick, M. R. (1968). *Statistical theories of mental test scores.* Reading, MA: Addison-Wesley.

MacDonald, R. P. (1999). *Test theory: A unified treatment.* Mahwah, NJ: Erlbaum.

Magnussen, D. (1966). *Test theory.* Reading, MA: Addison-Wesley.

Maruyama, G. M. (1998). *Basics of structural equation modeling.* Thousand Oaks, CA: Sage.

National Association of School Psychologists (2003). *Position statement on using large scale assessment for high stakes decisions.* Retrieved February 21, 2006 from http://www.nasponline.org/information/pospaper_largescale.html

Nunnally, J. C., & Bernstein, I. H. (1994). *Psychometric theory* (3rd ed.). New York: McGraw-Hill.

Rhoades, K., & Madaus, G. (2003). *Errors in standardized tests: A systemic problem.* Lynch School of Education, Boston College, Retrieved June 6, 2006 from http://www.bc.edu/research/nbetpp/statements/M1N4.pdf#search='Errors%20in%20Standardized%20tests%20Ford%20foundation'

Spearman, C. (1907). Demonstration of formulae for true measurement of correlation. *American Journal of Psychology, 18,* 161-169.

Spearman, C. (1913). Correlations of sums and differences. *British Journal of Psychology, 5,* 417-426.

Thorn, A. R., & Mulvenon, S. W. (2002). High stakes testing: An examination of elementary counselors' views and their academic preparation to meet this challenge. *Measurement and Evaluation in Counseling and Development, 36,* 195-206.

doi:10.1300/J370v23n02_03

High-Stakes Testing:
Does It Increase Achievement?

Sharon L. Nichols

University of Texas at San Antonio

SUMMARY. I review the literature on the impact on student achievement of high-stakes testing. Its popularity as a mechanism for holding educators accountable has triggered studies to examine whether its promise to increase student learning has been fulfilled. The review concludes there is no consistent evidence to suggest high-stakes testing leads to increases in student learning. Some evidence suggests it may have a negative effect for some student groups and in some important subject areas (e.g., reading). Implications for future research and for the practice of school psychology are discussed. doi:10.1300/J370v23n02_04 *[Article copies available for a fee from The Haworth Document Delivery Service: 1-800-HAWORTH. E-mail address: <docdelivery@haworthpress.com> Website: <http://www.HaworthPress.com> © 2007 by The Haworth Press, Inc. All rights reserved.]*

Address correspondence to: Sharon L. Nichols, College of Education and Human Development Department of Counseling, Educational Psychology, and Adult Higher Education, University of Texas at San Antonio, 501 West Durango Blvd., Suite DB 4.342, San Antonio, TX 78207-4415 (E-mail: sharon.nichols@utsa.edu).

The author would like to thank Tom Good for providing extensive feedback on earlier versions of this paper. The author also thanks David Berliner, Gene Glass, Michael Karcher, and Jeremy Sullivan for their helpful feedback and editorial suggestions on an earlier draft. Lastly, the author thanks Michelle Lynde for her extensive editorial help in preparing this manuscript.

[Haworth co-indexing entry note]: "High-Stakes Testing: Does It Increase Achievement?" Nichols, Sharon L. Co-published simultaneously in *Journal of Applied School Psychology* (The Haworth Press, Inc.) Vol. 23, No. 2, 2007, pp. 47-64; and: *High Stakes Testing: New Challenges and Opportunities for School Psychology* (ed: Louis J. Kruger, and David Shriberg) The Haworth Press, Inc., 2007, pp. 47-64. Single or multiple copies of this article are available for a fee from The Haworth Document Delivery Service [1-800-HAWORTH, 9:00 a.m. - 5:00 p.m. (EST). E-mail address: docdelivery@haworthpress.com].

Available online at http://japps.haworthpress.com
© 2007 by The Haworth Press, Inc. All rights reserved.
doi:10.1300/J370v23n02_04

KEYWORDS. Accountability, academic achievement, high stakes tests, educational policy, achievement tests

INTRODUCTION

The passage of the No Child Left Behind (NCLB) Act in 2002 increased the practice of high-stakes testing in America's schools. Although high-stakes testing is not new (Amrein & Berliner, 2002a; Linn, 2000), never before has the practice been so widely applied. In supporting NCLB, politicians from both sides of the aisle enthusiastically endorsed high-stakes testing as the mechanism for holding administrators, teachers, and their students accountable for what they learn. But is it working? In the years leading up to NCLB and since its passage, several studies have examined the effects of high-stakes testing on student achievement.

In contrast to the literature on the mostly deleterious and *un*intended effects of high-stakes testing, which is substantial and largely indisputable (Amrein & Berliner, 2002a; Jones, Jones, & Hargrove, 2003; Neill, Guisbond, & Schaeffer, 2004; Nichols & Berliner, 2005; Orfield & Kornhaber, 2001; Ryan, 2004; Valenzuela, 2005), research on the relationship between high-stakes testing and its *intended* impact on achievement is sparse. Studies have varied widely in scope and design making it difficult to reach a single conclusion about the effects of high-stakes testing policy on student achievement. Rapid policy changes also have made it difficult to replicate earlier analyses. Nevertheless, in this review I offer some tentative conclusions regarding the efficacy of high-stakes testing policy for increasing student achievement.

The purpose of this review is to describe what is known to date about the impact of high-stakes testing policy on student achievement. I review a few of the more prominent studies in this area and discuss not only their findings, but also important methodological issues. This review culminates with work by myself and colleagues that describes a unique methodological approach to measuring high-stakes testing pressure to look at the effects of this pressure on student achievement (Nichols, Glass, & Berliner, 2006). Our work in combination with other studies lead to the conclusion that high-stakes testing has not been successful in increasing what students learn in school.

Rationale for High-Stakes Testing

The theory of action undergirding the practice of high-stakes testing is that when faced with large incentives and threats of punishment teachers will work harder and be more effective, students will be more motivated, and parents will become more involved (e.g., McDonnell, 2005; Raymond & Hanushek, 2003). More specifically it is commonly held that high-stakes testing will be effective because:

- teachers need to be held accountable through high-stakes tests to motivate them to teach better, particularly to push the laziest ones to work harder;
- students work harder and learn more when they have to take high-stakes tests;
- scoring well on the test will lead to feelings of success, while doing poorly on such tests will lead to increased effort to learn;
- high-stakes tests are good measures of an individual's performance, little affected by differences in students' motivation, emotions, language, and social status; and
- teachers will use test results to provide better instruction for individual students (Amrein & Berliner, 2002b, pp. 4-5).

In short, the pressure of doing well on a test, it is argued, will spur everyone into action, thus improving American public schools significantly (Haertel & Herman, 2005; Peterson & West, 2003; Phelps, 2005). Regardless of these common sense assumptions, the answer as to whether high-stakes testing works to improve student learning is less clear.

HIGH-STAKES TESTING AND STUDENT ACHIEVEMENT

A literature search on this topic yields a wide array of work that varies in scope, design, and emphasis (Herman & Haertel, 2005). I review some of the more notable studies that illustrate the main findings and important methodological concerns that arise when studying high-stakes policy implementation and impact.

Lake Wobegon

One early exchange examining the impact of high-stakes testing on student achievement occurred in the late 1980s when John Cannell released an acrimonious report that examined how districts and states had reported their Iowa Test of Basic Skills (ITBS) results. Known as the Lake Wobegon effect, Cannell's (1988) analysis pointed out that states had reported ITBS results where more than 50% of students were performing above average. Seeing this as a statistical improbability, he argued that it was the pressure of public reporting that compelled states and districts to manipulate the data to look "more favorable." Questions regarding Cannell's analytic approach prompted scholars to replicate his analysis. Many began by simply asking whether it was statistically possible that, as in Garrison Keillor's fictional community of Lake Wobegon, all of our students were performing above average?

Linn, Graue, and Sanders (1990) examined ITBS data carefully and found that Cannell was right: "The overall percent of students above the national median is greater than 50 in all of the elementary grades in both reading and mathematics" (Linn et al., 1990, p. 6). They also found that the average number of students above the national median at the elementary school level was higher in math across the three-year study period than in reading, going from a low of 58% in grade 4 (1985-1986) to a high of 71% in grade 2 (1987-1988). By contrast, in reading it ranged from 52% in grade 5 (1985-1986) to 60% in grade 3 (1987-1988). A similar, but less dramatic, difference was found at the high school levels.

Although there was relative consensus that inflated reporting had occurred, there was much less agreement on why. Had the pressures of public reporting influenced administrators and teachers to fabricate learning gains? Were students becoming more proficient? Another explanation, offered by Linn et al. (1990), proposed that inflated ITBS results could be explained as a statistical artifact that is the natural outcome of the process of re-norming. They argue that it is natural to expect students' test performance to rise when newer test scores are being compared to older norms in part because students and teachers become increasingly familiar with test items and objectives. And, analyses of ITBS trends demonstrate just that. Norm referenced test performance tends to rise as the time period between its current administration and when the norming data were collected increases. But, this upward trend dips sharply in the year when new, and often times more stringent, norms are collected. Linn et al.'s (1990) analysis casts a shadow of doubt on Cannell's (1988) position that educators were purposely manipulating their data to look more favorable.

But another explanation emerged. Under conditions of pressure (i.e., being evaluated publicly by student test results), teachers and principals changed their behavior to focus instruction more intently on the test. Shepard (1990) collected interview and survey data from state officials regarding test and curriculum based instruction and found substantial reason to believe that increased pressure on the test compelled educators to engage in practices that could be considered as teaching to the test.

Although Linn et al.'s (1990) and Shepard's (1990) evidence was relatively strong, another analytic approach offered evidence that seemed to support more conclusively the contention that teaching to the test was occurring. Linn et al. (1990) compared ITBS scores with scores on the NAEP with the rationale that parallel increases in NAEP performance would be evidence of students' transfer of learning–evidence that student achievement gains were real. However, after statistically accounting for test related differences (issues of sampling, content), they found that ITBS scores rose higher and faster than scores on the NAEP. They argued that teaching-to-the test may have played a significant role in the test inflation worries of Lake Wobegon.

Although there remains no consensus on the Lake Wobegon studies, the empirical exchange unveiled an important issue that applies as well to current analyses of high-stakes testing and student achievement. Is it appropriate to use high-stakes test scores as evidence that high-stakes testing is working? Shepard (1990) persuasively showed that we must worry that as the stakes of testing rise, educators will focus more intently on preparing their students for it. This type of over preparation could compromise the validity of the test result. The importance of looking at a comparable no stakes test (such as the NAEP) for evidence that high-stakes policies are working to increase student learning was an important outcome of Lake Wobegon studies.

Texas Myth

During the 1990s, the accountability movement gained momentum and Texas was at the forefront, steadily increasing the stakes attached to testing of its students and teachers. Initially, Texas had received high praise and national accolades for the "success" of their policies as evidenced by increasing student achievement (Grissmer & Flanagan, 1998; Palmaffy, 1998). It appeared that accountability was working. However, the bubble burst when others examined their data and found that achievement increases were largely a "myth" (Haney, 2000) and not significantly different from achievement gains made in other states (Camilli, 2000). By looking carefully at reporting trends and again by comparing achievement on Texas's state test (then the Texas Assessment of Academic Skills or TAAS) with achievement on the NAEP, Haney (2000) and others (e.g., Klein, Hamilton, McCaffrey, & Stecher, 2000) found that the alleged and highly publicized success of high-stakes tests for increasing student learning was erroneous, largely the result of the same problems that were identified during the Lake Wobegon exchange. Namely, increases in the TAAS were more likely to be the result of teaching to the test and other problems (dropping lower scorers from taking the test, miscounting number of dropouts). Evidence seems to be mounting from Texas and elsewhere (e.g., Kentucky, see Koretz & Barron, 1998; Massachusetts, see Haney, 2002) that test validity is seriously compromised when high-stakes decisions are attached to test score performance (Haney, 2000; Pedulla et al., 2003).

Chicago's End to Social Promotion

During the 1996-1997 school year, in their quest to end social promotion, the Chicago Public School (CPS) district began tying serious consequences to ITBS.[1] This marked the first year students in grades 3, 6, and 8 could be held back for inadequate performance on a test and teachers could be reassigned or dismissed for their students' inadequate performance. Jacob (2002) and colleagues (Roderick, Jacob & Byrk, 2002) examined whether this policy had the intended effect of increasing student achievement by analyzing ITBS scores before and after the implementation of the policy. Jacob (2002) found significant increases on ITBS following the implementation of high-stakes testing. It appeared as if achievement levels rose and that perhaps the policy had something to do with it. But did it? Follow-up item level analyses revealed that ITBS math gains were largely the result of improvements on computation and number concept skills and not higher-level thinking skills such as problem solving and data interpretation. This finding raises questions about the validity of the argument that high-stakes testing increases learning. Here it appears as if it worked only to increase basic skills that are susceptible to teaching to the test practices.

Roderick, Jacob and Byrk (2002) also examined ITBS performance following the introduction of high-stakes testing in Chicago, looking specifically at achievement following the "gateway" school years when students could be held back for low test performance at grades 3, 6, and 8. They found that the introduction of high-stakes testing in Chicago had a varying effect on achievement. For example, they found that in reading, the lowest achieving students benefited by the policy (achievement went up). However, the opposite was found in math where high achieving students benefited most. They also found evidence of school-level effects where students in low performing schools showed larger gains in achievement after policy implementation than students of similar skill levels in better performing schools. Thus, it appears that in CPS, high-stakes testing had a mixed effect. Sometimes it was associated with gains made by low achievers, and other times it is was associated with gains made by high achievers. Similarly, sometimes it was related to gains among third graders and other times among sixth graders. Of course, follow-up studies are needed to see if these findings are sustained; however, from this study alone, the varied pattern of results makes it difficult to draw conclusions about how high-stakes testing impacts student learning and teacher instruction.

High-School Graduation Exams

Some have investigated the impact of high school graduation exams (tests students must pass in order to receive a diploma) on student achievement. Jacob (2001), for example, looked at twelfth-grade achievement in reading and math as reported on the National Educational Longitudinal Survey (NELS) in states with and without high school graduation exams. After accounting for prior achievement and other background characteristics (e.g., SES, ethnicity), Jacob found that the institution of high school graduation exams was not related to student achievement. The only exception was with lower achieving students in reading where there emerged a slightly positive effect associated with high school graduation exams. But, Jacob (2001) also found that states with high school graduation exams had more dropouts than those without such exams.

Marchant and Paulson (2005) looked at the effect of high school graduation exams on state level graduation rates, aggregated SAT scores, and individual student SAT scores. By comparing graduation rates and SAT scores in states with a graduation exam against states without a graduation exam, they found that states with graduation exams had lower graduation rates and lower aggregate SAT scores. They also found that the requirement of a high school graduation exam had a negative relationship with individual student SAT performance. Importantly, conclusions from this study are made with caution due to study limitations (e.g., reliability of graduation rate calculation, selectivity of SAT takers).

RESEARCH EVOLVES WITH CHANGING POLICY

Amrein and Berliner (2002b) triggered the most recent debate regarding the impact of high-stakes testing policy. They looked at state-level NAEP achievement trends over time since 1990. Using time trend analysis, Amrein and Berliner (2002b) looked at NAEP trajectories before and after high-stakes testing policies were introduced and compared them with a national average. This approach allowed them to determine if significant increases in fourth and eighth-grade NAEP performance occurred as a result of high-stakes testing policies being implemented. Across each of the 28 states included in their study, they found a random pattern of effects. Sometimes math performance went up; sometimes it went down. Similar results were found for reading performance. Sometimes gains were found in fourth grade, sometimes in eighth.

Rosenshine (2003) reanalyzed the same data set utilized by Amrein and Berliner (2002b) using a different design[2] and found that the overall average NAEP scores of states with high-stakes testing rose more rapidly than the average scores in states without any programs. But, when he looked at trends at the individual state level, there was no consistent effect detected. Rosenshine (2003, p. 4) concluded that "although attaching accountability to statewide tests worked well in some high-stakes states it was not an effective policy in all states." In a follow-up response to Rosenshine (2003), Amrein-Beardsley and Berliner (2003) used his design approach, but also included in their analysis NAEP exclusion rates.[3] They concluded that although states with high-stakes tests seemed to outperform those without high-stakes tests on the fourth-grade math NAEP exams, this difference disappeared when they controlled for NAEP exclusion rates.

Braun (2004) also critiqued Amrein and Berliner (2002b) on methodological grounds. In his analysis of fourth- and eighth-grade math achievement (he did not look at reading) from 1992 to 2000, he found that when standard error estimates are included in the analyses, NAEP gains were greater in states with high-stakes testing for eighth-grade math than in those without in spite of exclusion rate differences. However, the impact of high stakes testing is much lower when it comes to fourth grade math achievement and it is almost absent when looking at cohort achievement trends (1992 fourth-grade math and 1996 eighth-grade math; 1996 fourth-grade math and 2000 eighth-grade math). Cohort analyses are important because they minimize the validity threats due to selection bias in the groups compared, time, or experience. Students tested in fourth grade and then in eighth grade four years later theoretically have experienced the same kinds of changes in instruction and the same increases in high-stakes testing pressure. Thus, assuming it may take time for testing pressures to take effect, a significant finding of high-stakes testing producing greater achievement among a cohort of students would be a robust confirmation of the policy's impact.

Measuring High-Stakes Testing Policy on a Continuum

Carnoy and Loeb (2002) were among the first to craft an index that rated states along a continuum of accountability "strength" designed to measure the level of pressure of high-stakes testing (see Appendix A, Carnoy & Loeb, 2002). However, their innovative index (scale of 0-5) had some measurement problems in that the numerical distinctions were relatively vague. For example, to receive the highest strength of accountability score they note, "States receiving a 5 had to have students tested in several different grades, schools sanctioned or rewarded based on student test scores, and a high school minimum competency test required for graduation. Other states had some of these elements, but not others" (Carnoy & Loeb, 2002, p. 14).

Carnoy and Loeb (2002) examined how their accountability index related to NAEP achievement. Their findings were mixed. They found a significant increase in eighth grade math performance (among White, Black and Hispanic students) as a result of increased accountability pressure. By contrast, the increases for fourth-grade math performance were much smaller for Black and Hispanic students and nonexistent for White students. Thus, like Braun (2004), Carnoy and Loeb (2002) found that eighth grade math is positively related to increases in high-stakes testing pressure. Importantly, their analysis focused only on 1996-2000 math performance and did not look at progress before or after that time period, or in any other subject area.

Hanushek and Raymond (2005) used a regression model to estimate accountability as a function of how long states had enacted high-stakes testing policy. Their analysis looked at fourth through eighth grade NAEP changes across Black, Hispanic and White student groups. They found that the introduction of state accountability had a positive impact on student performance overall. But when disaggregated by ethnicity, they found that NAEP increases were much lower for Black and Hispanic students than for White students. Hanushek and Raymond conducted other analyses with similar results. They concluded that consequential based policy has a positive impact on NAEP achievement for some groups but not others. However, they caution the reader that theirs is a "blunt" measure of accountability that does not take into consideration state level variation in how accountability policy is enacted.

Our Measure of High-Stakes Testing Pressure

My colleagues and I were dissatisfied with extant research primarily because of weaknesses in their approaches to the measurement of high-stakes testing policy, largely explained by a rapidly changing political climate. States have been quickly adopting and transforming their high-stakes testing policies making it difficult to measure and isolate their effects. At the time of our work, every state had adopted some form of high-stakes testing. Because every state then had some form of high-stakes testing policy, it was impossible to make group comparisons between states with and without such policies. Although Carnoy and Loeb (2002) and Hanushek and Raymond (2005) created scales for capturing state level accountability differences, we felt these measures were inadequate for accounting for differences in policy implementation and impact on schools, students, and teachers.

We created an empirically derived rating scale that captured a more differentiated version of testing pressure embedded in 25 states' accountability systems (only states with complete or almost complete NAEP participation since 1990 were included). The determination of our Assessment Pressure Rating (APR) relied on a set of portfolios constructed to describe in as much detail as possible the past and current character of accountability practices for each state. These portfolios included a wide range of documents describing the politics, legislative activity, and impact of a state's high-stakes testing program as well as newspaper articles that served as a proxy for legislative implementation and impact (a full description of the selection strategy and portfolio examples can be found elsewhere, Nichols, Glass, & Berliner, 2006). Using these portfolios, we enlisted the help of over 300 graduate level student participants, each of whom rated a single pair of states. The method of "comparative judgments" was adopted for scaling our study states along a hypothetical continuum of high-stakes testing pressure (Torgerson, 1960).[4]

Our Study Findings

Our analytic approach included a series of correlations looking at APR and fourth and eighth grade NAEP in math and reading (overall and disaggregated by student ethnicity). We also did a series of antecedent-consequence analyses where we correlated earlier changes in high-stakes testing pressure (e.g., from 1994 to 1998) with later achievement changes (e.g., from 1998 to 2002), thus providing a relatively robust estimation of a causal relationship (see Gujarati, 1995). We found that pressure was related only to fourth grade math achievement; the greater the pressure, the higher the math performance for all groups of students. Second, among the dozens of correlations looking at eighth grade math, results were inconsistent (some were positive, some negative, most were absent). Third, there was little impact on reading achievement at either the fourth or eighth grade levels. However, in the few instances the relationship was statistically significant, the outcome was mostly negative suggesting high-stakes testing pressure may be eroding reading performance especially in the fourth grade. Thus, the pressure to improve teaching and learning through applying sanctions based on test results produced test score gains only where drill on basic skills might raise achievement, namely elementary school arithmetic. Lastly, like Braun (2004), we found no link between high-stakes testing pressure and cohort achievement in math or reading.

CONCLUSION

Overall, the findings from the most rigorous studies on high-stakes testing do not provide convincing evidence that high-stakes testing has the intended effect of increasing student learning. Moreover, the modest gains found in some studies should be viewed with caution since the findings indicate that increases in achievement could be the result of teaching to the test. Of course, as others have noted (e.g., Crocker, 2005; Mathews, 2006), teaching to the test in some form is desirable. In preparing students for a test, it seems reasonable that instruction will be aligned with the objectives that will be covered on the test. But teaching becomes counterproductive when academic activities are geared specifically for students to do better on a test. This is especially true when it comes at the cost of other kinds of instruction or subject matter coverage. Studies that consider performance on NAEP suggest that by and large, high-stakes testing does not lead to "real" learning gains, but rather manufactured ones that are more likely the result of greater attention to the material that will be tested.

The Amrein and Berliner (2002b), Rosenshine (2003), and Braun (2004) exchange highlights a few important issues. First, findings were simply too inconsistent to conclude high-stakes testing has any type of systematic effect (positive or negative) on learning. A second issue is the importance of including exclusion rates in analyses. Any time averaged test results are reported, one must ask the question of who participated in the testing and who did not. Evidence increasingly suggests that as pressure to perform increases, the lower test scorers are more likely to be removed from taking the test therefore inflating average test scores (Clarke et al., 2003; Nichols & Berliner, 2005). Any analysis attempting to connect high-stakes testing with achievement must account for the test taking pool. A third issue is how high-stakes testing is measured. Rosenshine (2003) found that achievement, when averaged across states, was higher in high-stakes testing states than in non stakes states. However, these findings disappeared when the data were disaggregated by state suggesting that implementation differences probably matter. That is, states with the same amount pressure may yield increases or decreases in learning–a result that could be attributed to the way the policy is implemented and received.

Implications and Future Directions

School psychologists must be aware of the inherent limitations of studies investigating high-stakes testing impact on student achievement. From Lake Wobegon, we learned about the potential problems associated with using the high-stakes test itself as a measure of high-stakes testing policy effectiveness. As Shepard (1990) and many others have now illustrated (e.g., Nichols & Berliner, in press-a; Pedulla et al., 2003), we must be suspicious of the validity of test scores when that test is used for making decisions about teachers and students. Studies of high-stakes testing policy must turn to "audit" tests such as the NAEP for an indication that learning has occurred.

A second critical element of these studies is how high-stakes testing policy is measured. Prior to NCLB and when only a selection of states had implemented accountability-based testing, it was appropriate to employ two group designs (comparing achievement trends in states with high-stakes against those without). However, now that all states employ some type of high-stakes testing policy, this approach is no longer relevant. Instead, researchers must find ways to measure the level of differentiation in their high-stakes testing policy from state to state as did Carnoy and Loeb (2002), Hanushek and Raymond (2005), and Nichols, Glass, and Berliner (2006). From these studies, we see that not all high-stakes testing policies are created equal. Some states' accountability practices are harder or more intense than others. The difference, however, is how this notion of state-level pressure was conceptualized. Carnoy and Loeb looked at the number of laws each state had, Hanushek and Raymond (2005) considered the length of time laws were on the books, and Nichols, Glass, and Berliner (2006) attempted to account for the implementation and impact of these laws. Thus, school psychologists must be critical consumers of the research on high-stakes testing and carefully weigh the efficacy of the conceptualization and measurement of high-stakes testing policy.

Although some of the gains on state developed standardized tests may be due to increased learning, there are data to suggest that much of the gains are a result of drilling and test preparation (Darling-Hammond & Rustique-Forrester, 2005; Jones & Egley, 2004; Shepard, 1990; Taylor et al., 2003). Thus, school psychologists could play a significant role in helping teachers avoid the pitfalls of teaching to the test when they are under pressure. The Center on Education Policy recommends that teachers avoid: (a) using the actual test questions from current test form and teaching students the answers, (b) giving students actual test questions for drill, review, or homework, or (c) copying distributing, or keeping past versions of a test that have not been officially released as a practice exam (Kober, 2002). As "obvious" as these tips seem, I remind readers that as the pressures of doing well on tests increase, so will the temptation to teachers and their students to engage in practices that might encroach on these warnings (Nichols & Berliner, in press-b). Thus, school psychologists must be prepared to support teachers when the stress increases and these temptations become more salient.

Additionally, school psychologists could also be helpful in assisting teachers to cope with their own test related anxiety and that of their students (see Kruger, Wandle, & Struzziero, 2007). As the pressure on teachers increases, they will find themselves increasingly in positions where the morality of their decision making will be challenged. For example, as NCLB marches on, more and more students are likely to fail the high-stakes test, putting more and more of our students in a vulnerable position where they may be retained in school, denied a diploma or scholarship monies. Teachers will be challenged by these dilemmas that ask them whether they should cross the line in order to "save" a struggling student or in order to save their job. These situations will inevitably trigger many difficult questions. Is following testing protocols worth it when students are so stressed out? How hard should I work to keep a struggling student in school when their lowered test score may threaten my livelihood? These are tough questions all teachers and school psychologists will have to face.

Additionally, school psychologists must be armed and ready to face a growing number of students with test related anxiety. As the stakes rise, so too does the likelihood for failure for more of our students. Thus, school psychologists must be prepared to help students cope with and manage their anxiety and fears related to taking any high-stakes test. As part of this, it seems important that school psychologists help all students and all teachers realize that the goals of schooling are much bigger than what the performance on a single test suggests. As all educators are fully aware, students are social beings with complex lives (McCaslin & Good, 1996). In helping students and teachers cope with test related anxieties, it is important to help them gain perspective on the overall importance of the test in the long run. I suspect this will become increasingly harder if we continue to increase the stakes to teachers and their students. Still, school psychologists must be prepared to counsel students that their livelihoods do not rest solely on the performance on a single test.

Although more research is needed to unpack the relationship between high-stakes testing and student achievement, the evidence available provides ample reason to suspect it is not having the intended effect of increasing what students learn. By contrast, the literature is replete with stories about how the pressures of tests transform instruction and curricula to focus almost entirely on preparing for the test (Nichols & Berliner, in press-a). If we continue to hold students and their teachers accountable for performance on a single test, we run the risk of narrowing students' schooling experiences and thereby transforming public education into nothing more than a drill and kill set of exercises and demands.

School psychologists are in a position to play a significant role in voicing the problems and pitfalls of high-stakes testing to administrators, teachers, and parents. Through their voice, perhaps more will come to understand the significant limitations of test scores for representing what students know. Perhaps even more importantly, however, is the need for school psychologists to join with others to voice their concerns to those who set policy. The more often we share with our representatives personal stories of the effects of high-stakes testing on schools, teachers, and students, the more impact we may have for improving the way our students are assessed and our teachers are evaluated.

NOTES

1. NAEP data are not available at the district level.
2. Rosenshine wanted to address what were viewed as flaws in Amrein and Berliner's analysis. Instead of comparing states with high-stakes testing policies against a national average, Rosenshine compared states with high stakes testing policy with those that had no such policies.
3. Exclusion rates are defined as those students excluded from the assessment because "school officials believed that either they could not participate meaningfully in the assessment or that they could not participate without assessment accommodations that the program did not, at the time, make available. These students fall into the general categories of students with disabilities (SD) and limited-English proficient students (LEP). Some identified fall within both of these categories." From Pitoniak, M. J., & Mead, N. A. (2003, June). Statistical methods to account for excluded students in NAEP. Educational Testing Service, Princeton, NJ. Prepared for U.S. Department of Education; Institute of Education Sciences, and National Center for Education Statistics; p. 1. Retrieved February 14, 2005 from http://nces.ed.gov/nationsreportcard/pdf/main2002/statmeth.pdf
4. APR Results (lower number represents lower pressure): KY = .54, WY = 1.00, CT = 1.60; HI = 1.76, ME = 1.78, RI = 1.90, MO = 2.14, CA = 2.56, AK = 2.60, UT = 2.80, MD = 2.82, AL = 3.06, VA = 3.08, WV = 3.08, MA = 3.18, SC = 3.20, NM = 3.28, AZ = 3.36, GA = 3.44, TN = 3.50, LA = 3.72, MS = 3.82, NY = 4.08, NC = 4.14, TX = 4.78.

REFERENCES

Amrein, A.L., & Berliner, D.C. (2002a). High-Stakes testing, uncertainty, and student learning. *Education Policy Analysis Archives, 10*(18). Retrieved January 7, 2004, from http://epaa.asu.edu/epaa/v10n18/

Amrein, A.L., & Berliner, D.C. (2002b). *The impact of high-stakes tests on student academic performance: An analysis of NAEP results in states with high-stakes tests and ACT, SAT, and AP test results in states with high school graduation exams.* Retrieved January 7, 2004, from Arizona State University, Education Policy Studies Laboratory Web site: http://www.asu.edu/educ/epsl/EPRU/documents/EPSL-0211-126- EPRU.pdf

Amrein-Beardsley, A., & Berliner, D. (2003, August 4). Re-analysis of NAEP math and reading scores in states with and without high-stakes tests: Response to Rosenshine. *Education Policy Analysis Archives, 11*(25). Retrieved February 5, 2005, from http://epaa.asu.edu/epaa/v11n25/

Braun, H. (2004, January 4). Reconsidering the impact of high-stakes testing. *Education Policy Analysis Archives, 12*(1). Retrieved February 5, 2005, from http://epaa.asu.edu/epaa/v12n1/

Camilli, G. (2000). Texas gains on NAEP: Points of light? *Educational Policy Analysis Archives,* 8 (42). Retrieved September 21, 2006, from http://epaa.asu.edu/epaa/v8n42.html

Cannell, J. J. (1988). Nationally normed elementary achievement testing in America's public schools: How all 50 states are above the national average. *Educational Measurement: Issues and Practice, 7*(2), 5-9.

Carnoy, M., & Loeb, S. (2002). Does external accountability affect student outcomes? A cross-state analysis. *Educational Evaluation and Policy Analysis, 24*(4), 305-331.

Clarke, M., Shore, A., Rhoades, K., Abrams, L., Miao, J., & Li, J. (2003). *Perceived effects of state-mandated testing programs on teaching and learning: Findings from interviews with educators in low-, medium-, and high-stakes states.* Retrieved January 7, 2004, from Boston College, National Board on Educational Testing and Public Policy Web site: http://www.bc.edu/research/nbetpp/statements/nbr1.pdf

Crocker, L. (2005). Teaching for the test: How and why test preparation is appropriate. In R. P. Phelps (Ed.), *Defending standardized testing* (pp. 159-174). Mahwah, NJ: Erlbaum.

Darling-Hammond, L., & Rustique-Forrester, E. (2005). The consequences of student testing for teaching and teacher quality. In J. L. Herman & E. H. Haertel (Eds.), *Uses and misuses of data for educational accountability and improvement. The 104th Yearbook of the National Society for the Study of Education, Part II* (pp. 289-319). Malden, MA: Blackwell.

Grissmer, D., & Flanagan, A. (1998). *Exploring rapid achievement gains in North Carolina and Texas.* Washington, D.C.: National Education Goals Panel.

Gujarati, D. N. (1995)(3rd ed.), *Basic econometrics.* New York: McGraw Hill.

Haertel, E. H., & Herman, J. L. (2005). A historical perspective on validity arguments for accountability testing. In J. L. Herman & E. H. Haertel (Eds.), *Uses and misuses of data for educational accountability and improvement. The 104th Yearbook of the National Society for the Study of Education, Part II* (pp. 1-34). Malden, MA: Blackwell.

Haney, W. (2000, August). The myth of the Texas miracle in education. *Education Policy Analysis Archives, 8*(41). Retrieved February 5, 2005, from http://epaa.asu.edu/epaa/v8n41/

Haney, W. (2002). Lake Woebeguaranteed: Misuse of test scores in Massachusetts. *Educational Policy Analysis Archives, 10*(24). Retrieved September 22, 2006, from, http://epaa.asu.edu/epaa/v10n24/

Hanushek, E., & Raymond, M. E. (2005). Does school accountability lead to improved student performance? *Journal of Policy Analysis and Management, 24*(2), 297-327.

Herman, J. L., & Haertel, E. H. (Eds.). (2005). *Uses and misuses of data for educational accountability and improvement. The 104th Yearbook of the National Society for the Study of Education, Part II.* Malden, MA: Blackwell.

Jacob, B. (2001). Getting tough? The impact of high school graduation exams. *Educational Evaluation and Policy Analysis, 23*(2), 99-121.

Jacob, B. (2002, May). *Accountability, incentives and behavior: The impact of high-stakes testing in the Chicago public schools.* (National Bureau of Economic Research Working Paper No. W8968). Abstract retrieved June 3, 2006, from http://ssrn.com/abstract = 314639

Jones, B. D., & Egley, R. J. (2004, August 9). Voices from the frontlines: Teachers' perceptions of high-stakes testing. *Education Policy Analysis Archives, 12*(39). Retrieved December 2, 2004, from *http://epaa.asu.edu/epaa/v12n39/*

Jones, M. G., Jones, B. D., & Hargrove, T. (2003). *The unintended consequences of high-stakes testing*. Lanham, MD: Rowman & Littlefield.

Klein, S. P., Hamilton, L. S., McCaffrey, D. F., & Stecher, B. M. (2000, October 26). What do test scores in Texas tell us? *Education Policy Analysis Archives, 8*(49). Retrieved February 22, 2005, from http://epaa.asu.edu/epaa/v8n49/

Kober, N. (2002, June). Teaching to the test: The good, the bad, and who's responsible. *Test talk for leaders, 1*. Retrieved June 30, 2006, from http://www.cep-dc.org/testing/testtalkjune2002.pdf

Koretz, D., & Barron, S. (1998). The validity of gains in scores on the Kentucky Instructional Results Information System (KIRIS). Rand Corporation.

Kruger, L. J., Wandle, C. & Struzzieto, J. (2007). Coping with the Stress of High Stakes Testing. *Journal of Applied School Psychology, 23* (2), 109-128.

Linn, R. L. (2000). Assessments and accountability. *Educational Researcher, 29*(2), 4-16.

Linn, R. L., Graue, M. E., & Sanders, N. M. (1990). Comparing state and district test results to national norms: The validity of claims that "everyone is above average." *Educational Measurement: Issues and Practice, 9*(3), 5-14.

Marchant, G. J., & Paulson, S. E. (2005, January 21). The relationship of high school graduation exams to graduation rates and SAT scores. *Education Policy Analysis Archives, 13*(6). Retrieved June 30, 2006 from http://epaa.asu.edu/epaa/v13n6/.

Mathews, J. (2006, February 20). Let's teach to the test. *The Washington Post*, p. A21.

McCaslin, M., & Good, T. (1996). The informal curriculum. In D. Berliner & R. Calfee (Eds.), *Handbook of educational psychology* (pp. 622-673). New York: Macmillan.

McDonnell, L. M. (2005). Assessment and accountability from the policymaker's perspective. In J. L. Herman & E. H. Haertel (Eds.), *Uses and misuses of data for educational accountability and improvement. The 104th Yearbook of the National Society for the Study of Education, Part II* (pp. 35-54). Malden, MA: Blackwell.

Neill, M., Guisbond, L., & Schaeffer, B. (with Madison, J. & Legeros, L.). (2004). *Failing our children: How "No Child Left Behind" undermines quality and equity in education and an accountability model that supports school improvement*. Cambridge, MA: Fairtest.

Nichols, S., & Berliner, D. C. (2007). *Collateral damage: How high-stakes testing corrupts America's schools*. Cambridge, MA: Harvard Education Press.

Nichols, S., & Berliner, D. C. (2007). The pressure to cheat in a high-stakes testing environment. In E. Anderman and T. Murdock (Eds.), *Psychological Perspectives on Academic Cheating* (pp. 289-312). NY: Elsevier.

Nichols, S. & Berliner, D. C. (2005, March). *The inevitable corruption of indicators and educators through high-stakes testing*. Retrieved March 23, 2005, from the Great Lakes Center Web site: http://www.greatlakescenter.org/pdf/EPSL-0503-101-EPRU.pdf

Nichols, S., Glass, G. V., & Berliner, D.C. (2006). High-stakes testing and student achievement: Does accountability pressure increase student learning? *Education Policy Analysis Archives, 14*(1). Retrieved June 9, 2006 from http://epaa.asu.edu/epaa/v14n1/

Orfield, G. & Kornhaber, M.L. (Eds.). (2001). *Raising standards or raising barriers? Inequality and high-stakes testing in public education*. New York: The Century Foundation Press.

Palmaffy, T. (1998). The Gold Star State: How Texas jumped to the head of the class in elementary school achievement. *Policy Review, 88*, p. 30-38.

Pedulla, J. J., Abrams, L. M., Madaus, G. F., Russell, M. K., Ramos, M. A., & Miao, J. (2003, March). *Perceived effects of state-mandated testing programs on teaching and learning: Findings from a national survey of teachers.* Retrieved January 7, 2004, from Boston College, National Board on Educational Testing and Public Policy Web site: http://www.bc.edu/research/nbetpp/statements/nbr2.pdf

Peterson, P. E., & West, M. R. (Eds). (2003). *No Child Left Behind? The politics and practice of school accountability.* Washington, DC: Brookings Institute.

Phelps, R. P. (Ed.) (2005). *Defending standardized testing.* Mahwah, NJ: Erlbaum.

Phillips, G. W. (1990). The Lake Wobegon effect. *Educational Measurement: Issues and Practice, 9*(3), 3, 14.

Raymond, M. E., & Hanushek, E. A. (2003). High-stakes research [Electronic version]. *Education Next 3*(3), pp. 48-55.

Roderick, M., Jacob, B. A., & Byrk, A. S. (2002). The impact of high-stakes testing in Chicago on student achievement in promotional gate grades. *Educational Evaluation and Policy Analysis, 24*(4), 333-357.

Rosenshine, B. (2003, August 4). High-stakes testing: Another analysis. *Education Policy Analysis Archives, 11*(24). Retrieved January 7, 2004, from http://epaa.asu.edu/epaa/v11n24/

Ryan, J. E. (2004). The perverse incentives of the No Child Left Behind Act. *New York University Law Review, 79*, 932-989.

Shepard, L. A. (1990). Inflated test scores gains: Is the problem old norms or teaching the test? *Educational Measurement: Issues and Practice, 9*(3), 15-22.

Taylor, G., Shepard, L., Kinner, F., & Rosenthal, J. (2003). *A survey of teachers' perspectives on high-stakes testing in Colorado: What gets taught, what gets lost.* (CSE Technical Report 588: CRESST/CREDE/University of Colorado at Boulder). Los Angeles: University of California.

Torgerson, W. S. (1960). *Theory and methods of scaling.* New York: John Wiley.

Valenzuela, A. (Ed.). (2005) *Leaving children behind: How "Texas-style" accountability fails Latino youth.* Albany, NY: State University of New York Press.

doi:10.1300/J370v23n02_04

The Unintended Outcomes of High-Stakes Testing

Brett D. Jones

Virginia Tech

SUMMARY. Although it is important to evaluate the intended outcomes of high-stakes testing, it is also important to evaluate the unintended outcomes, which might be as important or more important than the intended outcomes. The purpose of this paper is to examine some of the unintended outcomes of high-stakes testing, including those related to: (a) using tests as a means to hold educators accountable, (b) the effects on instruction, (c) the effects on student and teacher motivation, and (d) the effects on students who are at-risk of school failure. In examining the evidence, I conclude that while some unintended outcomes of high-stakes testing have been positive, many of the unintended outcomes have been negative. Hopefully, through a greater awareness of the unintended outcomes, school psychologists can work to minimize the negative effects of testing on students and educators. doi:10.1300/J370v23n02_05 *[Article copies available for a fee from The Haworth Document Delivery Service: 1-800-HAWORTH. E-mail address: <docdelivery@haworthpress.com> Website: <http://www.HaworthPress.com> © 2007 by The Haworth Press, Inc. All rights reserved.]*

Address correspondence to: Brett D. Jones, Virginia Tech, School of Education, 310 War Memorial Hall (0313), Blacksburg, VA 24061 (E-mail: brettjones@vt.edu).

[Haworth co-indexing entry note]: "The Unintended Outcomes of High-Stakes Testing." Jones, Brett D. Co-published simultaneously in *Journal of Applied School Psychology* (The Haworth Press, Inc.) Vol. 23, No. 2, 2007, pp. 65-86; and: *High Stakes Testing: New Challenges and Opportunities for School Psychology* (ed: Louis J. Kruger, and David Shriberg) The Haworth Press, Inc., 2007, pp. 65-86. Single or multiple copies of this article are available for a fee from The Haworth Document Delivery Service [1-800-HAWORTH, 9:00 a.m. - 5:00 p.m. (EST). E-mail address: docdelivery@haworthpress.com].

Available online at http://japps.haworthpress.com
© 2007 by The Haworth Press, Inc. All rights reserved.
doi:10.1300/J370v23n02_05

KEYWORDS. High stakes tests, unintended outcomes, accountability, instructional effects, motivation

INTRODUCTION

Educators and researchers have noted the unintended outcomes of standardized testing for many years (e.g., Smith, 1991), especially those that have negative effects on students. Recently, however, the widespread use of standardized tests for high-stakes decisions regarding students and educators has magnified the impact of the unintended consequences and created other unforeseen consequences. The purpose of this paper is to examine some of the unintended outcomes of high-stakes testing with a particular focus on those that affect students who are at-risk of school failure. In the first part of this paper, I describe some of the unintended outcomes related to: (a) using tests as a means to hold educators accountable, (b) the effects on instruction, and (c) the effects on student and teacher motivation. In the second part, I discuss the unintended effects on students with learning or behavioral problems, students from economically impoverished families, students from minority groups, and students with limited English proficiency.

Although I refer to the outcomes in this article as *unintended*, it is impossible to determine whether these outcomes were intended or unintended. Therefore, it might be more accurate to define unintended outcomes as those that were not the primary intended outcome according to the *Statement of Purpose* provided in Title I of the *No Child Left Behind Act of 2001* (NCLB, 2002): "The purpose of this title is to ensure that all children have a fair, equal, and significant opportunity to obtain a high-quality education and reach, at a minimum, proficiency on challenging state academic achievement standards and state academic assessments" (Title I, Sect. 1001, 20 USC 6301, para. 1).

UNINTENDED OUTCOMES
FOR STUDENTS AND EDUCATORS

The Use of Standardized Tests for Accountability

One of the main purposes of NCLB (2002) was to increase accountability related to student achievement by mandating states to implement statewide assessments (U.S. Department of Education, n.d.). Some teachers have suggested that such accountability was needed. For example, one Florida teacher reported: "I believe that the [testing] has made teachers accountable for teaching the Sunshine State Standards. We had the Sunshine State Standards, but until there was the accountability, not all teachers were using them" (Jones & Egley, 2004c, *Themes 1 and 6*, para. 14). The viewpoint presented by this teacher suggests that using test scores to hold teachers accountable is working as intended. In fact, 90% of teachers in one study reported that teachers should be accountable for their teaching (Reese, Gordon, & Price, 2004).

Many educators and researchers, however, believe that using high-stakes test scores to hold students, teachers, and schools accountable is improper and unfair (Abrams, Pedulla, & Madaus, 2003; Haney, 2002; Popham, 1999, 2000). Some educators claim that it is unfair to compare students on a one-time standardized test because children develop at different rates and come from different backgrounds. They claim that many factors related to student achievement are out of their control, such as students' parental involvement, socioeconomic status, and home life (Jones & Egley, 2004c). For this reason, they report that it is particularly unfair to compare schools that serve different populations (Jones & Egley, 2004a). Empirical evidence appears to support these concerns. For instance, Reeves (2000) found that 30-40% of the variation in test scores between districts in Kentucky could be attributed to contextual effects that were not under the direct control of teachers and administrators. Similarly, Wilkins (2000) found that nearly 50% of the variance in test passing rates in Virginia was determined by factors unrelated to schooling such as household income and parental education (cited in English, 2002).

Several professional organizations, such as the National Association of School Psychologists (NASP), the American Psychological Association, and the American Educational Research Association (AERA) also support the position that a single test score should not be used to make high-stakes decisions for students. For example, NASP stated that: "NASP strongly opposes the use of large-scale testing as the *sole determinant* for making critical, high stakes decisions about individual students and educational systems, including access to educational opportunity, retention or promotion, graduation or receipt of a diploma" (NASP, 2003, para. 2). AERA made a similar statement: "Decisions that affect individual students' life chances or educational opportunities should not be made on the basis of test scores alone" (2004, para. 6). Clearly, these organizations are opposed to using test scores alone to make high-stakes decisions; yet, this is exactly how these scores have been used.

One of the problems with relying solely on test scores to make high-stakes decisions is that it involves making inferences about the quality of teachers, administrators, and schools. Popham (2000) explains, from a measurement perspective, why it is unacceptable to make these inferences about educational quality using standardized test scores:

> When standardized achievement tests are employed to ascertain educational quality it really is like measuring temperature with a tablespoon. Tablespoons have a different measurement mission than indicating how hot or cold something is. Standardized achievement tests also have a different measurement mission than indicating how good or bad a school is. Standardized achievement tests should be used to make the comparative interpretations that they were intended to provide. They should not be used to judge educational quality. (p. 400)

Despite these types of warnings by educators and measurement experts, student test scores have consistently been used to rate the quality of schools, especially in states such as Florida where schools are given a letter grade (i.e., A, B, C, D, F) based on students' test scores. In fact, the Governor of Florida, Jeb Bush, has called using test scores to assess schools a "key innovation" (Bush, 2003).

Because the school ratings are reported publicly in newspapers and on state websites (e.g., http://fcat.fldoe.org/), the rating becomes a label for the school. Limiting a school's quality to a rating oversimplifies the complexity of factors that contribute to a quality education. For instance, in Florida, half of a school's grade is based on students' reading test scores, one-third is based on students' mathematics test scores, and one-sixth is based on students' writing test scores. By limiting a school's rating to these academic areas, other important factors are excluded from the rating, such as student work samples, student dropout rate, types and number of courses offered, number of advanced placement courses taken, extracurricular activities available, and students' attitude toward and interest in school (Popham, 2004). As an example of how limiting this view of educational quality is, a parent at one Florida school found the "F" rating of her child's school surprising: "When people look at the grade, they're going to think that the teachers are failing the students. That has absolutely not been my experience" (Gilmer, 2002, p. B6).

Student test scores are also being used to judge teachers. For example, some school districts (e.g., Denver, Houston) have begun to tie teacher pay to students' test scores, a practice that involves the use of second-level inferences that Popham has warned against (Popham, 2000). In Houston, if students improve on state and national tests, teachers are given as much as $3,000 in extra pay (HISD Connect, n.d.). Teachers who motivate students or help students develop socially or emotionally are not rewarded under such a system. The unintended outcome, therefore, is that the test scores have become the sole measure of teacher and school quality, which severely limits what is considered to be quality teaching and a quality education.

Effects on Instruction

There is strong evidence that high-stakes testing has coerced teachers into aligning their curriculum to the areas tested (e.g., Firestone, Mayrowetz, & Fairman, 1998). On one hand, this may be considered a positive consequence of high-stakes testing in that teachers should be responsible for teaching the state curriculum. As an example, teachers and administrators in one Ohio district found that testing helped the school system align the curriculum between grade levels, helped educators identify curricular weaknesses, and made educators more conscious of educational outcomes (DeBard & Kubow, 2002). Similarly, some teachers in Florida were pleased that the testing had standardized the curriculum across the state and that it had given teachers a standard to which to teach (Jones & Egley, 2004c).

On the other hand, state curricula are too extensive to be accurately measured with a one-time standardized test. As a result, standardized tests are generally limited to only a few subjects such as reading, writing, and mathematics. A possible negative outcome, therefore, is that the curriculum is limited to the subjects tested. Other subjects such as social sciences, health, music, art, and physical education take a back seat and may be excluded completely from the curriculum (Jones, Jones, & Hargrove, 2003).

A related curriculum concern is that the goal of schooling is being restricted to passing standardized tests. School has become limited to developing basic academic and cognitive skills and, in some cases, thinking skills. As a result, the emphasis on other major goals such as developing students' creativity, self-concept, interpersonal relations, ability to be self-directed, ability to become involved in a democracy, emotional and physical well-being, moral and ethical character, and ability to contribute to the development of a better society (Goodlad, 1979), might be diminishing. For instance, Horn (2003) found that the 10th grade English Language Arts test in Massachusetts was ensuring proficiency in only a subset of skills that have been defined as essential for work in the new millennium.

Some teachers believe that the limited curriculum has made their lessons less engaging for students. Consider this teacher's statement:

> Before [standardized testing] I was a better teacher. I was exposing my children to a wide range of science and social studies experiences. I taught using themes that really immersed the children into learning about a topic using their reading, writing, math, and technology skills. Now I'm basically afraid to NOT teach to the test. I know that the way I was teaching was building a better foundation for my kids as well as a love of learning. Now each year I can't wait until March is over so I can spend the last two and a half months of school teaching the way I want to teach, the way I know students will be excited about. (Jones & Egley, 2004c, *Themes 2 and 7: Effects on the Curriculum*).

A related point made by this teacher is that testing can have a negative effect on students' in-depth learning and understanding. Because some educators believe that the tests cover a wide range of topics in the curriculum areas tested, they might be less likely to devote the time needed for in-depth exploration of a topic. This can be problematic because researchers have found that learning with understanding (as opposed to rote memorization) takes time (National Research Council, 2000). This issue may be worse in states that administer their tests in February and March, a couple of months prior to the end of the school year. In these states, teachers must fit the entire year's worth of curriculum into about two-thirds of the academic year.

In many cases, state standardized testing has not only affected *what* is taught, but also *how* it is taught. Although there does not appear to be any systematic effect of testing on teaching that can be generalized to all teachers and states (Cimbricz, 2002; Jones, Jones, & Hargrove, 2003), several negative effects have been noted. The most commonly cited one on teaching and learning is that teachers feel compelled to teach to the test. Doing so can lead to a focus on low-level knowledge and skills through the use of rote level, discrete, individual drill and skill practice

(Barksdale-Ladd & Thomas, 2000; Hoffman, Assaf, & Paris, 2001). As a teacher in Texas reported: "We try to do hands-on kinds of things actively involving students, but we realize we have to spend lots of time on drill and practice with paper and pencil because of the way the test is formatted" (Gordon & Reese, 1997). In fact, teachers in Florida reported spending an average of 40% of their instructional time practicing test-taking strategies specifically designed to help students score higher on tests (Jones & Egley, 2004b).

The "three-point-five essay" is one example of how Florida's tests have affected instruction. This type of essay gets its name from the fact that a student's response to a prompt on the writing test consists of three points in five paragraphs. Some educators teach this formula to help students pass Florida's 45 minute writing test. The administrator of Florida's Department of Education's Assessment and School Performance Office admits that a three-point-five essay will allow a student to pass the writing test (cited in Catalanello, 2004). The writing project coordinator for one school district in Florida calls it "test-writing"; and unfortunately, she sees it as having negative effects. She states: "We teach the love of writing right out of kids" (cited in Catalanello, 2004). However, with the pressure for students to pass the test, it is understandable why a teacher would choose to use this proven and acceptable method.

Teachers have reported that formulaic approaches have stifled their teaching ability and creativity, including limiting their ability to meet the learning needs of students (Jones & Egley, 2004c). Teachers have noted that students are often not ready for the knowledge and skills they are teaching, but that they have to rush through the curriculum to cover the content before the test. This issue is exacerbated in some districts in states such as North Carolina and Florida that have implemented "pacing calendars" to show which topics should be covered on any particular day. For example, 8,800 third-graders in one Florida school district were scheduled to read *Little Grunt and the Big Egg* from October 13 to October 21 in 2004 (Tobin & Winchester, 2004, October 4). Such a rigid schedule does not allow the flexibility that might be needed to meet the individual needs of students.

Effects on Student and Teacher Motivation

To understand how testing has affected student and teacher motivation, it is helpful to consider some of the various ways in which motivation has been defined and measured in educational settings (see Pintrich & Schunk, 2002, for a complete discussion). One useful definition divides a student's motivation into either intrinsic or extrinsic. Students are intrinsically motivated when they engage in an activity because they enjoy it or are interested in it; whereas, students are extrinsically motivated when they engage in an activity as a means to an end (Pintrich & Schunk, 2002).

High-stakes tests are inherently extrinsic motivators because they focus students on the end result: passing the test. The main reward for passing a high-stakes test is that the student will be allowed to pass to the next grade level and/or that her school will be rated highly (which may result in public praise and monetary rewards for the school). Other rewards have also been given to students who score highly, including limousine rides (George, 2001), new bicycles (George, 2001), and pizza parties (Firestone & Mayrowetz, 2000). These types of rewards make it clear to students that an important aim of schooling is to do well on high-stakes tests (Triplett, Barksdale, & Leftwich, 2003); thus, promoting extrinsic motivation.

Unfortunately, few studies have assessed the impact of testing on student motivation by querying students or by distinguishing between intrinsic and extrinsic motivation. As a result, it is impossible to make definitive statements about how testing has affected students' intrinsic or extrinsic motivation. However, one of the few studies to ask students about their motivation found that 83% of elementary and 45% of secondary students in an Ohio school district agreed that testing had motivated them to study (DeBard & Kubow, 2002). This seems to suggest that at least some students are extrinsically motivated by testing. While this might appear to be a laudable outcome of high-stakes testing, research suggests that extrinsic rewards decrease intrinsic motivation in the long term when perceived as controlling (Deci, 1971; Lepper, Greene, & Nisbett, 1973). The unintended outcome, therefore, is that students might enjoy school subjects less in the future even though they appear to be more motivated in the short term by extrinsic rewards.

In fact, from the inception of the high-stakes testing movement, researchers have warned that high-stakes testing could undermine students' intrinsic motivation (Kellaghan, Madaus, & Raczek, 1996). Researchers who have asked teachers about how testing had affected students' "love of learning" (which is one measure of students' intrinsic motivation) have found that most teachers find testing to have a negative effect on students' love of learning or no effect at all on it (Jones et al., 1999; Rapp, 2002; Yarbrough, 1999). This makes sense given that the focus of testing is on the end result of passing the test with little incentive for teachers to foster students' natural curiosity and intrinsic motivation. One teacher noted: "School is becoming a drudgery for teachers and students alike. Yes, standards are important and schools should work to ensure every child's success, however, not at the expense of the love of learning" (Jones & Egley, 2004c, *Student Motivation*, para. 2). More research is needed to better understand how testing has affected students' intrinsic motivation and which students are most affected.

There is much evidence, however, to suggest that testing has created a stressful environment for students. Both students and teachers have reported negative effects on students related to testing such as worry, anxiety, nervousness, sweat, tears, stomach aches, irritability, vomiting, headaches, and loss of sleep (DeBard & Kubow, 2002; Hoffman, Assaf, & Paris, 2001; Jones et al., 1999; Triplett, Barksdale, & Leftwich, 2003). In an interesting study, Wheelock, Bebell, and Haney (2000) found that students who were asked to draw a self-portrait in testing situations depicted themselves as anxious, angry, bored, pessimistic, and withdrawn from high-stakes tests.

Maybe the most serious outcome of these negative effects on student motivation is that students may drop out of school altogether. Although students drop out for various reasons, high school graduation exams appear to increase the number of student retentions, which has increased the dropout rate (Amrein & Berliner, 2003; Haney, 2000; Jacob, 2001). Testing has increased retention rates by requiring students to pass tests to be promoted to the next grade and by pressuring some teachers to retain students who they doubt will pass the tests in the following year without being retained (Amrein & Berliner, 2003; McNeil, 2000). Retaining more students has likely increased dropout rates due to the fact that students who are retained are significantly more likely to drop out of school (Goldschmidt & Wang, 1999). Sadly, some teachers choose to spend less attention on students who are not likely to pass the tests, focusing instead on the "bubble kids" who can pass with a little extra help and who will give the teacher and school the biggest return on their investment (Booher-Jennings, 2006). Exactly who is dropping out and to what extent has been hotly debated because researchers have used different sets of data and different methods for calculating dropout rates (see Bracey, 2006, for a discussion). Consequently, it is difficult to state with certainty the extent of the dropout problem, although there is mounting research to suggest that testing policies have had an adverse effect on it (Wheelock, 2003).

Many *teachers* have also experienced increased stress from the pressure of the tests which has led some teachers to report negative attitudes towards the profession, lower teacher morale, less enjoyment in their job, and an increase in teacher attrition (Center on Education Policy, 2006; DeBard & Kubow, 2002; Jones & Egley, 2004c). With respect to attrition, 85% of Texas teachers in one study agreed that some of the best teachers are leaving the field because of high-stakes testing (Hoffman, Assaf, & Paris, 2001) and 52% of teachers surveyed in two large Florida districts reported having thought about leaving the teaching profession in the past year (Tobin & Ave, 2006). Interestingly, some teachers who stay in the profession have reported that they wanted to transfer out of tested grades (Abrams, Pedulla, & Madaus, 2003). Moreover, some Florida administrators, especially those in rural schools, have reported that their school rating had negatively affected their ability to attract high quality teachers (Egley & Jones, 2004a). Teacher resignations and difficulty in teacher recruitment are two possible consequences that could severely affect the quality of education provided by schools. It is worth noting that the research about the effects of testing on teachers presented here is based on teacher perceptions, which is appropriate for assessing teachers' level of stress, attitudes towards the profession, morale, and enjoyment of their job. However, an analysis of actual attrition rates would be useful in verifying teachers' beliefs about teacher recruitment and retention.

Other Effects on Education

Educators, policy makers, and the general public have cited other negative effects of testing beyond those discussed previously in this paper. Among them is that testing is costly to implement and takes money away from more critical needs. For example, the cost for developing, administering, scoring, and reporting all components of the state testing program in Florida is about $42 million per year (Florida Department of Education, 2003). The Connecticut State Department of Education estimated that the costs of NCLB to the State Department of Education would be about $112.2 million in staff time and actual dollar outlay from 2002 through 2008 (Connecticut State Department of Education, 2005). Because the State of Connecticut only expected to receive $70.6 million from the federal government to cover these costs, the burden has fallen on the state to pay the $41.6 million difference. Consequently, the Commissioner of Education in Connecticut reported that that this money could have been spent on more critical education needs: "In sum, the $41.6 million in staff time and additional financial resources the State of Connecticut needs in order to meet specific NCLB demands could be spent in much better ways–ways that would *truly* leave no child behind" (Connecticut State Department of Education, 2005, p. 29).

Finally, some educators believe that the testing has created a negative image of public education (Jones & Egley, 2004a, 2004c). As one teacher explained, "The [testing] makes schools look bad instead of celebrating many of their successes" (Jones & Egley, 2004c, *Theme 5*, para. 7). The following two newspaper headlines serve as examples of how the media can use test results to help create a negative image of public schools: "Few schools find reason to celebrate: Half of high schools get a D" (Tobin, 2004, June 16, p. B1; in Florida, schools are graded an A, B, C, D, or F); and "Pinellas schools losing their luster" (Tobin & Winchester, 2004, November 21).

UNINTENDED OUTCOMES FOR STUDENTS AT-RISK

One of the purposes of NCLB (2002) is to ensure that *all* children have a high-quality education. To this end, the policy requires that "assessment results and State progress objectives must be broken out by poverty, race, ethnicity, disability, and limited English proficiency to ensure that no group is left behind" (U.S. Department of Education, n.d., *Increased Accountability*). Clearly, the stated intent of NCLB is to focus on at-risk populations that might otherwise be forgotten or treated unfairly. A positive outcome of NCLB is that it has, in some cases, brought much needed attention to these disadvantaged groups. The purpose of the following sections is to examine some of the unintended consequences on these groups that have resulted from the implementation of high-stakes testing.

Students with Learning or Behavioral Problems

Much anecdotal evidence exists about the effects of high-stakes testing on students with disabilities, but the empirical evidence available is limited (see Ysseldyke et al., 2004 for a review). Many of the intended consequences of high-stakes testing appear to be positive in that some evidence suggests that for students with disabilities: scores have increased on high-stakes tests (Filbin, 2002; Gloeckler, 2001; Thompson & Thurlow, 2001), participation in the testing has increased (Schulte, Villwock, Whichard, & Stallings, 2001; Thompson & Thurlow, 2001), and educator and parental expectations have been raised (Gloeckler, 2001; Thompson & Thurlow, 2001).

Nonetheless, students with disabilities continue to underperform on high-stakes tests as compared to their nondisabled counterparts, regardless of the type of accommodations received (Horn, 2003; Koretz & Hamilton, 2001). One explanation for this underperformance is provided by Disability Rights Advocates (2001):

> One reason that high-stakes assessments have a discriminatory impact on students with learning disabilities is because often when the tests were developed, little or no attention was given to how the tests would impact learning disabled test takers. The sample population that is used by test developers to set the average scores for the tests usually does not include students with disabilities. When disabled students are included in the sample population, it is often unintentional, and the performance of these individuals is not separately tracked. Most testing publishers also do not give students with disabilities accommodations they need when testing a sample population, thus leading to a dearth of information and research about the true effect of an accommodation on a testing situation. (p. 3)

As a result of the lack of research about how testing accommodations affect test score validity, test publishers might label the accommodations as "non-standard" or "modifications" because they do not know how they affect test score validity (Disability Rights Advocates, 2001, p. 9). Even with accommodations, standardized testing conditions can unfairly disadvantage students with learning disabilities. For instance, multiple choice tests might not provide the sufficient context needed for dyslexic students who rely heavily on context to identify words (Disability Rights Advocates, 2001).

Many of the unintended outcomes noted previously in this article also apply to students with disabilities. For example, the effects of narrowing the curriculum to the subjects tested can have an equal if not greater negative impact on students with disabilities. As Ysseldyke et al. (2002) note: "The curriculum for students with disabilities may be narrowed in the sense that their remedial courses may prevent them from selecting other coursework that may help direct future vocational goals" (Nelson, 2002, p. 85).

Another often-cited unintended consequence for students with disabilities is an increase in anxiety, although many of these claims are anecdotal (Nelson, 2002, cited in Ysseldyke et al., 2002, p. 89). Even so, it is hard to ignore stories about students whose motivation and self-esteem have been negatively affected by high-stakes tests. Holbrook (2001) describes a few such cases of students who are learning disabled and are unable to pass the pass the Massachusetts Comprehensive Assessment System (MCAS) tests because of their lack of reading ability. Holbrook wrote that "For my fourth-graders, the present MCAS is a ridiculous waste of time, emotion, and self-esteem" (p. 784). Teachers such as Holbrook question why students with documented disabilities are required to take tests that they cannot pass given their disability or current level of cognitive development.

In sum, there appear to be some positive intended outcomes and some negative unintended outcomes associated with high-stakes testing for students with disabilities. Unfortunately, research has not addressed many other important questions related to high-stakes testing and students with disabilities, such as: How has testing affected the practice of "tracking" students with disabilities? Or, how has testing affected how students are provided supplementary services (e.g., summer school, remedial programs, mentors)?

Students from Economically Impoverished Families

Many reasons have been provided for why schools with students from economically impoverished families are less likely to demonstrate Adequate Yearly Progress (as defined by NCLB [2002]) than schools in more affluent areas (Smith, 2005). Of course, this issue is confounded by the fact that many low socioeconomic status (SES) students are also minorities, English Language Learners (ELLs), or both, all of whom tend to score lower on standardized tests. Nonetheless, factors associated with poverty create unique challenges for educators, as is evidenced by the fact that the gap between poor students and non-poor students has failed to close since the implementation of NCLB (Lee, 2006).

A clear correlation exists between poverty and low academic achievement (Berliner, 2006). So much so that English (2002) claims that the achievement gap will never be resolved because SES is a crucial variable in explaining test score variance. In this respect, high-stakes testing could be useful in highlighting the connection between poverty and low test scores and the need for more resources in these high-poverty schools. Unfortunately, what typically has happened is that high-stakes tests have been used to blame educators in high-poverty schools for their lack of success. As one Florida teacher explained, "The [high-stakes test] seems to be a way to make teachers scapegoats for problems plaguing society" (Jones & Egley, 2004c, *Theme 5*, para. 7). Instead of blaming educators for poor test scores, Berliner (2006) argues that our whole society needs to be held as accountable for providing healthy children ready to learn. "One-way accountability, where we are always blaming the schools for the faults that we find, is neither just, nor likely to solve the problems we want to address" (Berliner, 2006, *Conclusion*, para. 3).

Few studies address the effects of testing specifically on the instruction of poor students. However, in studying school districts in New Jersey, Firestone et al. (2002) found that teaching to the test occurred most often in the poorest New Jersey districts. Similarly, in their study of Florida teachers, Jones and Egley (2004b) found that teachers at poorer schools reported spending more time teaching test-taking strategies. Furthermore, poor students are at a disadvantage because teacher quality has a large effect on student achievement (Darling-Hammond, 1999) and poor students are typically taught by less qualified teachers (e.g., Shen, Mansberger, & Yang, 2004).

Other negative effects of testing on low SES students relate to the fact that these students do not have access to resources in their home life to adequately prepare them for certain standardized tests. For instance, students from economically impoverished families may depend more heavily on their school to provide access to cultural, vocational, and enrichment activities because they have little access to these activities outside of school. Yet, as discussed previously, these types of activities have been disappearing from schools as educators narrow the curriculum to focus more on the basic skills in tested subjects such as reading, writing, and mathematics. Further, these limited experiences affect the background knowledge from which students can draw to answer test questions. The following example demonstrates the disadvantage to which low SES students can be subjected when their day-to-day life revolves around survival:

> Teachers gave several examples of the class bias in the SAT-9. Nicole mentioned that there might be a question about airplane travel, yet only two of her students have ever been to an airport. Mary mentioned a reading comprehension question on a passage about a woman who worked in the health profession. The students were required to make an inference on why the woman chose this job. The answer the test creator was looking for was that she enjoyed helping people. However, Mary noticed that her few students who could actually read and comprehend the passage chose

the answer, "because she needed the money." (Wright, 2002, *Social, cultural, and class bias*)

Schools attended by poorer students have also been impacted by high-stakes testing. Hodges (2002) noted that rural schools face unique challenges because they may lack educational service centers, have service centers that lack personnel, or are located in geographically isolated areas. This lack of services can lead to the following types of problems: (a) not having faculty trained in assessment, its administration, or its interpretation; (b) not having access to quality staff development to assess the causes of low test scores, to train teachers to alleviate these causes, or to follow up on success of new methods or programs; (c) not having time and personnel to align state and local standards to the test; and (d) not being able to prepare rural students for the tests or to provide them with information as to the importance of the tests (Hodges, 2002). Some school administrators in rural Florida also claimed that testing had a negative effect on their ability to attract high-quality teachers (Egley & Jones, 2004).

Students from Minority Groups

African-American and Hispanic students continue to score well below White students on academic achievement tests (National Center for Education Statistics, 2004). This finding has often been labeled the "achievement gap" because of the large gap between the higher test scores of White students and the lower test scores of some minority groups. Although some progress has been made in some areas (Center on Education Policy, 2006; Coley, 2003), the achievement gap has failed to substantially close over several decades. Discouragingly, NCLB has not had a significant effect on closing the racial gap (Lee, 2006) and the gap has actually widened for African-American students on the SAT (*The Journal of Blacks in Higher Education*, 2005).

In addition to factors associated with SES, African-American students might be at a disadvantage on high-stakes tests due to a phenomenon known as stereotype threat. Stereotype threat refers to the risk associated with confirming a negative stereotype based on group membership (Steele, 1997; Steele & Aronson, 1995). On high-stakes tests, African-American students might score lower than would be expected based on their abilities due to a fear that they will confirm the negative stereotype that African-American students score lower on high-stakes tests than White students (Kellow & Jones, 2005). For instance, when ninth-grade African-American students were told that a test they were about to take was predictive of their ability on a high-stakes test, they scored lower than when they were told that African-American students typically scored the same on the test as White students (Kellow & Jones, 2005). These findings indicate that one factor in the achievement gap might be the stereotype threat felt by African-American students during high-stakes tests. Consequently, compared to White students, African-American students may be at a disadvantage because they are unable to demonstrate their true abilities on tests in which African-Americans have been shown to consistently score lower than White students. The negative outcome of stereotype threat is not only that African-American students score lower than would be expected on tests, but also that they may be retained or prevented from graduating high school based on these inaccurate test scores.

Students with Limited English Proficiency

Because English Language Learners (ELLs) are often minorities from low-income families (Cosentino de Cohen, Deterding, & Clewel, 2005), NCLB requires that these students are assessed for Adequate Yearly Progress (AYP) in three subgroups: the ELL subgroup, a racial/ethnic subgroup, and the low-income subgroup. Unfortunately, ELL students have consistently scored lower on high-stakes tests when compared to other students (Horn, 2003), which becomes a serious concern for educators who are worried about their school making AYP. As a result, states and districts consider the NCLB requirement for ELL students one of the law's greatest challenges because of the instructional time and resources that it consumes (Center on Education Policy, 2006). Much of the cost and difficulty in administering it is related to the fact that it requires one teacher or administrator to work with a single student (Center on Education Policy, 2006).

Others have questioned whether test scores for ELL students are reliable or valid (Adebi, 2003; Heubert & Hauser, 1999). Some educators are especially concerned that high-stakes tests do not accurately measure student learning and development (Jones & Egley, 2004c; Wright, 2002). In fact, Pedulla et al. (2003) found that nine out of ten teachers did not regard their state test as an accurate measure of what ELL students know or can do. A possible negative effect of such inaccurate test results is that it leads to frustrated students and teachers who do not believe that they have a fair chance to succeed in school according to these types of external measures.

Although many teachers have noted how testing has narrowed the curriculum and forced them to spend excessive time on test preparation, these concerns are paramount for some ELL teachers who have difficulty in designing individualized literacy instruction based on their professional judgment, experience, and expertise because of the amount of time it takes to implement district mandated reading programs (Wright, 2002). For instance, Wright (2002) describes how the curriculum in California shifted to a highly scripted one-size-fits-all model that relies on drills and worksheets leaving little time for reading. The curriculum was adopted because its use had raised student test scores on the SAT-9 in Texas and other parts of California. Such findings have led Wiley and Wright (2004) to conclude that "current federal education policy for language-minority students in need of English language development no longer mandates, nor even encourages, bilingual education" (p. 162).

CONCLUSION

In this article, I discussed several of the unintended outcomes of testing that have been reported, either empirically or anecdotally. It is difficult to generalize the findings from any one state, district, school, or classroom to another because contextual factors mediate the extent of these effects. Even within states, student and educator perceptions can vary significantly. Nonetheless, patterns in the data are beginning to emerge that can help us better understand the effects of high-stakes testing on public education. Unfortunately, many of the outcomes of testing have been negative. Certainly, positive effects of testing have been noted; however, we must continually ask whether the benefits outweigh the negative effects.

Because high-stakes testing has placed a tremendous focus on a single test score as a measure of a student's ability, one of my aims in writing this article was to present some of the many factors that can affect a student's test score. School psychologists should consider these factors when making decisions about students and when discussing the results of high-stakes tests with parents and other educators. School psychologists can use their position to educate students, parents, other educators, and the general public about the limitations of using high-stakes test scores as the sole evaluation of a student's ability. They can advocate for using these scores in combination with other indicators of a student's ability, such as grades, classroom behaviors, and scores on other types of tests and measurements. The use of other measures is especially important for at-risk students given the multitude of factors that can affect their standardized test scores and the often limited test score reliability and validity information available for these subgroups. In using the results of high-stakes tests appropriately and in educating others about the need for multiple measures of students' abilities, school psychologists can help to lessen the intense focus on and importance of high-stakes test scores.

REFERENCES

Abrams, L. M., Pedulla, J. J., & Madaus, G. F. (2003). Views from the classroom: Teachers' opinions of statewide testing programs. *Theory Into Practice, 42*(1), 18-29.

Adebi, J. (2003) Standardized achievement tests and English language learners: Psychometric issues. *Educational Assessment, 8*(3), 231-258.

American Educational Research Association. (2004, December). *High-stakes testing in PreK-12 education.* Retrieved March 30, 2006, from http://www.aera.net/policyandprograms/?id=378

Amrein, A. L., & Berliner, D. C. (2003). The effects of high-stakes testing on students' motivation and learning. *Educational Leadership, 60*(5), 32-38.

Barksdale-Ladd, M., & Thomas, K. (2000). What's at stake in high-stakes testing: Teachers and parents speak out. *Journal of Teacher Education, 51*(5), 384-397.

Berliner, D. C. (2006). Our impoverished view of educational reform. *Teachers College Record, 108*(6), 949-995.

Booher-Jennings, J. (2006). Rationing education in an era of accountability. *Phi Delta Kappan, 87*(10), 756-761.

Bracey, G. W. (2006). Dropping in on dropouts. *Phi Delta Kappan, 87*(10), 798-799.

Bush, J. (2003). *Lessons learned in the Sunshine State.* Hoover Digest, 3. Retrieved April 18, 2006, from http://www.hooverdigest.org/033/bush.html

Catalanello, R. (2004, February 1). Kicking "FCAT essay" habit. *St. Petersburg Times.* Retrieved February 6, 2004, from http://www.sptimes.com.

Center on Education Policy. (2006, March). *From the capital to the classroom: Year 4 of the No Child Left Behind Act.* Retrieved March 30, 2006, from http://www.cep-dc.org/nclb/Year4/Press/

Cimbricz, S. (2002). State-mandated testing and teachers' beliefs and practice. *Education Policy Analysis Archives, 10*(2). Retrieved April 18, 2005 from http://epaa.asu.edu/apaa/v10n2.html

Coley, J. (2003). *Growth in school revisited: Achievement gains from the fourth to the eighth grade.* Princeton, NJ: Educational Testing Service.

Connecticut State Department of Education. (2005, March 2). *Cost of Implementing the Federal No Child Left Behind Act in Connecticut: State-Level Costs, Part I.* Retrieved July 19, 2006, from http://www.state.ct.us/sde/NCLB_Study_2_28_05.pdf

Cosentino de Cohen, C., Deterding, N., & Clewel, B. C. (2005). *Who's left behind: Immigrant children in high and low LEP schools.* Washington, DC: The Urban Institute

Darling-Hammond, L. (1999). *CTP research report: Teacher quality and student achievement: A review of state policy evidence.* Seattle, Washington: Center for the

Study of Teaching and Policy. Retrieved July 10, 2006 from http://depts.washington.edu/ctpmail/PDFs/LDH_1999.pdf

DeBard, R., & Kubow, P. K. (2002). From compliance to commitment: The need for constituent discourse in implementing testing policy. *Educational Policy, 16*(3), 387-405.

Deci, E. L. (1971). Effects of externally mediated rewards on intrinsic motivation. *Journal of Personality and Social Psychology, 18*, 105-115.

Disability Rights Advocates. (2001). *Do no harm–High stakes testing and students with learning disabilities*. Oakland, CA: LD Access Foundation. Retrieved May 3, 2006, from http://www.dralegal.org/publications/do_no_harm.php

Egley, R. J., & Jones, B. D. (2004). Rural elementary administrators' views of high-stakes testing. *The Rural Educator, 26*(1), 30-39.

English, F. W. (2002). On the intractability of the achievement gap in urban schools and the discursive practice of continuing racial discrimination. *Education and Urban Society, 34*(3), 298-311.

Filbin, J. (2002). No more field trips on test days: How students with disabilities benefit from the CSAP. *Inside Special Education, 3*(2), 2. Retrieved April 18, 2006, from http://www.cde.state.co.us/cdesped/download/pdf/inside_fall2001.pdf

Firestone, W. A., & Mayrowetz, D. (2000). Rethinking "high stakes": Lessons from the United States and England and Wales. *Teachers College Record, 102*(4), 724-749.

Firestone, W. A., Mayrowetz, D., & Fairman, J. (1998). Performance-based assessment and instructional change: The effects of testing in Maine and Maryland. *Educational Evaluation and Policy Analysis, 20*(2), 95-113.

Firestone, W. A., Monfils, L., Camilli, G., Schorr, R. Y., Hicks, J. E., & Mayrowetz, D. (2002). The ambiguity of test preparation: A multimethod analysis in one state. *Teachers College Record, 104*(7), 1485-1523.

Florida Department of Education. (2003). *FCAT Myths vs. Facts*. Retrieved July 13, 2006, from http://www.firn.edu/doe/sas/fcat/pdf/myths-facts.pdf

George, P. S. (2001). A + accountability in Florida? *Educational Leadership, 59*(1), 28-32.

Gilmer, K. R. (2002, June 13). 48 A's...and two F's. *St. Petersburg Times*, B1, B6.

Gloecker, L. C. (2001). The door to opportunity: Let's open it for everyone. *State Education Standard, 2*, 21-25.

Goldschmidt, P., & Wang, J. (1999). When can schools affect dropout behavior? A longitudinal multilevel analysis. *American Educational Research Journal, 36*(4), 715-738.

Goodlad, J. I. (1979). *What are schools for?* Bloomington, IN: Phi Delta Kappan.

Gordon, S. P., & Reese, M. (1997). High-stakes testing: Worth the price? *Journal of School Leadership, 7*, 345-368.

Haney, W. (2000, August 19). The myth of the Texas miracle. *Educational Policy Analysis Archives, 8*(41). Retrieved March 30, 2006, from http://epaa.asu.edu/epaa/v8n41/

Haney, W. (2002, May 6). Lake Woebeguaranteed: Misuse of test scores in Massachusetts, Part I. *Educational Policy Analysis Archives, 10*(24). Retrieved July 10, 2006, from http://epaa.asu.edu/epaa/v10n24/

Heubert, J. P., & Hauser, R. M. (Eds.). (1999). *High stakes: Testing for tracking, promotion, and graduation*. Washington, DC: National Academy Press.

HISD Connect (no date). *Teacher Performance Pay*. Retrieved March 29, 2006 from http://www.houstonisd.org/

Hodges, V. P. (2002). High stakes testing and its impact on rural schools. *Rural Educator, 24*(2), 3-7.
Hoffman, J., Assaf, L., & Paris, S. (2001). High-stakes testing in reading: Today in Texas, tomorrow? *The Reading Teacher, 54*, 482-492.
Holbrook, P. J. (2001). When bad things happen to good children: A special educator's views of MCAS. *Phi Delta Kappan, 82*(10), 781
Horn, C. (2003). High-stakes testing and students: Stopping or perpetuating a cycle of failure? *Theory Into Practice, 42*(1), 30-41.
Jacob, B. A. (2001). Getting tough? The impact of high school graduation exams. *Education Evaluation and Policy Analysis, 23*(2), 99-121.
Jones, B. D., & Egley, R. J. (2004, April 15). *Learning to understand or learning to achieve? Effects of high-stakes testing on student learning.* Paper presented at the annual meeting of the American Educational Research Association, San Diego.
Jones, B. D., & Egley, R. J. (2004a). Is testing the right direction? Administrators share their thoughts. *ERS Spectrum, 22*(3), 16-25.
Jones, B. D., & Egley, R. J. (2004b, April 15). *Learning to understand or learning to achieve? Effects of high-stakes testing on student learning.* Paper presented at the annual meeting of the American Educational Research Association, San Diego.
Jones, B. D., & Egley, R. J. (2004c). Voices from the frontlines: Teachers' perceptions of high-stakes testing. *Education Policy Analysis Archives, 12*(39). Retrieved August 23, 2004, from http://epaa.asu.edu/epaa/v12n39/
Jones, M. G., Jones, B. D., Hardin, B., Chapman, L., Yarbrough, T., & Davis, M. (1999). The impact of high-stakes testing on teachers and students in North Carolina. *Phi Delta Kappan, 81*(3), 199-203.
Jones, M. G., Jones, B. D., & Hargrove, T. Y. (2003). *The unintended consequences of high-stakes testing.* Lanham, MD: Rowman & Littlefield Publishers, Inc.
Kellaghan, T., Madaus, G. F., & Raczek, A. (1996). *The use of external examinations to improve student motivation.* Washington, D.C.: American Educational Research Association.
Kellow, J. T., & Jones, B. D. (2005). Stereotype threat in African-American high school students: An initial investigation. *Current Issues in Education, 8*(20). Retrieved October 25, 2005, from http://cie.asu.edu/volume8/number20
Koretz, D., & Hamilton, L. (2001). *The performance of students with disabilities on the New York Regents comprehensive examination of English* (CSE technical report 540). University of California, Los Angeles: Center for the Study of Evaluation. Retrieved March 25, 2006, from http://www.cse.ucla.edu/CRESST/pages/reports.htm
Lee, J. (2006). *Tracking achievement gaps and assessing the impact of NCLB on the gaps: An in-depth look into national and state reading and math outcome trends.* Cambridge, MA: The Civil Rights Project at Harvard University.
Lepper, M. R., Greene, D., & Nisbett, R. E. (1973). Undermining children's intrinsic interest with extrinsic rewards: A test of the "Overjustification Hypothesis." *Journal of Personality and Social Psychology, 28*, 129-137.
McNeil, L. M. (2000). *Contradictions of school reform: Educational costs of standardized testing.* New York: Routledge Kegan Paul.
National Association of School Psychologists (2003). *Position statement on using large scale assessment for high stakes decisions.* Retrieved July 13, 2006, from http://www.nasponline.org/information/pospaper_largescale.html
National Center for Educational Statistics (2004). *National assessment of educational progress: 2004 long-term trend assessment results.* Retrieved August 4, 2005, from http://nces.ed.gov/nationsreportcard

National Research Council. 2000. *How people learn*. Washington, D.C.: National Academy Press.

Nelson, J. R. (2002). *Closing or widening the gap of inequality: The intended and unintended consequences of Minnesota's Basic Standards Tests for Students with Disabilities*. Unpublished doctoral dissertation, University of Minnesota, Minneapolis.

No Child Left Behind Act of 2001. (2002, January 8). Public Law 107-110, 115 Stat. 1425. Retrieved April 18, 2006, from http://www.ed.gov/policy/elsec/leg/esea02/107-110.pdf

Pedulla, J. J., Abrams, L. M., Madaus, G. F., Russell, M. K., Ramos, M. A., & Miao, J. (2003). *Perceived effects of state-mandated testing programs on teaching and learning: Findings from a national survey of teachers*. Boston College: National Board on Educational Testing and Public Policy.

Pintrich, P. R., & Schunk, D. H. (2002). *Motivation in education: Theory, research, and applications*. Upper Saddle River, NJ: Merrill Prentice Hall.

Popham, W. J. (1999). Why standardized tests don't measure educational quality. *Educational Leadership, 56*(6), 8-15.

Popham, W. J. (2000). *Modern educational measurement: Practical guidelines for educational leaders*. Boston: Allyn & Bacon.

Popham, W. J. (2004). *America's "failing" schools: How parents and teachers can cope with* No Child Left Behind. New York: Routledge Falmer.

Rapp, D. (2002). National board certified teachers in Ohio give state education policy, classroom climate, and high-stakes testing a grade of F. *Phi Delta Kappan, 84*(3), 215-218.

Reese, M., Gordon, S. P., & Price, L. R. (2004). Teachers' perceptions of high-stakes testing. *Journal of School Leadership, 14*(5), 464-496.

Reeves, E. B. (2000). High-stakes accountability and contextual effects: An empirical study of the fairness issue. *Research in the Schools, 7*(2), 49-58.

Schulte, A., Villwock, D. V., Whichard, S. M., & Stallings, C. (2001). High-stakes and expected progress standards for students with learning disabilities: A five-year study of one district. *School Psychology Review, 30*, 487-506.

Shen, J., Mansberger, N. B., & Yang, H. (2004). Teacher quality and students placed at risk: Results from the baccalaureate and beyond longitudinal study 1993-1997. *Educational Horizons, 82*(3), 226-235.

Smith, M. L. (1991). Put to the test: The effects of external testing on teachers. *Educational Researcher, 20*(5), 8-11.

Smith, E. (2005). Raising standards in American schools: The case of No Child Left Behind. *Journal of Education Policy, 20*(4), 507-524.

Steele, C. M. (1997). A threat in the air: How stereotypes shape intellectual identity and performance. *American Psychologist, 52*(6), 613-629.

Steele, C. M., & Aronson, J. (1995). Stereotype threat and the intellectual test performance of African Americans. *Journal of Personality and Social Psychology, 69*(5), 797-811.

The Journal of Blacks in Higher Education (2005). The widening racial scoring gap on the SAT college admissions test. *The Journal of Blacks in Higher Education, 49*. Retrieved March 25, 2006, from http://www.jbhe.com/features/49_college_admissions-test.html

Thompson, S., & Thurlow, M. (2001). *2001 State special education outcomes: A report on state activities at the beginning of a new decade*. Minneapolis, MN: University of Minnesota, National Center on Educational Outcomes. Retrieved July 10, 2006, from http://education.umn.edu/NCEO/OnlinePubs/2001StateReport.html

Tobin, T. C. (2004, June 16). Few schools find reason to celebrate: Half of high schools get a D. *St. Petersburg Times*, pp. B1, B4.

Tobin, T. C. & Ave, M. (2006, May 14). Teachers troubled with job, poll says. *St. Petersburg Times*, pp. A1, A6.

Tobin, T. C., & Winchester, D. (2004, October 4). New FCAT push accelerates teaching pace. *St. Petersburg Times*, pp. A1, A6.

Tobin, T. C., & Winchester, D. (2004, November 21). Pinellas schools losing their luster. *St. Petersburg Times*, pp. A1, A10.

Triplett, C. F., Barksdale, M. A., & Leftwich, P. (2003). Children's perceptions of high stakes testing. *Journal of Research in Education, 13*(1), 15-21.

U.S. Department of Education (no date). *Executive Summary*. Retrieved April 18, 2006, from http://www.ed.gov/nclb/overview/intro/execsumm.html

Wheelock, A. (2003). Myopia in Massachusetts. *Educational Leadership, 61*(3), 50-54.

Wheelock, A., Bebell, D. J., & Haney, W. (2000). What can student drawings tell us about high-stakes testing in Massachusetts? *Teachers College Record*. Retrieved July 10, 2002 from http://www.tcrecord.org/Content.asp?ContentID = 10634

Wiley, T. G., & Wright, W. E. (2004). Against the undertow: Language-minority education policy and politics in the "Age of Accountability." *Educational Policy, 18*(1), 142-168.

Wilkins, J. (2000, April). *Characteristics of demographic opportunity structures and their relationship to school-level achievement: The case of Virginia's standards of learning*. Paper presented at the American Educational Research Association, New Orleans.

Wright, W. E. (2002). The effects of high-stakes testing on an inner-city elementary school: The curriculum, the teachers, and the English language learners. *Current Issues in Education, 5*(5). Retrieved March 25, 2006, from http://cie.asu.edu/volume5/number5

Yarbrough, T. L. (1999). *Teacher perceptions of the North Carolina ABC program and the relationship to classroom practice*. Ph.D. dissertation, University of North Carolina at Chapel Hill.

Ysseldyke, J., Nelson, R. J., Christenson, S., Johnson, D. R., Dennison, A., & Triezenberg, H. et al. (2004). What we know and need to know about the consequences of high-stakes testing for students with disabilities. *Exceptional Children, 71*(1), 75-94.

doi:10.1300/J370v23n02_05

SECTION 2:
NEW ROLES
FOR SCHOOL PSYCHOLOGISTS

Providing Academic Support for Teachers and Students in High Stakes Learning Environments

Judy Elliott, PhD

Long Beach Unified School District

SUMMARY. The pressures and demands of educating students have never been greater. Providing effective instruction for all students may be the single greatest challenge facing educators today. This article examines the impact of No Child Left Behind and the Individuals with Disabilities Act on assessment, accountability and instruction for all stu-

Address correspondence to: Judy Elliott, PhD, Assistant Superintendent of School Support Services, Long Beach Unified School District, 1515 Hughes Way, Long Beach, CA 90810 (E-mail: jelliott@lbusd.k12.ca.us).

[Haworth co-indexing entry note]: "Providing Academic Support for Teachers and Students in High Stakes Learning Environments." Elliott, Judy. Co-published simultaneously in *Journal of Applied School Psychology* (The Haworth Press, Inc.) Vol. 23, No. 2, 2007, pp. 87-107; and: *Multicultural Issues in School Psychology* (ed: Louis J. Kruger, and David Shriberg) The Haworth Press, Inc., 2007, pp. 87-107. Single or multiple copies of this article are available for a fee from The Haworth Document Delivery Service [1-800-HAWORTH, 9:00 a.m. - 5:00 p.m. (EST). E-mail address: docdelivery@haworthpress.com].

Available online at http://japps.haworthpress.com
© 2007 by The Haworth Press, Inc. All rights reserved.
doi:10.1300/J370v23n02_06

dents, including students with disabilities and English language learners. This article focuses on what we know about effective instruction and the need for systemic efforts to link classroom instruction to students' learning. Test preparation and the use of accommodations are also discussed within the context of high stakes learning environments. Implications for school psychologists as instructional change agents are provided. doi:10.1300/J370v23n02_06 *[Article copies available for a fee from The Haworth Document Delivery Service: 1-800-HAWORTH. E-mail address: <docdelivery@haworthpress.com> Website: <http://www.HaworthPress.com> © 2007 by The Haworth Press, Inc. All rights reserved.]*

KEYWORDS. Academic support, instruction, academic achievement, achievement tests, high stakes tests

The Individuals with Disabilities Act (IDEA) and the legislation associated with No Child Left Behind (NCLB) have had a substantial impact on the regulations for assessment and accountability programs for all students, including students with disabilities and those learning English as a second language. However, it is amazing to note the variation in degree of implementation from state to state and district to district even in the same state. As we head into another reauthorization of NCLB, it can be said that we, as a nation, have not fully implemented what we were legislated to do five years ago. In the same spirit, we have accomplished a great deal for the betterment of educating all students under both IDEA and NCLB.

Implementation issues pertaining to NCLB can be found daily in national education news. Issues range from the cost associated with the mandated changes to the size of subgroups included in annual progress reports, the lack of progress toward the 2014 mandated proficiency of all students, and the inclusion of students with disabilities and English Language Learning (ELL) students in Adequate Yearly Progress (AYP) reports. There are many questions and discussions swirling around the educational work place–questions that just a few years ago would not have been the topic of discussion. "Is the school you work in a Program Improvement School? Has your school and district met Adequate Yearly Progress (AYP)? What subgroup(s) did and did not make AYP?" Within each of these questions looms the bigger question about what is to be done when accountability goals are not met. And, how can ELL students and students with disabilities show the academic performance that is required for schools and districts to be considered successful under NCLB?

Although this article will emphasize the impact of NCLB and IDEA on special populations, it is also important to note the impact of these laws on all students. Before NCLB, many general education students, including those at risk for failure, and special education students routinely did not participate in state and district assessment and accountability systems. Many reasons exist for this. Some argued that students with disabilities and 'at-risk' students were not learning the content covered on tests. Others suggested that testing would cause undo anxiety and stress for students. The expectations for learning and assessment results were not set at high levels for all students (Elliott & Thurlow, 2004).

In the mid to late 1990's as accountability and assessment systems became more inclusive, the field of education began to look more closely at all student learners. As the emphasis on high test scores began to rise, students who were struggling to learn continued to be referred for individual assessment for special education. During this time, there was no law that mandated that the performance of specific subgroups of students, such as those with disabilities, must be reported both separately and in the aggregate in state-wide assessment and accountability systems. Therefore, students not progressing in the general education curriculum continued to be placed into special education programs. However, the bigger issue was whether they were curriculum disabled or learning disabled. Little emphasis was placed on pedagogy and progress monitoring. As Reid Lyon, former Chief of the Child Development and Behavior Branch within the National Institute of Child Health and Human Development (NICHD) once said, special education was receiving the 'spillage' of general education failures (personal communication). Today, under NCLB and IDEA, all students regardless of how they learn or where they learn are a part of assessment and accountability systems. Under these laws, all students are important participants in the educational process count in policy decisions at the federal, state, and local levels.

The reauthorization of IDEA 1997 in 2004, called the Individuals with Disabilities Education Improvement Act of 2004 (IDEIA 2004) confirmed the participation of students with disabilities in the AYP accountability requirements. The key elements of IDEA and NCLB have created a whirlwind of activities in schools, districts, and states. To a large extent, the whirlwind reflects a need to respond to some very new and innovative requirements–access to the general curriculum, participation in state and district assessments, public reporting of disaggregated results of students with disabilities and ELL students, development of alternate assessments for those students with disabilities unable to participate in regular assessments, accountability that requires targeting AYP toward a goal of 100% of students proficient by 2014 (all students and each subgroup), and a 1% cap on the percentage of students in an alternate assessment who can demonstrate proficiency based on alternate achievement standards. There is also the most recently added provision of allowing up to an additional 2% of students with disabilities to take an alternate assessment based on modified achievement standards. Still pending at the time this article was written are the regulations that will allow this provision initially announced in April 2005 to be implemented. Both IDEA and NCLB have had dramatic effects in their own ways for students with disabilities, ELL and those at-risk for failure–essentially putting them on the educational radar for all to see and, more importantly, to address their needs.

Today's teachers, staff, and administrators all work in high-stakes environments that emphasize the need to produce results. Absolutely key to obtaining these results is the need for ongoing sustained professional development and resources to maximize student performance on high-stakes tests. In this article we will take a look at instruction, test-taking and study strategies, the use of data to drive instruction and the need for accommodations for some students with disabilities. This article will focus on how school psychologists can help teachers with their instructional practices as they work to increase student achievement and performance on district and state tests of accountability.

INTEGRATING STANDARDS, ASSESSMENT, AND INSTRUCTION

An important sequence should be followed to address the achievement of all students, including those most at risk for poor performance. The first and most basic step is for teachers and others, including school psychologists, to know what standards students need to work toward as well as the nature of the assessment that tests those standards. This step is critical to planning instruction on certain skill sets that will be heavily emphasized on a district or state assessment. Of course, next is the delivery of quality instruction that is directly linked to the standards and skills that will be assessed.

Why Is This Sequence Important to School Psychologists?

School psychologists should be familiar enough with this sequence as well as instruction and professional development to support change and to engage in meaningful conversations with teachers and administrators regarding a student's strengths, weaknesses, and the need and appropriateness of robust instructional interventions. In addition, it is important for school psychologists to be aware of and participate in professional development that teachers are required to attend. It is important to know what teachers and administrators are learning, the district's or school site's initiatives, and how to use that information in conversations about student learning when consulting with building staff.

Having targeted discussions about effective instruction and intervention as they relate to concepts, skills, and/or strategies being taught, is critical to ensure equal access and opportunity to learning as well to avoid inappropriate referrals and misdiagnoses. An anticipated outcome of high stakes testing is increased referrals for psycho-educational testing, especially in those states that have exit or graduation exams. Approximately 23 states require all students to pass a graduation exam in order to receive a diploma (Education Week, 2006). Sixteen of these states provide alternate routes to a diploma for students with disabilities. Ten states provide alternate routes for general education students, and yet different alternate routes to a diploma for students with disabilities (Krentz, Thurlow, Vitaliy, & Scott, 2005). For example, on the California High School Exit Exam (CAHSEE), students with disabilities and those on 504 plans are allowed to use any accommodation they need in order to take the test as long as they are written on IEPs and 504 plans. If they use a non-standard accommodation, also referred to as a modification, and they receive a passing score (referred to as a "modified passing score"), then they are granted a regular high school diploma. In June 2006, the first class of seniors were required to pass the CAHSEE to graduate. Last minute urgency legislation in January 2006 provided exemptions for students on IEPs and 504 plans. In other words, any students on an IEP or 504 plan were exempt from having to pass the CAHSEE to graduate (students did need to meet credit/course requirements under the exemption rule).

It is easy to see how these situations might increase the referrals for special education eligibility assessments in all grades, including high school! It is also clear to see why it is so important for school psychologists to have a deep understanding of standards, instruction, assessment, and the larger accountability system for the state and district in which they work. The lack of access to core content and poor instruction can increase student failure and the number of inappropriate referrals for special education eligibility assessments.

For ELL students, protections are virtually non-existent. There is no law mandating accommodation requirements or allowing exemptions, for example, similar to the laws for students on IEPs and 504 plans. Therefore, the issues of standards, instruction, and assessment are magnified for ELL students. The role of the school psychologist as a child advocate and interventionist for ELL students is critical to ensure that these students are not inappropriately referred for testing due to poor academic performance, when perhaps it is an issue of language acquisition or even poor instruction. ELL students with disabilities comprise approximately 9.2% of all students who are ELLs, according to a study conducted in 2001-2002 (Golden & Sacks, 2001). Since this finding was made public there has been much discussion as to whether this may be an underestimate of the true population of these students (National Research Council, 2002). More and more educators are working with students who might speak a different language, who might or might not be literate in their first language, and who might or might not have ever been exposed to a written language, or even have been in an educational setting before. The population of ELL students has grown dramatically in the United States during the past 10 years, much more rapidly than the total student population (National Research Council, 2000).

The impact of language acquisition on learning is only too familiar for school psychologists. ELL students have social and academic languages. Proficiency in both is pivotal to academic success. Two common terms related to ELL students are basic interpersonal communication skills (BICS) and cognitive academic language proficiency (CALP). It is generally accepted that students must reach a threshold of BICS before CALP can develop. Additionally, the development of CALP is dependent on academic reasoning skills which are more likely to exist or develop more quickly if a student has strong language skills in his or her first language (August & Hakuta, 1997; Gersten, Baker, & Marks, 1998). Therefore, if a student is not strong in her first language, she may present as a student with a learning disability when the real issue is language acquisition.

Why Is This Important for School Psychologists?

Whereas it is generally considered that CALP needs more time to develop for success in reading, social studies and science, less time for

CALP development is needed for success in math and language. Now ask yourself–"What is the number one reason for student referral for individual assessment by school psychologists?"–reading of course! There is a strong connection between language acquisition, ELL, performance in core content areas, and referrals. But is poor performance really due to a lack of proficiency in CALP, poor instruction, or a true disability? Regardless of the cause, if an ELL student is referred the likelihood of finding a language deficit may be high. And, if you live in a state where there are different rules or expectations for students on IEPs and 504 plans, there can be an incentive to refer, test, and place ELL students. However, with the recently released regulations for IDEA 2004, we now can use the response to interventions (RtI) to increase the likelihood that robust interventions are used and that progress is monitored, instead of simply conducting assessments for the purpose of determining if a discrepancy between ability and achievement exists. Response to Intervention (RtI) is best defined as the practice of providing high quality instruction and intervention matched to students needs. RtI uses learning rate over time and the level of performance to make important data-based educational decisions (Batsche et al., 2005).

THE REALITIES

Have you ever heard any of the following statements: "These state assessments are too hard for special education students!" "How can we expect ELL students to take these tests when they don't have command of their primary language?" "Why would we make students with disabilities take these tests?"

There are at least three reasons why individuals think that state assessments are too difficult for students with disabilities and ELL students: (a) students have not learned the academic concepts or content, (b) the format of the test is such that it impedes the students from demonstrating what they know, and (c) students need accommodations not allowed on the test.

First, we need to ask why students have not learned the concepts or content. It is due to lowered expectations? Is it the result of a lack of opportunity to learn or of access to the curriculum related to the standards? And, if this is the case, one must ask why? If the goal is for students to graduate with a high school diploma, why are they not learning the same content? There are several states that do allow students on IEPs and/or 504 plans to graduate with a diploma if they meet their IEP goals. An unintended outcome of this might be that educators are less likely to feel responsible for the learning of these students because whether or not these students learn the content they receive the same diploma.

States, districts, and teachers struggle with the barriers posed by the format of the test. That is, we can impact the delivery of instruction and the use of needed accommodations, but we cannot alter or change the format of the state assessments. Simply put, not all accommodations are allowed on state tests. ELL students do not have the same rights as students with IEPs or 504 plans to use accommodations they may in fact need to show what they know and can do. For students with IEPs and 504 plans, it is important that appropriate decisions about the need for assessment accommodations are written into IEPs and 504 plans. Recent reviews of research on accommodations have identified the complex relationships between accommodations and test performance (Bolt & Thurlow, 2004; Sireci, Li, & Scarpati, 2003; Thompson, Blount, & Thurlow, 2002; Tindal & Fuchs, 1999). For example, research has explored what accommodations might have a negative impact on student performance, and what accommodations might have minimal impact on construct validity. While there is much research underway, clearly, more is needed to clarify the impact of accommodations on test performance. Research is needed on the use of accommodations with respect to specific types of test items. Although not all accommodations are allowed on state assessments, and some accommodations may alter or modify the construct being assessed, there have been several landmark legal cases that have challenged the denial of student use of accommodations on state assessments (Elliott & Schrag, 2002; Disability Rights Advocates, 2001, Juleus Chapman et al. v. California Department of Education, 2001).

The trend now is to provide students their civil right to use needed accommodations on assessments and then figure out how to score, disaggregate, or report these assessment results. A complicating element is that in some states, such as California for example, if a student uses a non-standard accommodation or modification, then the assessment is automatically scored as 'far below basic.' Therefore, while we advocate for what a student needs in order to show what s/he knows and can do, the non-standard accommodation might negatively impact the school's or district's scores.

Why Is This Important for School Psychologists?

The importance of school psychologists in facilitating appropriate accommodations should be obvious. Helping teachers and other IEP team members understand the importance of the use of accommodations in instruction and assessment is pivotal to providing students an even footing when they take classroom, district or state assessments. Checklists and resources exist (Elliott & Thurlow, 2004; Thurlow, Elliott, & Ysseldyke, 2003) to provide assistance in making good decisions about accommodations as well as to provide professional development to IEP teams (ASES SCASS, 2005a; ASES SCASS, 2005b).

IMPLICATIONS FOR SCHOOL PSYCHOLOGISTS

There are several things school psychologists can do to help identify accommodations individual students need for classroom instruction, testing and other assessments.

- Talk to the students. Ask each student about what helps them learn, what works, and what does not.
- Ask parents/guardians what they do to help students complete tasks at home. Although they may not speak in accommodation terms, parents have great insight about what their children need and use.
- Use your assessment expertise to identify what strengths and weaknesses a student may have that are directly linked to the curriculum, test, or standard being taught or assessed.
- Teach students how to use their accommodations. Teach students when to use accommodations and when to ask for them.
- Teach the students the importance of self-advocacy. Work with them to feel confident to ask for needed accommodations.
- Help the students understand the impact of the needed accommodations on performance when it is and isn't used.

School psychologists can also help guide careful and complete decisions about accommodations for students on IEPs and 504 plans. In this regard, school psychologists should consider the following guidelines:

1. The decisions about providing accommodations and type of accommodations should not be determined by the student's membership in a particular group, type of disability, the availability of accommodations, or how well a student is performing.

2. Whether an accommodation is needed and the specific accommodations that are needed by a student might change over time as a function of the student's age or skills.

Students who neither have an IEP nor a 504 plan, should also be considered for accommodations as necessary. While most states require students to have IEPs or 504 plans, several states allow any student an accommodation for state and district testing. For students who do not have IEPs or 504 plans but are at-risk for failure, it is imperative to work toward teaching compensatory skills. This teaching should focus on how the student can work toward proficiency without an accommodation. If this cannot be accomplished through effective instruction, intervention, and progress monitoring, then the student might need to be referred for more intensive assessment.

WHAT DO WE KNOW ABOUT EFFECTIVE INSTRUCTION?

Teachers are expected to raise test scores and close achievement gaps of an increasingly diverse group of students, teach huge amounts of content and manage a wide range of behaviors, almost certainly with limited resources. The good news is that research on what works in terms of highly effective instruction has yielded helpful findings. While most of this research has focused on general education settings, recent research has identified, with no surprise, similar trends for special needs students.

A cross-case analysis in Massachusetts urban public schools (Donahue Institute, 2004) identified practices essential for students with special needs. The following is a list of general practices that were identified in this study:

- Pervasive emphasis on curriculum alignment to state standards
- Effective system to support curriculum alignment
- Emphasis on inclusion and access to curricula
- Culture and practices that support high standards and student achievement
- Well disciplined academic and social environment
- Use of student assessment data to inform decision making
- Unified practice supported by targeted professional development
- Access to resources to support key initiatives
- Effective staff recruitment, retention, and deployment

- Flexible leaders and staff who work effectively in a dynamic environment
- Effective leadership that is essential to success

Nationally, the focus on assessment under NCLB has created heightened stress on the teaching force. In addition, the pressure has caused some districts to look for loopholes in reporting requirements (see, e.g., Jones, 2007). That is, some school districts attempt to move students in and out of programs and schools to keep the numbers of certain types of students (e.g., students with disabilities, ELL students) sufficiently low so that they do not create a subgroup large enough to be counted for the purposes of accountability and test scores. A long standing and pervasive argument since the inception of high stakes testing is that the breadth and depth of what is getting taught in the classroom is directly related to what gets tested (Algozzine, Ysseldyke, & Elliott, 1997; Elliott & Thurlow, 2004; Thurlow et al., 2003). If this is in fact true, then why is it that so many students are still performing lower than expected? Individuals can only blame the state or district assessments for so long (e.g., it is too difficult or too long) before they direct their attention to what matters: effective high quality instruction. Although there is no one correct way to teach all students, empirically supported ways exist for increasing student performance through the implementation of effective instructional strategies (Algozzine et al., 1997; Elliott, Algozzine, & Ysseldyke, 1998).

Algozzine et al. (1997) provide a four part conceptual framework for effective instruction that communicates the basic tenets of research-based instruction in a teacher-friendly, strategy-based way. The outline of the framework is provided in Table 1.

In most cases, when a student does not progress at the expected rate, the presumed deficits of the student are assessed. In other words, the problem is believed to reside within the child and testing takes place to see what skills a student lacks. Seldom does an evaluation of the student's classroom take place to examine what classroom factors may in fact be directly related to the reported lack of progress. Without a comprehensive evaluation of the student within the context of the instructional environment, it is often difficult to reliably and validly indicate the environmental causes of poor student progress (see Ysseldyke & Christenson, 2002). Psycho-educational evaluations most often do not include an analysis of variables directly related to academic success such as academic engaged time, opportunities to respond, teacher pre-

TABLE 1. Components of Effective Instruction

Planning instruction	The degree to which teaching goals and teacher expectations for student performance and success are stated clearly and are understood by the student
Managing instruction	The degree to which classroom management is effective and efficient
	The degree to which there is a sense of positiveness in the school environment
Delivering instruction	The degree to which there is an appropriate instructional match
	The degree to which lessons are presented clearly and follow specific instructional procedures.
	The degree to which instructional support is provided for the individual student
	The degree to which sufficient time is allocated to academics and instructional time is used efficiently.
	The degree to which the student's opportunity to respond is high
Evaluating instruction	The degree to which the teacher actively monitors student progress and understanding
	The degree to which student performance is evaluated appropriately and frequently

Source: Reprinted with permission from Sopris West Educational Services (Algozzine, Ysseldyke, & Elliott, 1998)

sentation style, teacher-student monitoring procedures, academic learning time, and teacher expectations.

Teaching Is Complex

Teachers make thousands of decisions every day. Deciding what to teach and how to teach each student makes teachers' jobs even more complex. One way to conceptualize the task is by means of the planning pyramid. Introduced by Schumm, Vaughn, and Leavell (1994) the instructional planning pyramid provides a visualization of the context, topic, and instructional practices that are needed by students (see Figures 1 and 2).

The planning pyramid is based on the idea that teachers need to consider what all students must learn, what some students can and should learn, and what few students will learn. That is, some students will naturally need extensions or more-in-depth coverage of topics, and others

FIGURE 1. The Instructional Planning Pyramid

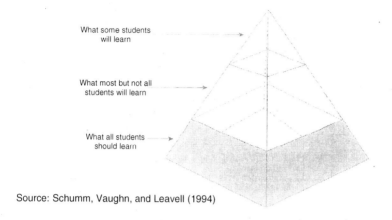

Source: Schumm, Vaughn, and Leavell (1994)

FIGURE 2. A Tiered Approach to Intervention

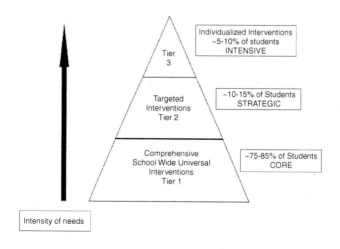

will strive to learn the basic elements of a fact, concept or strategy. One of the strengths of the pyramid is that it provides a way to think and plan within the context of standards based instruction and students' abilities. Whether a student learns at the base, middle, or top of the pyramid is not determined by a student's ability. Rather the planning pyramid takes into consideration a student's prior knowledge, interests, and motivation to learn. Awareness of these factors helps a teacher plan instruction more efficiently.

Students' interests influence their excitement to learn and the ease with which they acquire or learn information. For example, some are more excited to learn about biophysics than others. Still others are more motivated to learn how to make the perfect soufflé. Another important piece is the context in which learning takes place. Learning how to make change in a store is more real than doing so in a classroom lecture format. Knowing where, when, why, and how to make change is contextually important. Instructional practices then, among other things should reflect the student, topic, and context of instruction. Box 1 provides ideas on how the planning pyramid might be used to guide instruction.

The instructional planning pyramid is only one way to look at the breadth and depth of what is taught and its relevance for all students. Because of standards-based instruction and accountability, it is important to obtain tools that allow us to teach all, some, and a few of the skills they need to be successful learners.

RtI also uses a pyramid to guide thinking about intervention planning. However, the RtI pyramid identifies different groups of students. As a general rule of thumb, in this pyramid, the base represents the core instruction that 75-85% of students should be learning. The middle of the pyramid, also known as strategic interventions, is reserved for 10-15% of students needing an additional instruction or methodology to get to where they need to be. The top of the pyramid, also known as intensive instruction is for 5-10% of the student population who need small group and very specific, intense instructional interventions to learn what is required. (Tier 3 does not equal special education!)

In Tier 3, students may be deficient in skills necessary to engage in meaningful learning. These deficits may be due to poor instruction, lack of opportunity to learn, lack of mastery in necessary hierarchical skills to allow further successful learning, and the like. The point here is that Tier 3 is meant to deliver targeted and focused small group instructional or behavioral interventions. Although not the focus of this article, there

BOX 1. Guiding Questions for the Instructional Planning Pyramid

The following questions can be used in a self-questioning process to guide decision making when considering topics of instruction, readiness to teach the material, and student readiness to receive the instruction.

Questions Pertaining to the Topic

- Is the material new or review?
- What prior knowledge do students have of this topic?
- How interesting is the topic to individual students? To me?
- How many new concepts are introduced?
- How complex are the new concepts?
- How clearly are concepts presented in the textbook?
- How can this material be connected to previous instruction? Can it?
- How important is this topic or parts of the topic for students to learn?

Questions Pertaining to the Teacher

- Have I taught this material before?
- How can I evaluate whether students are learning what I am teaching?
- How interesting is the topic to students? To me?
- How can students' cultural and linguistic backgrounds be connected to the topic?
- How much time do I have to plan for the unit and individual lessons?
- What resources do I have available to me for this unit?

Questions Pertaining to Students

- Will students' communication skills make comprehension of a particular topic or concept difficult?
- Will students with reading difficulties be able to work independently while learning about the concept from the text?
- Will a student with behavior or attention problems be able to concentrate on this material?
- Which students will likely have high interest in or prior knowledge of this concept or be anxious to explore this topic in greater breadth and depth?
- What experiences have the students had that will relate to this concept?
- Is there some way to relate this concept to the cultural and linguistic backgrounds of the students?

---

are many good resources and research articles on RtI for school psychologists. A recent publication by the National Association of State Directors of Special Education offers the most comprehensive overview and research based resources available at present (Batsche et al., 2005).

Implications for School Psychologists

School psychologists need to know much more about the instructional environment than ever before. This knowledge is inextricably linked to NCLB and IDEA in many ways. One major unanticipated outcome of these laws is the additional testing accommodations students on IEPs and 504 plans have that other students do not have. Some think that these allowances such as accommodations will help a student's test performance. While there is research to refute that assumption (e.g., see Tindal & Fuchs, 1999; Thompson et al., 2002), perception drives reality and some students might be referred to testing in the hopes that they will qualify for an IEP or 504 plan, and thereby receive accommodations. It is important for school psychologist to educate administrators as well as teachers about the components of effective instruction. It is also very important that school psychologists help other educators avoid making referrals based on erroneous assumptions.

Helping the Student Prepare for Testing

Test preparation is an overlooked aspect of improving test performance as well as instruction. Many test-preparation skills are not identified as critical, because they come naturally to students who do not have disabilities or who are not at risk for failure. Test-taking strategies are beneficial for all students; however, many of these strategies do not appear in typical test-preparation books. School psychologists are in a good position to support teachers to ensure these skills are taught as a part of daily instruction, especially if we know that skill deficits in these areas can result in poor academic performance on classroom assessments. Some of the most common causes for lack of test performance related to test preparation include (Abbamont & Brescher, 1997; Arter, 2003; Elliott & Thurlow, 2004; Rubenstein, 2003):

- Lack of test-taking strategies
- Lack of problem-solving skills
- Lack of strategies to address the psychological stress that comes with testing
- Physical fatigue and stamina
- Lack of personal coping strategies for stressful situations
- Lack of content knowledge of the curriculum being assessed

Implications for School Psychologists

School psychologists can help identify common causes for poor test performance, such as those due to lack of proper test preparation. There are simple strategies for working with teachers and students in regard to addressing these causes. The first strategy is to begin by actively preparing students for testing programs. In doing so, it is important to (a) review basic skills that will be tested (e.g., math concepts, grammar, punctuation); (b) teach students problem-solving skills and provide a variety of practice; (c) teach students test taking strategies that are necessary to address pacing under timed conditions, such as question selection (e.g., making sure one reads all questions and answers those that are easiest first) and setting priorities in terms of where to put test taking efforts; (d) provide full length practice tests to build familiarity, stamina and pacing while desensitizing students to stress that comes with testing; (e) integrate the types of test problems (e.g., multiple choice, short answer, etc.) into classroom assessments; and (f) incorporate test taking skills and strategies into daily instruction. (For a complete discussion, see Elliott & Thurlow, 2004.)

THE CHANGING ROLE OF THE SCHOOL PSYCHOLOGIST

School psychologists are in a prime position to impact many of the variables discussed in this article. Assessment of learning and/or behavior strengths and weaknesses, and identifying robust interventions are key roles in the daily routine of school psychologists. Therefore, knowing all the components that comprise a successful learning environment–standards, effective instruction, curriculum, and assessment–is a great place to start in supporting teachers who have increasingly diverse student populations and real pressures of meeting assessment and accountability benchmarks. Making sure no student is placed on an IEP or 504 plan without real cause is central, and for this to occur one might need to have courageous conversations with teachers, administrators and parents.

LEADERSHIP

It is one thing to have knowledge about components of the learning environment, but it is another thing to take the lead in discussing what needs to happen to ensure that all students have equal and equitable access to standards and effective instruction. It is about leadership. The ability to lead in this arena makes the role of a school psychologist even more valued than ever before. Most often when teachers or parents refer a student for testing it is because they want help for that individual. If people still believe that testing is the only way to get help for a student, then we have not done our jobs in supporting and advocating for what the research on effective instruction has so clearly delineated. Some of the key ways school psychologists can lead in this arena are:

- Ensure there are valid, reliable and well-trained problem-solving teams at the site(s) in which you work. If there is not one, work to set up training to make this happen.
- Do a needs assessment with the teachers and principals you work with to find out what areas of student academic performance and behavior need improvement, Provide training in these areas. Collaborate with curriculum and/or assessment personnel to deliver a credible message.
- Capitalize on the data demands that now exist under IDEA and NCLB. Provide teachers with opportunities to learn or hone their progress monitoring skills. Help build that capacity in your work sites. We have become so dependent on summative data (district/state tests) that often the formative assessments are forgotten. Help teachers understand the importance of frequent data collection and progress monitoring to inform and drive instruction.
- Get in classrooms (and not just for testing purposes). It is necessary that school psychologists be seen as a credible and knowledgeable resource about students learning and instruction. Knowledge about instruction can be a challenge for school psychologists if they have not previously been teachers. However, in order to stem the tide of inappropriate referrals, credible conversations about instruction and robust implementation of research-based interventions must take place. It is more helpful to the students to be called on for your expertise in learning and behavior, rather than simply being asked 'Can you test this student?' You are more likely to be called upon as an interventionist and instructional resource when you have credibility that comes from being in the classroom.
- Finally, familiarity with instruction planning and RtI is pivotal to provide an umbrella under which all interventions take place.

Indeed the role of the school psychologist has changed during the last decade, more dramatically than ever before. It is an exciting and challenging time. With the release of the IDEA 2004 regulations, states and districts will no longer have to focus on a discrepancy model to find a student in need of intervention or special education. Rather, targeted interventions and outcome-based discussions about what students and teachers need to be successful will take place much earlier in the assessment-intervention process. This proactive approach will support teachers' and students' learning in a high stakes learning environment.

REFERENCES

Abbamont, G. W., & Brescher, G. (1997). *Test smart!: Ready to use test-taking strategies and activities for grades 5-12.* John Wiley & Sons: New York, NY.

Advocates for Special Kids (ASK) v. Oregon State Board of Education, Federal District Court,1999, No. CV99-263 K1.

Algozzine, B., Ysseldyke, J., & Elliott, J. (1997). *Strategies and tactics for effective instruction.* (2nd ed.). Longmont, CO: Sopris West.

Arter, J. (2003). Assessment for learning: Classroom assessment to improve student achievement and well-being. In J. Wall & G. Walz (Eds.), *Measuring up: Assessment issues for teachers, counselors, and administrators* (pp. 463-484). (ERIC Document Reproduction Service No. ED 480379).

ASES SCASS (2005a). *How to select, administer, and evaluate the use of accommodations for instruction and assessment of students with disabilities.* Washington, DC: Council of Chief State School Officers.

ASES SCASS (2005b). *The Professional Development Guide.* Washington, DC: Council of Chief State School Officers.

August, D., & Hakuta, K. (1997). Improving schooling for language-minority children: A research agenda. *National academy of sciences–National research council.* Washington, DC: Board on Children, Youth and Families.

Batsche, G., Elliott, J., Graden, J., Grimes, J., Kovaleski, J. F., Prasse, D. et al. (2005). *Response to Intervention: Policy considerations and implementation.* Alexandria, VA: National Association of State Directors of Special Education.

Bolt, S., & Thurlow, M. (2004). Five of the most frequently allowed testing accommodations in state policy. *Remedial and Special Education,* 25(3), 141-152.

Disability Rights Advocates. (2001). *Do no harm: High stakes testing and students with learning disabilities.* Oakland, CA: Disability Rights Advocates.

Donahue Institute. (2004). *A study of MCAS achievement and promising practices in urban special education: Report of field research findings.* Hadley, MA: University of Massachusetts Donahue Institution.

Education Week. (2006). Quality counts at 10: A decade of standards-based education. *Education Week, 25*(17).

Elliott, J., Engelhard, G., Schrag, J., & Vogel, S. (2000). "Students with learning disabilities and the Oregon statewide assessment system." (Report of the Blue Ribbon Panel for Advocates for Special Kids [ASK] v. Oregon State Board of Education.) Portland, OR: Federal District Court.

Elliott, J., Algozzine, B., & Ysseldyke, J. (1998). *Timesavers for educators.* Longmont, CO: Sopris West.

Elliott, J., & Thurlow, M. (2004). *Improving test performance of students with disabilities on district and state assessments.* (2nd ed.). Thousand Oaks, CA: Corwin Press.

Elliott, J., & Schrag, J. (2002, February). *Assessment and accommodation: Lessons learned in Oregon.* International Dyslexia Association.

Gersten, R., Baker, S. K., & Marks, S. U. (1998). Teaching English language learners with learning difficulties: Guiding principles and examples from research-based practice. *Disabilities and gifted education.* Reston, VA: Council for Exceptional Children.

Golden, L. & Sacks, L. (2001, November). *An overview of states' policies for reporting the performance of English-language learners on statewide assessments.* Paper presented at the workshop on reporting test results for accommodated examinees: Policy, measurement, and score use considerations, Washington, DC.

Jones, B. (2007). The unintended outcomes of high stakes testing. *Journal of Applied School Psychology, 23*(2), 67-88.

Juleus, Chapman et al. v. California Department of Education et al., 2001, No. C01-1780.

Krentz, J., Thurlow, M., Vitaliy, S., & Scott, D. (2005). *Alternative routes to the standard diploma. (Synthesis Report 54).* Minneapolis, MN: University of Minnesota, National Center on Educational Outcomes.

National Research Council. (2000). *Testing English-language learners in U.S. schools.* Washington, DC: National Academy Press.

National Research Council. (2002). *Reporting test results for students with disabilities and English-language learners.* Washington, DC: National Academy Press.

Rubenstein, J. (2003). Test preparation: What makes it effective? In J. Wall & G. Walz (Eds.), *Measuring up: Assessment issues for teachers, counselors, and administrators* (pp. 397-415). (ERIC Document Reproduction Service No. ED 480063).

Sireci, S.G., Li, S., & Scarpati, S. (2003). *The effects of test accommodation on test performance: A review of the literature. (Research Report No. 485).* Amherst, MA: Center for Education Assessment.

Thompson, S., Blount, A., & Thurlow, M. (2002). *A summary of research on the effects of test accommodations: 1999 through 2001. (Technical Report 34).* Minneapolis, MN: University of Minnesota, National Center on Educational Outcomes.

Thurlow, M., Elliott, J., & Ysseldyke, J. (2003). *Testing student with disabilities: Practical strategies for complying with district and state requirements.* (2nd ed.). Thousand Oaks, CA: Corwin Press.

Tindal, G., & Fuchs, L. (1999). *Summary of research on test changes: An empirical basis for defining accommodations.* Retrieved September 13, 2006, from mid-south regional resource center: www.ihdi.uky.edu/msrrc/pdf/tindal&fuchs.pdf.

Ysseldyke, J., & Christensen, S. (2002). *Functional assessment of academic behavior: Creating successful learning environments.* Longmont, CO: Sopris West.

doi:10.1300/J370v23n02_06

Coping with the Stress of High Stakes Testing

Louis J. Kruger, PsyD
Northeastern University

Caroline Wandle, PhD
Tufts University

Joan Struzziero, PhD
Scituate Public Schools

SUMMARY. High stakes testing puts considerable pressure on schools, teachers, and students to achieve at high levels. Therefore, how schools and individuals cope with this major source of stress may have important implications for the success of high stakes testing. This article reviews relevant theory and research on stress as they relate to public schools and high stakes testing. Particular attention is given to the negative consequences of stress when the external pressure exceeds the ability of the school or individual to cope with the pressure. The article also reviews strategies that can be used by schools, teachers, and students to cope with stress. doi:10.1300/J370v23n02_07 *[Article copies available for a fee from The Haworth Document Delivery Service: 1-800-HAWORTH. E-mail address: <docdelivery@haworthpress.com>*

Address correspondence to: Louis J. Kruger, School Psychology Program, 203 Lake Hall, Northeastern University, Boston, MA 02115 (E-mail: kruger@neu.edu).

[Haworth co-indexing entry note]: "Coping with the Stress of High Stakes Testing." Kruger, Louis J., Caroline Wandle, and Joan Struzziero. Co-published simultaneously in *Journal of Applied School Psychology* (The Haworth Press, Inc.) Vol. 23, No. 2, 2007, pp. 109-128; and: *High Stakes Testing: New Challenges and Opportunities for School Psychology* (ed: Louis J. Kruger, and David Shriberg) The Haworth Press, Inc., 2007, pp. 109-128. Single or multiple copies of this article are available for a fee from The Haworth Document Delivery Service [1-800-HAWORTH, 9:00 a.m. - 5:00 p.m. (EST). E-mail address: docdelivery@haworthpress.com].

Available online at http://japps.haworthpress.com
© 2007 by The Haworth Press, Inc. All rights reserved.
doi:10.1300/J370v23n02_07

Website: <http://www.HaworthPress.com> © 2007 by The Haworth Press, Inc. All rights reserved.]

KEYWORDS. Stress management, high stakes tests, test anxiety, coping, prevention

THE PROBLEM OF STRESS

Almost two decades ago, Elias (1989) provided an analysis of how educational reform efforts were having the paradoxical effect of creating greater barriers to the academic and social development of students. He argued that schools were becoming too narrowly focused on academics, and concomitantly more pressure was being put on students for academic success, including test-based accountability. Given the current wide spread use of high stakes tests in the United States and other countries, the vexing question about the role of stress in education is more prominent than ever. Some states have linked grade promotion or high school diplomas to scores on high stakes tests. These requirements might be particularly stressful for students who historically have performed less well on achievement tests, including students with learning or behavioral problems, students from economically impoverished families and from minority groups, and students who are English language learners.

Stress has been conceptualized as a reaction to external events or chronic conditions that threaten the physical, psychological, or general well-being of an individual (Grant, Behling, Gipson, & Ford, 2005). Successfully coping with stress is related to good academic performance (e.g., Struthers, Perry, & Menec, 2000). Therefore, it is imperative that school psychologists and other educators understand how high stakes testing and other factors might interact to impact an individual's or an organization's ability to cope with stress, and how stress might be reduced to manageable levels. In order to facilitate this understanding, we first review the research on stress with respect to schools, teachers and students. In the second part of this paper, we focus on stress prevention and intervention strategies with consideration of implications for the practice of school psychology.

School Level

High stakes testing can be viewed as another stressor for schools. Depending on the number of years a school fails to make adequate yearly progress (AYP) in improving high stakes test scores, the No Child Left Behind Act (NCLB) of 2001 mandates successively more intrusive sanctions. Sanctions can range from labeling a school as "needing improvement" to restructuring the school and replacing its staff. Some states also have instituted their own sanctions if schools do not make AYP in improving high stakes test scores, such as putting schools on probation or removing their accreditation (Nichols, Glass, & Berliner, 2006). In addition to federal and state sanctions, many schools that are performing poorly also are confronted by increased scrutiny by the mass media. For example, the Boston Globe provides an annual ranking of the performance of all schools in Massachusetts on that state's high stakes test (Boston Globe, 2005). Such public scrutiny increases the pressure and competition among schools.

Systems theory (Katz & Kahn, 1978) can be used to understand how an organization might respond to a stressful external environment, such as high stakes testing, and when external demands threaten to exceed the organization's ability to meet those demands. In an open system, the organization accepts informational inputs from the external environment and uses these inputs to accomplish its aims and adapt to the external environment. However, if the external demands are excessive, then it is theorized that the organization attempts to cope by restricting the flow of information with the external environment and exerting more control over the internal environment.

Although we could not locate any studies specifically on how schools cope with the stress of high stakes testing, we did find one study (Griffith, 2004) that applied the open systems theoretical framework to stress at the school level. In this study (Griffith, 2004), schools were considered to be under more stress if they had a (a) large percentage of students who were from groups that typically scored low on achievement tests, (b) large student population, and (c) high ratio of actual enrollment to planned enrollment.

The assumption was that these factors would tax a school's ability to cope with external demands, such as making AYP on scores of high stakes tests. The results partially supported the theory. Schools which were experiencing more stress did tend to have less information exchanged with the external environment than schools under less stress. Specifically, these schools had less parental involvement. Thus, the schools which were under the most stress also had the least input from a major stakeholder group who might help the school successfully cope with the external demands. However, there was no evidence from this study that the schools under the most stress also exerted most control over their internal environments. Indeed, the schools which were under the most stress also tended to have more internal disruptions, such as rapid turnover of principals.

Teacher Level

Whereas very little research has focused on the impact of stress on schools at the organizational level, much more research exists with respect to teacher stress. This research (e.g., Johnson et al., 2005) indicates that teaching is one of the more stressful occupations. It has been estimated that somewhere between 5 and 15 percent of teachers are suffering from the effects of chronic stress (Farber, 1991). The job demands-resources theory has been the most influential perspective on understanding occupational stress, including teacher stress (Guglielmi & Tatrow, 1998; Hakanen, Bakker, & Schaufeli, 2006). This theory predicts that individuals can avoid the negative effects of stress if they have access to resources to meet the demands. Thus, high demands, in of themselves, do not necessarily lead to negative outcomes from stress, such as burnout, if the resources are commensurate to meet the demands. Of the different possible resources that might protect individuals against stress, considerable research support has been found for the importance of job autonomy and control (Guglielmi & Tatrow, 1998). Teachers who perceive that they have more autonomy over their curriculum and general teaching are less likely to experience the negative effects of stress (Pearson & Moomaw, 2005).

High-stakes testing poses two problems for teacher stress. First, it potentially heightens the level of stress in an already stressful occupation. Possible teacher sanctions for poor student performance include being labeled a "bad teacher," being associated with a school that needs improvement, receiving mandated supervision, and/or losing one's job (Nichols et al., 2006). In a study of teachers in North Carolina, more than three quarters of respondents reported that their jobs were more stressful as a result of participation in high-stakes testing (Jones et al., 1999). A qualitative analysis of interviews of teachers in two other states, which implemented high-stakes testing, indicated that they experienced pressure associated with the tests from memos, in-school conversations, and media accounts (Barksdale-Ladd & Thomas, 2000). Importantly, stress on teachers may continue even after a good performance on high stakes tests because there may be ongoing pressure to sustain or raise high scores. For example, beginning in 2007, teachers' raises and bonuses in Florida will be directly linked to how their students perform on that state's high stakes test (Whoriskey, 2006).

In addition to increasing the stress on teachers, high stakes testing might constrain autonomy, one of the principal moderating influences on stress (Guglielmi & Tatrow, 1998). In a high-stakes environment, it is important that the curriculum be tightly coupled with the test content. Without such coupling, students are at risk for not being exposed to the content that will be covered on the test, and therefore will be at greater risk for failing the test. This situation inevitably constrains local decision making about curriculum. As Jones (1999) pointed out, in a high-stakes environment, many teachers feel compelled to teach to the test.

STUDENT LEVEL

Although there is no research that directly connects teacher stress with student stress, it is, nonetheless, evident that school-related issues are major sources of stress for children and adolescents. In two surveys conducted in different states in the United States (Anderson, Jimerson, & Whipple, 2005; Yamamoto & Byrnes, 1987), sixth grade students indicated that being retained in the same grade was one of the five most stressful life events. Moreover, in the more recent survey (Anderson et al., 2005), which was conducted in 2001, retention was rated as the most stressful event, even more stressful than losing a parent or going blind. Given the passage of NCLB in 2001, and the subsequent implementation in many states of serious consequences for failing the tests, including retention, the academic stress on students has likely increased.

Concerns about academics, such as tests, grades, and homework are some of the most prominent stressors among high school students (e.g., de Anda, Baroni, Boskin, Buchwald, Morgan, Ow, Gold, & Weiss, 2000). High levels of school-related stress are not confined to the United States. For example, adolescents in England (West, Willis, & Sharp, 1982) and Singapore (Isralowitz & Hong, 1990) also have reported school-related problems as their primary source of stress.

The few studies that have been conducted on the relationship between student stress and high stakes testing suggest that these tests might be a considerable source of stress for students (Cornell, Krosnick, & Chang, 2006; Jones, 2006; Jones & Egley, 2004; Jones et al., 1999). Students who fail high stakes tests constitute an especially vulnerable group. As part of a class action suit, Cornell, Krosnick, and Chang (2006) examined the emotional reactions of more than 900 Minnesota students who were erroneously told that they had failed a high stakes mathematics test. Notably, over 80% of the students reported adverse emotional consequences that included feelings of worry, depression and embarrassment. A survey conducted by Jones and Egley (2004) in Florida indicated that teachers were concerned about stress placed on them as well as their students as a result of high stakes testing. Also, many children in the United Kingdom reported a high level of anxiety and psychological strain when preparing to take that country's high stakes assessments (Denscombe, 2000).

Although relatively little of the stress research has focused on high stakes testing, research on other variables suggest how an additional major stressor in a student's life, such as high stakes testing, might impact an individual. For example, the cumulative effect of multiple stressful events can predispose adolescents for maladjustment (Kim, 2005; Printz, Shermis, & Webb, 1999). Stressors at home and school have been found to be related to students' shorter attention spans and lower academic motivation, factors that can impair academic performance (Pryor-Brown & Cowen, 1989). Furthermore, multiple stressful life events predict later psychological problems in adolescents (Grant, Compas, Thurm, McMahon, & Gipson, 2004).

Potential Protective Factors

Although research supports the relationship between stress and negative outcomes, such as dropping out of school (e.g., Hess & Copeland, 2001), other factors can either strengthen or weaken this relationship. Coping style, social support, and motivation can potentially protect students from the negative effects of stress.

An individual's coping style seems to have an important role in determining to what extent stress negatively impacts one's mental health (Compas, Champion, & Reeslund, 2005) and academic performance (Struthers et al., 2000). Coping can be defined as efforts to manage demands that are perceived to tax or exceed the person's resources or ability to meet those demands (Folkman & Lazarus, 1984). Compas et al. (2005) differentiated between voluntary engagement coping and voluntary disengagement coping. Voluntary engagement coping involves active attempts to (a) change some aspect of the stressful situation, (b) change one's emotional reactions to the stressor, or (c) adapt to the stressor. Voluntary disengagement coping involves emotional, physical, or cognitive avoidance of the stressor. Compas et al. (2005) reported that voluntary engagement coping is more likely than voluntary disengagement coping to result in positive outcomes for adolescents. Struthers et al. (2000), for example, found that college students who used problem-focused coping, a type of voluntary engagement coping that focuses on changing some aspect of the stressful situation, tended to attain higher grades. In addition, college students who used voluntary engagement coping strategies also tended to persist longer in college (Shields, 2001). In contrast, the use of avoidance, a type of voluntary disengagement coping, has led to negative outcomes. For example, Sandler, Tein, and West (1994) found that children who used avoidant coping strategies were more likely to report symptoms associated with depression, anxiety, and conduct problems than those who used active, problem-solving strategies. The negative outcomes associated with avoidant coping are particularly relevant for adolescents with learning disabilities, because they seem to be more likely to use that strategy in coping with school-related stress (Geisthardt & Munsch, 1996).

Another possible protective factor is social support. Social support involves the communication of assurance and acceptance, as well as providing information or assistance (Albrecht & Adelman, 1987). Although social support, in general, has been shown to have an inverse relationship to the negative effects of stress (Albrecht & Adelman, 1987), the evidence has been inconsistent across studies (Grant et al., 2004). Printz, Shermis and Webb (1999), for example, found that social support by itself did not mediate the relationship between stress and adolescent adjustment. However, when adolescents used problem solving (a type of voluntary engagement coping) in combination with social support they were less likely to experience the negative effects of stress. Thus, the presence of multiple protective factors might decrease the likelihood that stress will have deleterious effects.

Another factor that seems to be an important mediator between stress and academic performance is motivation. Keogh, Bond, and Flaxman (2005), for example, found that changes in academic motivation mediated between the effects of a stress management program and the students' subsequent performance on a high stakes test in the United Kingdom. Similarly, Struthers et al. (2000) found that academic motivation mediated between a high level of stress and academic performance in college students. Linnenbrink and Pintrich (2002), in their review of the research of academic motivation, identified four dimensions of motivation that were related to academic achievement: (a) academic self-efficacy, (b) attribution of success to personal traits, such as ability, (c) intrinsic motivation, and (d) student goals for mastering new skills. Not only is academic self-efficacy related to students' test scores (Vrugt, Langereis, & Hoogstraten, 1997), but also to their persistence (Linnenbrink & Pintrich, 2002). Persistence might be an important factor in helping at-risk students pass high stakes tests. Most states that have a high school exit exam afford students multiple opportunities to pass the test. In regard to the Massachusetts high school graduating class of 2007, for example, only 55% of students with learning disabilities, 34% of students with limited English proficiency, and 59% of African-American and 54% Latino students passed that state's high stakes test on their first attempt (Massachusetts Department of Education, 2006). Thus, in order for high percentages of students from these at-risk groups to pass this exit test, they must be sufficiently resilient and motivated to retake the test one or more times.

Anxiety as a Risk Factor

Whereas coping style, social support and, to a lesser extent, motivation have been found to mediate between stress and a broad range of outcomes, anxiety is an important factor mediating the relationship between stress and test performance. Most of the recent research on test anxiety builds upon the theoretical assumption that test anxiety is a situation-specific trait that predisposes the individual to respond with elevated anxiety in response to a test or another performance task (Hodapp, Glanzman, & Laux, 1995). Estimates of the prevalence of test anxiety range from one-quarter to one-half of all students (Harvey, 2001; McDonald, 2001). These estimates suggest that millions of students may be affected by test anxiety.

In a comprehensive review of over 500 studies, Hembree (1988) found convincing evidence that test anxiety causes poor performance on achievement tests. Two of the subject areas, English and mathematics, which showed the strongest relationships to test anxiety (Hembree, 1988), are the areas most often included on high stakes tests. Furthermore, Hembree found that students who had weak academic ability were more likely to suffer from test anxiety. Thus, many of the students with disabilities who take high stakes tests may have three disadvantages: weak academic skills, poor coping strategies, and high test anxiety. Although most of the obtained negative correlations between anxiety and test performance are relatively modest (between $-.2$ and $-.3$), it is important to note that a correlation of only −.2 could result in an additional 20% of students who fail a test (McDonald, 2001).

Developmental differences in test anxiety also are apparent. Test anxiety becomes increasingly evident in grades three to five, stabilizes during the middle and high school years, and then declines in college (Hembree, 1988). Unfortunately, test anxiety seems to peak during adolescence, when students may be particularly vulnerable to the pressure of high stakes testing.

Worry and emotionality are two important dimensions of test anxiety (e.g., Keogh et al., 2005). Worry is a cognitive component that represents concerns about being negatively evaluated or about one's ability to perform on a test. Emotionality refers to affective responses to perceived autonomic reactions to the test situation, such as nervousness and rapid heart rate. Research has consistently supported a direct relationship between high levels of worry and poor test performance (e.g., Eysenck & Calco, 1992; Hembree, 1988; Hong, 1999). In other words, students who have difficulty controlling their negative thoughts (e.g., "I'm going to fail this test") immediately before and during a test situation are more likely to underachieve on the test. In a study of college students, the dimension of worry seemed to mediate the relationship between the perceived difficulty of the test and subsequent test performance (Hong, 1999). The relationship between emotionality and test performance is less clear. Emotionality appears to affect performance only under specific conditions, such as when the individual also is experiencing a high level of worry (e.g., Hodapp et al., 1995).

PREVENTION AND INTERVENTION

Despite the pressure exerted on schools, teachers, and students from high stakes testing and the potential negative consequences of that pressure, there are empirically supported strategies that can facilitate coping with stress. Interventions intended to reduce the negative impact of excessive stress associated with high stakes testing can occur at the school, teacher, and student levels.

School Level

Interventions intended to help the school cope with the stress associated with high stakes testing should focus on either maintaining or increasing the resources available to meet the demands of high stakes testing. In this regard, two resources might be particularly important: (a) collaboration with parents and others outside the school system, and (b) the organization's problem solving capacity. Unfortunately, as indicated by Griffith's (2004) research, schools that are under considerable stress might be more likely to reduce rather increase their contact with individuals outside the schools, such as parents. To prevent this occurrence, it would seem advisable for schools to undertake systematic efforts to make their boundaries more permeable by collaborating with parents, and building such collaborations into their institutional routines. As Sarason (1971) pointed out, schools will never have all the human resources they need to meet the demands placed on them. Therefore, it is imperative that schools reach out to parents and others and view them as partners and collaborators. Multiple benefits can be derived from home-school collaborations, including higher student achievement (Epstein, 1995). Specifically in regard to high stakes testing, parents can provide their children with support and help them develop appropriate coping strategies and test-taking strategies. Home-school collaborations also can support and enhance the parent's role as a teacher.

Esler, Godber, and Christenson (2002) provide ideas for facilitating home-school collaboration. These ideas are organized with respect to (a) communicating with parents, (b) enhancing learning, (c) shared decision-making, and (d) collaborating with the community. In regard to communication, for example, they recommend maintaining a positive orientation by using multiple strategies, including phoning parents with good news about their children. School personnel and parents can collaborate on enhancing learning by developing a personalized educational plan for all students. In regard to shared decision-making, schools should provide training to parents and staff on best practices in collaboration and decision-making practices. Collaboration with the community can focus on many areas, including strategies for publicizing the school's successes in different media outlets.

Increasing an organization's ability to solve problems can also help it cope with external demands, such as the demands associated with high stakes testing. One possible means of increasing the organization's problem solving capacity is systems level consultation (Curtis & Stollar, 2002). Although the consultant can be either internal or external to the system, an external consultant for systems level problems has two distinct advantages. First, systems level consultation entails close collaboration with school administrators, who have formal authority over other personnel in the systems, including individuals who might serve as consultants, such as school psychologists. This power differential can have an inhibiting influence on an internal consultant's behavior or recommendations, thereby reducing effectiveness of the consultation. In contrast, an external consultant can share information that might make administrators feel uncomfortable without fear of jeopardizing his/her job security. Second, an external consultant is less likely to be biased because of personal relationships and experiences within the school system, therefore, making it easier for the consultant to be objective in his/her assessments and recommendations.

Another means of increasing the organization's problem solving capacity is to develop a problem-solving team. Unlike the typical problem solving teams in schools, which are focused on student concerns, this type of problem solving team should be focused on organizational level problems. Maher and Kruger (1992) provide a case study of one such a team, the quality circle, which was comprised of school psychologists and designed to take a problem solving approach to resolve work-related concerns. The evaluation results indicated that the team was able to successfully resolve multiple work-related problems and team members were satisfied with problem solving process. A quality circle team could provide leadership in problem solving about stress-related factors, such as a high ratio of actual enrollment to planned enrollment. This factor, which was included in Griffith's (2004) study, might pose a threat to a school's ability to cope with the stress related to high stakes testing.

Teacher Level

In addition to helping the entire organization more effectively cope with stress, quality circle teams can focus on job enrichment strategies. These strategies are oriented toward making the job more rewarding for the teacher. Given the concern about the impact of high stakes testing on teacher autonomy and the important buffering role autonomy has in regard to stress (Guglielmi & Tatrow, 1998), it would seem advisable for teachers and administrators to brainstorm how the teachers' work autonomy can be expanded. Problem solving teams also might help reduce teacher stress by focusing their efforts on acquiring resources, such as consultation services, that are most likely to help teachers cope with the demands of high stakes testing. Administrators and colleagues also can have important roles in reducing teachers' stress by providing them with support. For example, Russell, Altmaier, and Van Velzen (1987) found that teachers who reported high levels of support from administrators and positive feedback from colleagues were less likely to experience burnout.

Stress management programs can be implemented for teachers. Stress management interventions often begin with awareness training (Brown & Uehara, n.d.). In particular, participants are informed about the causes and symptoms of stress. Forman (1981), for example, implemented a program that informed the participants about the causes of stress in schools, the prevalence of stress, and its impact on individuals in the schools. After the initial awareness is established, a more active and participatory training component is typically implemented. This latter component might include identifying the specific stressors that are affecting the participants, and finally, developing and implementing preventative measures (Brown & Uehara, n.d.).

Training in physiological coping also is a common component of stress management programs. This type of training can emphasize any one of several specific strategies, such as (a) muscle relaxation, (b) biofeedback, (c) meditation, (d) breathing techniques, or (e) aerobic activity (Brown & Uehara, n.d.). The purpose of these different strategies is to control the physiological symptoms that accompany high levels of stress. Finally, many stress reduction interventions also include a cognitive appraisal component (Brown & Uehara, n.d.). The assumption is that stress is often maintained by self-defeating cognitions. Therefore, if these cognitions can be replaced by more constructive thoughts, then these individuals might more successfully cope with stress. This approach to stress reduction is consistent with the notion that the individual's interpretation of the event is related to whether the event is experienced as a challenge or a threat (Baum, Singer & Baum, 1981).

Student Level

In addition to helping the school and teachers cope with the stress related to high stakes testing, school psychologists can take steps to prevent mental health difficulties among students that may arise as one of the unintended outcomes of high stakes testing. Prevention and intervention efforts intended to help students cope with the stress associated with high stakes testing may be conceptualized within a positive behavioral support model (Sugai & Horner, 2002) that provides a continuum of supports for the individual student, classroom, school and district (OSEP Technical Assistance Center on Positive Behavioral Interventions and Supports, n.d.). Within this model, consistent with prevention and mental health literature (OSEP Technical Assistance Center, n.d.;

Kutash, Duchnowski & Lynn, 2006), it is assumed that much of the stress associated with high stakes testing can be managed and modified by implementing a series of proactive interventions at the systems level. At the systems level, interventions are universal and focused on providing all children, teachers and administrators, families and community members coping strategies to prevent the development of more serious or persistent stress responses. At the secondary or selective level, students who have been identified as being at risk for developing more serious or persistent stress responses are provided more intensive and selective group level interventions.

Students often identified as being at particular risk include: students with disabilities, students who are English language learners, and students from economically impoverished families (Geisthardt & Munsch, 1996; Hembree, 1988; Hodge, McCormick, & Elliott, 1997). Selective (i.e., targeted) level intervention seeks to provide support and teach strategies so that students do not require more intensive, individual interventions (Kutash et al., 2006). For those students for whom selective, secondary interventions are unsuccessful and for those students who are identified as being at particularly high risk due to extremely low or failing scores on high stakes tests, tertiary interventions may be appropriate. Tertiary interventions are intensive, individualized interventions focused on teaching strategies to cope with the impact of stress associated with high stakes testing. Within a prevention model, schools that proactively adopt strategies to help children, teachers, and parents manage the stress associated with high stakes testing should find relatively fewer children requiring intensive, individualized, tertiary interventions. Additionally, some researchers suggest that students should be taught particular types of engagement coping strategies in a manner consistent with the situation-specific type of stressor experienced (Compas et al., 2005). For example, when the stressor is perceived as controllable, students should be encouraged to use primary control coping strategies, such as problem solving, emotional expression or emotional regulation. In contrast, when the stressor is perceived as being outside the students' control, they should be encouraged to use secondary control coping strategies, such as acceptance, distraction, and positive thinking. Both strategies could be used to help students cope with high stakes testing because there are aspects of high stakes testing that are both within and outside the control of students. For instance, students cannot control the fact they must take the test. Therefore, training students in positive thinking might help them cope with this aspect of the testing. However, students can control how they approach the test, and therefore might benefit from being taught how to apply a systematic problem solving approach to answering test questions.

At the systems level, school psychologists can provide school-wide universal interventions such as relaxation training and desensitization to minimize the stressful test situation for children. Such behavioral approaches are well recognized as acceptable interventions for reducing stressful responses (Merrell, 2001) and may provide students with the capacity to cope proactively with the stress of high stakes testing. Relaxation training, including the use of an anxiety exposure hierarchy, has been successful in reducing test anxiety among high school and college students (Gonzales, 1995; Kennedy & Doepke, 1999).

Universal interventions for stress reduction with children generally adopt behavioral and cognitive-behavioral (CB) approaches. One such program, Friends for Life (2006), uses a CB approach originally based on Kendall's Coping Cat (1992) program. This approach has been used as both a systems level intervention (Lowry-Webster, Barrett, & Dadds, 2001) and a secondary-selective intervention (Dadds, Holland, Barrett, Laurens, & Spence, 1999) for anxiety in several countries. The content of the program is integrated into the activities of the classroom. Students are taught cognitive-behavioral strategies for coping with a variety of common, stressful experiences. The program also has a parent education component. Such a component might be one part of an overall plan to prevent the school from closing its boundaries to important external resources, such as parents, who can help students and the entire school cope with the stress related to high stakes testing.

School psychologists also should consider other methods of providing information to parents so that parents can help their children cope with stress related to high stakes testing. In particular, school psychologists can offer workshops for parents in which universal interventions, such as relaxation training and desensitization, are taught. School psychologists may provide printed materials and website links through community newspapers and other media that offer information about topics, such as managing stress and best practices in preventing test anxiety. Additionally, school psychologists may provide resources to teachers on practical strategies to encourage ongoing, active coping and positive classroom climate (Fallin, Wallinga, & Coleman, 2001). In regard to classroom climate, teachers can implement strategies to reduce the level of academic competition among students in a school. Research indicates that the threat of academic competition is related to high test anxiety (Zatz & Chasin, 1985). One strategy, for example, that has been successful in reducing competition in the classroom and increasing academic achievement is cooperative learning (Johnson, Johnson, & Stanne, 2000). In cooperative learning, students are placed in small groups and work toward achieving shared academic goals. Finally, prevention activities can target the development of academic self-efficacy, an important factor in academic motivation (Linnenbrink & Pintrich, 2002).

At the selective level, school psychologists should provide interventions targeted towards students, who have been identified as being at high risk for maladaptive stress responses. While behavioral and cognitive behavioral approaches continue to be modes for interventions, interventions at this level target small groups of students who have been identified as needing additional help in dealing with the stress of high stakes testing. Several of the empirically supported programs for stress at the secondary level that are noted in Kutash et al. (2006) include: Coping with Stress for 13 to 18 year students; Stress Inoculation Training I for 16-18 year old students, and Stress Inoculation II for 13-18 year old students. All of these programs employ behavioral and C-B techniques within a group model. The use of a group context allows for strategies such as modeling and role playing (Merrell, 2001). Self-control training, self-instruction, and social skills training may be added (Merrell, 2001). A recent study at the secondary level by Keogh et al. (2005) conducted in the United Kingdom, used a CB stress management, small group intervention with adolescent students facing high stakes tests who had previously been identified as having test anxiety. Interestingly, this ten-week intervention led to an increase in the functionality of the cognitions of the students, indicating improved mental health, as well as an increase in motivation and significantly better performance on the standardized academic measure (Keogh et al., 2005). Such findings, if replicable, hold promise for interventions that impact both mental health and academic targets. Additionally, at the selective level, school psychologists should consider more actively involving parents in intervention plans to help alleviate the symptoms of stress and promote active coping strategies. Children who received school-based CB counseling in school for anxiety, and whose parents also received training in CB approaches, benefited more than those children who received CB programs in school without parent training (Bernstein, Layne, Egan, & Tennison, 2005).

At the tertiary level, school psychologists should provide individualized approaches for students whose level of stress linked to high stakes testing requires intensive intervention. One evidence-based program, reviewed by Yannacci and Rivard (2006), is the CB focused Coping Cat program (Kendall, 1992) that can be used for older children and adolescents. Another group program for children between the ages 7 and 14 is the Queensland Early Intervention and Prevention of Anxiety Project (QEIPAP) (Kutash et al., 2006) that is described as a modification of the Coping Cat program. At the tertiary level, school psychologists will find that it is essential to involve parents in the intervention. Both Coping Cat (Howard & Kendall, 1996) and QEIPAP (Kutash et al., 2006) include parent components. Additionally, because research (Struthers et al., 2000; Shields, 2001) suggests that active, problem-focused coping may increase motivation and persistence leading to improved academic performance, school psychologists should use such approaches with students. Finally, school psychologists should provide ongoing consultation for classroom teachers, particularly for teachers of groups of students who need tertiary level services due to special characteristics such as disabilities. For these teachers, the stress of having their students repeatedly challenged by high stakes testing is likely to lead to both professional and personal stress. School psychologists should consider providing special, intensive stress management workshops for teachers of these high-risk groups.

CONCLUSION

Stress impacts the educational system at the school, teacher, and student levels. Although there is considerable research on the debilitating effects of chronic and excessive stress in general on mental health and academic outcomes, there is much less research on stress and high stakes testing. Nonetheless, the research that is available suggests that there is good reason for concern. This concern is built upon the well-documented aspect of the cumulative nature of stress (Kim, 2005; Printz et al., 1999). That is, the negative effects of stress are exacerbated when additional stressors appear in one's life. The additional stressor that many schools, teachers and students are now confronted with is high stakes testing, and its attendant consequences, which vary from state to state.

School psychologists can be proactive in reducing the potential negative impact of this source of stress. In particular, they can take a leadership role in implementing preventative strategies, such as collaborative problem solving with parents and staff, as well as stress-reduction relaxation programs. In addition, they can identify the stress-related problems associated with high stakes testing in their schools, and implement more specific interventions that are tailored to the needs of at-risk groups or individual students. Such interventions may lead to more positive outcomes for students, families and schools confronting the stress associated with high stakes testing.

REFERENCES

Albrecht, T. L. & Adelman, M. B. (1987). Communication networks as structures of social support. In T. L. Albrecht & M. B. Adelman (Eds.), *Communicating social support* (pp. 40-63). Newbury Park, CA: Sage.

Anderson, G. E., Jimerson, S. R., & Whipple, A. D. (2005). Student ratings of stressful experiences at home and school loss of a parent and grade retention as superlative stressors. *Journal of Applied School Psychology, 21,* (1), 1-20.

Baum, A., Singer, J. E., & Baum, C. S. (1981). Stress and environment. *Journal of Social Issues, 37,* 4-35.

Bernstein, G. A., Layne, A. E., Egan, E. A, & Tennison, D. M. (2005). School-based interventions for anxious children. *Journal of American Academy of Child and Adolescent Psychiatry, 44,* 1118-1127.

Boston Globe (2005). *2005 MCAS Results.* Retrieved on August 18, 2006 from http://www.boston.com/news/education/k_12/mcas/.

Braden, J. F. (2007). Using data from high-stakes testing in program planning and evaluation. *Journal of Applied School Psychology, 23* (2), 129-151.

Brown, Z. A., & Uehara, D. L. (n.d.). Coping with teacher stress: A research synthesis for Pacific educators. Retrieved June 20, 2006 from http://www.prel.org/products/Products/Coping-teacherStress.htm.

Compas, B. E., Champion, J. E., & Reeslund, K. (2005). Coping with stress: Implications for preventive interventions with adolescents. *The Prevention Researcher, 12,* 17-20.

Cooley, E., & Yovanoff, P. (1996). Supporting professionals-at-risk: Evaluating interventions to reduce burnout and improve retention of special educators. *Exceptional Children, 62*(4), 336-355.

Cornell, D. G., Krosnick, J. A., & Chang, L. (2006). Student reactions to being wrongly informed of failing a high-stakes test: The case of the Minnesota Basic Standards Test. *Educational Policy, 20,* 718-751.

Crocker, L., Schmitt, A., & Tang, L. (1988). Test anxiety and standardized achievement test performance in the middle school years. *Measurement and Evaluation in Counseling and Development, 20*(4), 149-157.

Curtis, M.J. & Stollar, S. (1995). System-level consultation and organizational change. In A. Thomas and J. Grimes (Eds.), *Best practices in school psychology III* (pp. 51-58). Washington, D. C: National Association of School Psychologists.

Dadds, M. R., Holland, D., Barrett, P. M., Laurens, K., & Spence, S. (1999). Early intervention and prevention of anxiety disorders in children: Results at 2-year follow-up. *Journal of Consulting and Clinical Psychology, 67,* 145-150.

de Anda, D., Baroni, S., Boskin, L., Buchwald, L., Morgan, J., Ow, J., Gold, J. S., & Weiss, R. (2000). Stress, stressors and coping among high school students. *Children and Youth Services Review, 22*, 441-463.

Epstein, J. (1995). School/family/community partnerships: Caring for the children we share. *Phi Delta Kappan, 76*, 701-712.

Esler, A. N., Godber, Y., & Christenson, S. L. (2002). Supporting home-school collaboration. In A. Thomas & J. Grimes (Eds.), *Best practices in school psychology* (4th ed.) (pp. 389-411). Washington, DC: National Association of School Psychologists.

Fallin, K., Wallinga, C. & Coleman, M. (2001). Helping children cope with stress in the classroom. *Childhood Education, 78*, 17.

Farber, B. A. (1991). *Crisis in education: Stress and burnout in the American teacher.* San Francisco: Jossey-Bass.

Forman, S. (1981). Stress-management training: Evaluation of effects on school psychological services. *The Journal of School Psychology, 19*, 233-241.

Friends for Life. (2006, February). Evidence base abstracts. Retrieved June 7, 2006, from www.friendsinfo.net/downloads/FRIENDSAbstractsBooklet.pdf.

Geisthardt, C., & Munsch, J. (1996). Coping with school stress: A comparison of adolescents with and without learning disabilities. *Journal of Learning Disabilities, 29*, 225-336.

Gonzales, H. P. (1995). Systematic desensitization, study skills counseling, and anxiety coping training in the treatment of test anxiety. In C. D. Spielberger & P. R. Vaggs (Eds.), *Test anxiety: Theory, assessment and treatment* (pp. 117-132). Washington, DC: Taylor & Francis.

Grant, K. E., Compas, B. E., Thurm, A. E., McMahon, S. D., Gipson, P. Y., Campbell, A. J. et al. (May 2006). Stressors and child and adolescent psychopathology: Evidence of moderating and mediating effects. *Clinical Psychology Review, 26*(3), 257-83.

Grant, K. E., Compas, B. E., Thurm, A. E., McMahon, S. D., & Gipson, P. (2004). Stressors and child and adolescent psychopathology: Measurement issues and prospective effects. *Journal of Clinical Child and Adolescent Psychology, 33*, 412-425.

Griffith, J. (2004). Ineffective schools as organizational reactions to stress. *Social Psychology of Education, 7*, 257-287.

Guglielmi, R. S., & Tatrow, K. (1998). Occupational stress, burnout and health in teachers: A methodological and theoretical analysis. *Review of Educational Research, 68*, 61-99.

Hakanen, J., Bakker, A., Schaufeli, W. B. (2006). Burnout and work engagement among teachers. *Journal of School Psychology, 43*, 495-513.

Hembree, R. (1988). Correlates, causes, effects and treatment of test anxiety. *Review of Educational Research, 58(1)*, 47-77.

Hodapp, V., Glanzmann, P. G., & Laux, L. (1995). Theory and measurement of test anxiety as a situation-specific trait. In C. D. Spielberger & P. R. Vagg (Eds.), *Test anxiety: Theory, assessment, and treatment* (pp. 47-59). Washington, DC: Taylor & Francis.

Hodge, G. M., McCormick, J., & Elliott, R. (1997). Examination induced distress in a public examination at the completion of secondary schooling. *British Journal of Educational Psychology, 67*, 185-197.

Hong, E. (1999). Test anxiety, perceived test difficulty, and test performance: Temporal patterns of their effects. *Learning and Individual Differences, 11*, 431-447.
Howard, B. & Kendall, P. C. (1996). *Cognitive-behavioral family therapy for anxious children: Therapist manual.* Ardmore, PA: Workbook Publishing.
Isralowitz, R. E., & Hong, O. T. (1990). Singapore youth: The impact of social status on perceptions of adolescent problems. *Adolescence, 25*, 357-362.
Johnson, S., Cooper, C., Cartwright, S., Donald, I., Taylor, P., & Millet, C. (2005). The experience of work-related stress across occupations. *Journal of Managerial Psychology, 20*(2), 178-187.
Johnson, D. W., Johnson, R. T., & Stanne, M. B. (May 2000). *Cooperative learning methods: A meta-analysis.* Retrieved July 14, 2006 from http://www.co-operation.org/pages/cl-methods.html.
Jones, M. G., Jones, B. D., Hardin, B., Chapman, L., Yarbrough, T., & Davis, M. (1999). The impact of high-stakes testing on teachers and students in North Carolina. *Phi Delta Kappan, 81*(3), 199. Retrieved June 24, 2006, from Questia database: http://www.questia.com/PM.qst?a = o&d = 5001848258.
Kendall, P.C. (1992). *Coping cat workbook.* Ardmore, PA: Workbook Publishing.
Kennedy, D. V., & Doepke, K. J. (1999). Multicomponent treatment of a test anxious college student. *Education and Treatment of Children, 22*, 203-217.
Keogh, E., Bond, F. W. & Flaxman, P. E. (2005). Improving academic performance and mental health through stress management intervention: Outcomes and mediators of change. *Behavior Research and Therapy, 44*, 339-357.
Kim, K. J. (2005). Interconnected accumulation of life stresses and adolescent maladjustment. *The Prevention Researcher, 12*(3), 13-16.
Kutash, K., Duchnowski, A. J. & Lynn, N. (2006). *School-based mental health: An empirical guide for decision-makers.* Tampa, FL: University of South Florida, The Louis de la Parte Florida Mental Health Institute, Department of Child & Family Studies, Research and Training Center for Children's Mental Health.
Lowry-Webster, H. M., Barrett, P. M. & Dadds, M. R. (2001). A universal prevention trial of anxiety and depressive symptomatology in childhood: Preliminary data from an Australian Study. *Behaviour Change, 18*, 36-50.
Massachusetts Department of Education. (2006). Progress report on students attaining the competency determination. Statewide and by School and District: Classes of 2006 and 2007. Retrieved June 19, 2006, from www.doe.mass.edu/mcas/2006/results/CDreport_0606.doc.
McDonald, A. (2001). The prevalence and effects of test anxiety in school children. *Educational Psychology, 21(1)*, 89-101.
Merrell, K. W. (2001). *Helping students overcome depression and anxiety.* New York: Guilford Press.
Nichols, S. L., Glass, G. V., & Berliner, D. C. (2006). High-stakes testing and student achievement: Does accountability pressure increase student learning? *Education Policy Analysis Archives, 14*(1). Retrieved August 11, 2006, from http://epaa.asu.edu/epaa/v14n1/.
No Child Left Behind Act (NCLB) of 2001. Retrieved February 25, 2006, from http://www.ed.gov/policy/elsec/leg/esea02/107-110.pdf.

OSEP Technical Assistance Center on Positive Behavioral Interventions and Supports. (n.d.). U.S. Office of Special Education. Retrieved June 6, 2006, from www.pbis.org.

Pearson, L., & Moomaw, W. (2005). The relationship between teacher autonomy and stress, work satisfaction, empowerment, and professionalism. *Educational Research Quarterly, 29*(1), 37-53.

Printz, B.L., Shermis, M. D., & Webb, P. M. (1999). Stress-buffering factors related to adolescent coping: A path analysis. *Adolescence, 34*(136), 715-733.

Pryor-Brown, L., & Cowen, E. L. (September 1989). Stressful life events, support, and children's school adjustment. *Journal of Clinical Child Psychology, 18*(3), 214-220.

Russell, D., Altmaier, E., & Van Velzen, D. (1987). Job-related stress, social support, and burnout among classroom teachers. *Journal of Applied Psychology, 72,* 269-274.

Sarason, S. B. (1971). *The culture of the school and the problem of change.* Boston: Allyn and Bacon.

Shields, N. (2001). Stress, active coping, and academic performance among persisting and nonpersisting college students. *Journal of Applied Biobehavioral Research, 6,* 65-81.

Struthers, C. W., Perry, R. P, & Menec, V. H. (2000). An examination of the relationship among academic stress, coping, motivation, and performance in college. *Research in Higher Education, 41,* 581-592.

Sugai, G., & Horner, R. H. (2002). Introduction to the special series on positive behavior support in schools. *Journal of Emotional and Behavioral Disorders, 10,* 130-135.

Vrugt, A. J., Langereis, M. P., & Hoogstraten, J. (1997). Academic self-efficacy and malleability of relevant capabilities as predictors of exam performance. *Journal of Experimental Education, 66*(1), 61-72.

West, C. K., Willis, C. L., & Sharp, A. (1982). Academic stress among early adolescents in England and in the United States. *Journal of Early Adolescence, 2,* 145-150.

Whoriskey, P. (2006, March 22). Florida to link teacher pay to students' test scores. *Washington Post.* Retrieved August 15, 2006 from http://www.washingtonpost.com/wp-dyn/content/article/2006/03/21/AR2006032101545_pf.html.

Yamamoto, K., & Byrnes, D. A. (1987). Primary children's ratings of the stressful experiences. *Journal of Research in Childhood Education, 2,* 117-121.

Yannacci, J., & Rivard J. C. (2006, April). *Matrix of children's evidence-based interventions.* Center for mental health quality and accountability: NASMHPD research institute, inc.

Zatz, S. & Chassin, L. (1985). Cognitions of test-anxious children under naturalistic testing-taking conditions. *The Journal of Consulting and Clinical Psychology, 53,* 393-401.

doi:10.1300/J370v23n02_07

Using Data from High-Stakes Testing in Program Planning and Evaluation

Jeffery P. Braden

North Carolina State University

SUMMARY. This article intends to help school psychologists understand the nature of high stakes tests, methods for analyzing and reporting high stakes test data, standards for tests and program evaluation, and application of appropriate practices to program planning and evaluation. Although it is readily acknowledged that high stakes test data are not sufficient for effective program planning and evaluation, the availability of test results, and their salience for federally mandated accountability programs, argues in favor of using such data for program planning and evaluation. A decision-making model, which begins with high stakes test data, but also requires additional data from teachers and classrooms, is proposed to help practitioners evaluate program effectiveness, and make plans to improve student outcomes. doi:10.1300/J370v23n02_08 *[Article copies available for a fee from The Haworth Document Delivery Service: 1-800-HAWORTH. E-mail address: <docdelivery@haworthpress.com> Website: <http://www.HaworthPress.com> © 2007 by The Haworth Press, Inc. All rights reserved.]*

Address correspondence to: Jeff Braden, Department of Psychology, PO Box 7650, North Carolina State University, Raleigh, NC 36795-7650 (E-mail: jeff_braden@ncsu.edu).

[Haworth co-indexing entry note]: "Using Data from High-Stakes Testing in Program Planning and Evaluation." Braden, Jeffery P. Co-published simultaneously in *Journal of Applied School Psychology* (The Haworth Press, Inc.) Vol. 23, No. 2, 2007, pp. 129-150; and: *High Stakes Testing: New Challenges and Opportunities for School Psychology* (ed: Louis J. Kruger, and David Shriberg) The Haworth Press, Inc., 2007, pp. 129-150. Single or multiple copies of this article are available for a fee from The Haworth Document Delivery Service [1-800-HAWORTH, 9:00 a.m. - 5:00 p.m. (EST). E-mail address: docdelivery@haworthpress.com].

Available online at http://japps.haworthpress.com
© 2007 by The Haworth Press, Inc. All rights reserved.
doi:10.1300/J370v23n02_08

KEYWORDS. High stakes tests, program planning, evaluation, school psychology, data-based decision making

The phrase "high stakes test" is used often in public and professional literature to describe annual testing programs states conduct to comply with No Child Left Behind Act of 2001 (NCLB). Classic definitions of "stakes" or test consequences emphasize the immediacy and social salience of test consequences as factors in determining what makes stakes high or low (Heubert & Hauser, 1999). The test itself does not have any stakes per se; rather, it is the consequences institutions assign to test outcomes that determine the stakes of the test (Braden, 2002; Braden & Tayrose, in press).

In this light, annual testing required by NCLB is a low stakes enterprise for students, and a medium- to high-stakes enterprise for teachers and schools. NCLB does not require any consequences for test takers beyond the requirement that states must inform parents of their children's test scores. Currently, 23 of the states attach graduation decisions to high school tests, and only 8 use tests for grade promotion purposes (Education Week, 2006). Consequences for educators and schools are more profound, although consequences for failing to meet adequate yearly progress (AYP) goals for multiple consecutive years only apply to schools receiving Title I funds under NCLB. However, some states attached additional consequences to AYP determinations; 37 states provide additional assistance to any school identified in need of improvement, and 16 states provide rewards or incentives for schools that meet performance or improvement targets. Only 5 states withhold funds from schools failing to make AYP, suggesting that the assumption that NCLB tests lead to less funding for the lowest performing schools is inaccurate. In fact, all 5 states that withhold funds initially provide additional funds to improve failing schools (Education Week, 2006).

It is ironic to point out that, in an issue devoted to high stakes tests, tests themselves do not have stakes. Rather, it is the consequences that social institutions attach to test results that create "stakes," and stakes vary by stakeholders. The tests states use to implement NCLB mandates have low stakes for most students (i.e., less than half of states mandate consequences for students on such tests), and have medium stakes for educators (i.e., consequences such as loss of autonomy accrue indirectly and only over time). However, tests may have high stakes for some educators (e.g., North Carolina provides annual bonuses to teachers in schools meeting excellence criteria), and if the school fails to make AYP for many consecutive years, the consequences for educators may be substantial (e.g., loss of pay or job). The phrase "high stakes test" is used in this article to refer to tests states use to implement AYP decisions under NCLB.

USING TEST DATA TO EVALUATE SCHOOLS

Although NCLB mandates the use of test data for determining whether schools and LEAs meet AYP targets, the data generated by annual testing may be used for other purposes. Different purposes often require different methods to analyze and present data. Currently, three broad models are recognized for evaluating schools or LEAs: (a) status models, (b) improvement models, and (c) growth models (Council of Chief State School Officers [CCSSO], 2005). Each of these models is described in the following sections.

Status Models

A "status model" of accountability sets a target for student performance at a given point in time, without regard to past or future performance. The primary definition of AYP in NCLB is a status model. That is, each state must measure students' achievement of standards, and each state must identify objective criteria to determine whether students are proficient for their grade level. "Proficiency" is a criterion-referenced judgment that varies by grade level (e.g., students in eighth grade must score higher on a mathematics test to be proficient than students in third grade). NCLB requires states to judge schools AYP on the basis of the proportion of students who score at or above this "proficient" level. Although start points and annual targets vary by state, and within states by subject matter and grade level, schools must ensure that a certain proportion of their students (within each of nine groups) meets or exceeds the target. All states must set the target for 2014 at 100%, meaning all states must require all students to attain 100% proficiency.

For example, in 2005-2006, schools in North Carolina must have at least 76.7% of students in grades 3-8 proficient in reading, and 81% proficient in mathematics. In 2007-2008, the targets increase to 84.4% and 87.3%; in 2010-2011, they jump to 92.2% and 93.7%. It does not matter whether there are changes in the student body, or how well the school has done in the past, nor whether students in one school start at a different place than students at another school. The status model simply sets the target for a given year, then determines whether the target was met for the groups for which the school is responsible (which is determined by grade, demographic status, and group size).

The status model has the virtues of simplicity of calculation, ease of understanding, and defining and enforcing similar outcomes for all groups. However, the status model is insensitive to improvement in students and schools and is highly influenced by non-school factors (e.g., students' SES, parental education, ethnicity), which renders it a poor indicator of school quality (McCall, Kingsbury, & Olson, 2004; Raudenbush, 2004). Indeed, there is little evidence to support the argument that status models are even loosely associated with school quality (Haertel, 1999), and so the model is not widely supported by scholars, researchers, and organizations associated with assessing school quality (Linn, 2005).

Improvement Models

In contrast to status models, improvement models use the performance of students in a previous year or years, along with performance of students in the current year, to decide whether a school is making appropriate progress. This model is considered an improvement model because it may allow a school not meeting a status target to nonetheless meet AYP goals because a larger proportion of students in the current year are proficient compared to cohorts in previous years. The current "safe harbor" provision of NCLB outlines an improvement model alternative for schools to meet AYP. That is, if a school falls short of the status model target for a given group, if the proportion of students in that group scoring below proficient is reduced by 10% from the previous school year, and the group made progress on other academic indicators (e.g., attendance or graduation rate), the school may be considered to be making AYP.

The advantages of the improvement model include acknowledging that some schools have more challenging students than others, and that annual improvements in school performance should be recognized in an accountability system. The problems with the improvement model include setting different standards for different groups (e.g., why should a lower proportion of proficiency be accepted for a group even if it is better than the previous year's performance?) and comparing different cohorts across different years. The latter problem is particularly vexing for schools that experience changes in student demographics. For example, newly available subsidized housing, changes in the numbers of students attending a school, or district reassignment of pupils to schools, could substantially change the proportion of students who are proficient across different years, yet improvement models do not consider such changes in deciding whether improvement occurred (CCSSO, 2005; McCall et al., 2004).

Growth Models

Growth models attempt to measure change (i.e., "growth") over one or more years within the same students attending the same school. Therefore, a student's change from third to fourth grade, or from sixth to eighth grade, might be used to evaluate school effectiveness. The argument posits that schools that produce greater rates of growth among their students are better than schools producing lower rates of growth.

Growth models may also consider nonschool factors in evaluating school performance. This is important, because students do not have the same rates of growth when compared across different demographic and ability groups (Meyer, 1996). For example, students from poor families have lower rates of growth than students from wealthy families; likewise, students who have more knowledge at the beginning of a school year tend to improve more than students with less knowledge. Growth models that statistically control for nonschool factors (e.g., student demographics, ability) in evaluating growth are often called "value added" models, because they attempt to remove such variables from judgments about the degree to which schools "add value" to students in successive years (see CCSSO, 2005, for a discussion).

Although intuitively appealing, growth models have a number of drawbacks. The most critical of these drawbacks include the statistical and logistical capacity to measure and model growth. Not only are growth calculations complex, but the ability to produce and use a continuous scale to measure student achievement across two or more years, set growth targets, and otherwise implement growth models is a significant challenge (CCSSO, 2005). Some tests may have scales that lend themselves to reflecting more rapid growth in moving from low to average performance, whereas other tests may be more sensitive to growth from average to high performance (see Ferrara, Johnson, & Chen, 2004; Lissitz & Huynh, 2003; and Reckase & Martineau, 2004, for measurement challenges). Additionally, growth models may be criticized for failing to define and enforce equal expectations across groups, particularly if value-added models are used that adjust for no-school effects (i.e., by adjusting for ethnicity and SES, one is essentially setting a different standard for schools with high vs. low concentrations of ethnic/SES groups). A final limitation of growth models is that one must have multiple data points (ideally, three or more) to reliably predict and then measure growth. Given the costs of annual assessments, most states do not test in grades other than those required under NCLB (i.e., grades 3-8 and once in high school). To use NCLB data for growth modeling, a school should have three of these grades, meaning only elementary (grades 3-5) and middle schools (grades 6-8) are likely to be poised to use growth models for accountability and evaluation. Because most secondary schools only test students in one grade (usually tenth), or only in certain courses, multiple data points are not available for growth model evaluations of secondary schools.

Despite these problems, most scholars and educators agree that growth models are more fair than status or improvement models for measuring school quality, because growth models more directly determine which schools are doing better (or worse) than expected given the student bodies that they serve. That is, some schools that fail AYP under a status model actually improve student learning more than average, and some schools with excellent rates of proficiency do little to enhance student growth (McCall et al., 2004). Although NCLB does not currently allow for the use of growth models in determining AYP, the US Department of Education (2006) recently announced that two states, Tennessee and North Carolina, could begin using growth models as an alternative to status models for deciding whether a school meets AYP. Preliminary results in North Carolina using the growth model found that slightly less than 60 schools that failed to make AYP using the current status and improvement (i.e., "safe harbor") models would make AYP under the new growth model system. Although this is heartening news, it is a relatively small portion (about 6%) of the 968 schools that failed to make AYP in that year. Therefore, although growth models may produce different judgments of school quality than status models in some cases, it does not appear that a large proportion of schools failing under a status model are producing high or unexpected rates of growth within their students.

Status vs. Improvement vs. Growth Models: An Example

Figure 1 illustrates school data to illustrate the different kinds of conclusions one might draw from high stakes test data using status, improvement, and growth models. The figure shows reading test data for students with low income enrolled in a North Carolina elementary

FIGURE 1. Data Contrasting Status, Improvement, and Growth Models for a North Carolina School.

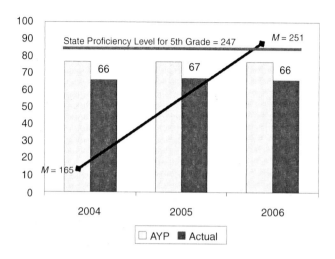

school in 2004, 2005, and 2006. The AYP annual targets for the school are a constant 76.7% each year (represented by the horizontal line). The school's percent proficient in grades 3-5 is represented in the solid dark vertical bar, and varies from 66-67%. Therefore, a status model would hold that the school did not meet AYP goals in any of the three years. Likewise, because the percent proficient across the three years does not show reliable or substantial increases, the school will not meet AYP targets using a "safe harbor" or improvement model.

The solid black line illustrates the mean scale score on the state test achieved by a cohort of students that were in the third grade (in 2004), and stayed with the school through fifth grade (in 2006). The state mandated level for proficiency in fifth grade is represented by the horizontal line (a scale score value of 247). It is clear that, in third grade, this cohort is well below fifth grade proficiency. However, by fifth grade, the cohort has progressed to the point where their average is above the state's proficiency cutoff, so most members score in the proficient range. The growth in this cohort implies that the school is highly effective at moving low scoring students to a level of proficiency by the time they complete fifth grade. A number of reasons might explain why the percent proficient in the years sampled does not change despite improvement in this cohort, such as student mobility or changes in student demographics (e.g., increasing numbers of low scoring students in third grade might offset gains in later grades).

In this example, it is clear that the model used to evaluate school performance leads to substantially different conclusions about the quality of the school. Status and improvement models identify the school as ineffective, whereas the growth model suggests the school is remarkably effective. Note that this example, although realistic, is not representative. Most of the schools with high and low status also exhibit high and low growth (McCall et al., 2004). However, some schools are characterized differently by the three models, with low status/high growth schools (such as the one in this example) being misrepresented as failing, and high status/low growth schools being misrepresented as successful. For a detailed comparison of status and growth models that uses high stakes test data to evaluate special education programs, see Schulte and Villock (2004).

Growth models also make it possible for schools to use data to evaluate the quality of the experiences they provide. In contrast to status and improvement models, which do not allow schools to determine what they add to student achievement, growth models could help schools identify which programs and practices within the school are most (and least) effective for promoting student growth. Issues of appropriateness, capacity, and consequences must be considered carefully in any use of test data. Therefore, the remainder of this article considers characteristics of test data that influence their value, and how to use such data to improve results.

CHARACTERISTICS THAT INFLUENCE THE VALUE OF HIGH STAKES TEST DATA

High stakes test data are similar to lights on an automobile dashboard: They alert the driver to a problem, but do not provide diagnostic information regarding what is causing the problem or what the driver should do about it. Drivers ignore such warnings at their peril, and good drivers will quickly seek additional information to diagnose and remedy the problem. Likewise, good educators will use annual test data to help identify problems, and will seek additional information to diagnose and remedy the problem.

There are four characteristics of test data that influence their value for program planning and evaluation: (1) breadth vs. narrowness of sampling, (2) timing of data availability, (3) the unit of analysis for aggregation of data, and (4) the metric in which data are reported. Each of these characteristics influences the value of test data for program planning and evaluation.

Breadth of sampling Most high stakes tests are designed to sample broad academic domains. Although broad representation of many skills increases the validity of tests as indicators of students' achievement of state standards, this same feature may limit value for program planning and evaluation. Knowing that a relatively high proportion of students are not proficient in "reading" is useful for identifying a problem, but not useful for understanding what to do about it. Deconstruction of broad domains into meaningfully inter-related units, such as the five components of reading (Armbruster, Lehr, & Osborn, 2001; National Reading Panel, 2000) or the seven domains of mathematics (National Council of Teachers of Mathematics, n.d.), is helpful in guiding instructional responses. However, high stakes tests may not have a sufficient number of items to adequately measure specific skills. For example, the proportion of students in Wisconsin considered proficient in Reading: Evaluation and Extend Meaning subskill went from 54% to 82% between the years of 2000 and 2001 (Department of Public Instruction, 2002) simply because one of the items used to estimate performance on that objective went from being a relatively easy to a relatively difficult item. Therefore, school psychologists should consider carefully issues of breadth, narrowness, and the influence of item changes in representing performance in academic objectives and skills.

Timing of test data. Two features of timing influence the uses and value of test data for program planning and evaluation. The first feature is the frequency with which data can be made available to those who need data to make programmatic and instructional decisions, and the second feature is the point at which data become available to those who use the data. Generally, higher frequency is better than lower frequency (e.g., Shinn, 2002), and formative data (i.e., data that can be used for planning) are better than summative data (i.e., those that only determine the degree to which an outcome has been achieved). Because high stakes test data are sampled annually, and usually are not available until the end of the academic year, they are of little or no value for program planning for test takers. However, their use for strategic planning (i.e., planning for the following academic year) will be discussed in the last section of this article.

Unit of analysis. High stakes test data are, by law, reported at the individual, group, school, and district level. However, these units do not necessarily correspond to the units that matter for program planning and evaluation. Rather, instructional groupings are more relevant. There are two ways to align data to instructional groups. The first is to aggregate test data to match existing structures (e.g., classrooms, individuals enrolled in a program). The second is to group students by test score data (i.e., assign students to groups based on test data). There are risks associated with both approaches; in the former, one risks unintended consequences (e.g., divisive comparisons between classrooms, teachers, and programs), whereas in the latter, one risks self-fulfilling prophecies with respect to low, medium, and high performing students.

Metric for reporting data. One of the more interesting features of NCLB is the requirement to report frequencies and proportions of students in a given group who score Proficient or Advanced on the state test. This requirement has two implications for metrics in which results are reported. The first implication is that tests must measure student performance on a criterion-referenced scale, rather than a norm-referenced scale (e.g., it is possible for the majority of students to be above proficient, but not above average). The second implication is that measures of central tendency, such as a mean or median, are irrelevant. Therefore, exceptionally high or low test scores mean the same as those just over or under the cutoff, which makes exceptionally high (or low) achievement irrelevant to AYP decisions. This may cause cynical educators to shift resources away from exceptional (i.e., high- or low-scoring) students in favor of students who score slightly below proficient to improve AYP performance.

The four features of high stakes test data (i.e., breadth, timing, unit of analysis, and reporting metric) influence the ways in which such data should–and should not–be used for program planning and evaluation. The following section attempts to outline practices that are intended to enhance the ability of school psychologists to plan and evaluate programs with the goal of enhancing students' academic performance.

USING RESULTS TO IMPROVE RESULTS

Given the limitations of high stakes test data, how can school psychologists use these data to enhance student success? The answer to this question is not well supported by research. However, research on effective schools (e.g., Newmann & Wehlage, 1995) and field studies of improving schools (e.g., Porter, 2002) suggests alignment of instruction and assessment is likely to improve outcomes. That is, schools that clearly identify what they want students to know and do, and then align instruction to ensure adequate opportunity for students to acquire such knowledge and processes, are more effective than schools that do not align their effort toward clearly identified goals. The standards-based reform movement was largely intended to help schools better align instruction to state standards (Swanson, 2006). Table 1 provides resources that may help psychologists use high stakes test data to improve educational outcomes.

Figure 2 provides a decision process for using high stakes test data to enhance instructional opportunities for students. The decision tree presumes that data are typically available for groups of students that make instructional sense (e.g., grades, classrooms, or groups targeted by a particular instructional program). Furthermore, decisions presume that data are available at or near the end of the school year, meaning that the purpose of the decisions is to inform instructional planning for the following year's cohort. Finally, decisions presume that those who will be executing instructional or programmatic changes are present and engaged in the process outlined in the tree. The school psychologist poses the questions and facilitates decisions, but the decisions should be made by those who are responsible for implementation.

Are Students Meeting AYP in the Subject Matter Area?

The answer to this question is fairly straightforward, and assumes failure to meet AYP is due to performance (i.e., score-related) criteria, rather than participation criteria. Should a school fail to make AYP because of missed participation goals, the focus of the response should be towards more effective inclusion of students and subgroups in the general curriculum (McDonnell, McLaughlin, & Morrison, 1997) and state tests (Elliott, Braden, & White, 2001). If the school fails to make AYP performance goals, one must ask if this is a general problem (i.e., Do many students fail to make AYP?) or a specific (i.e., only one or more subgroup) problem?

If most groups are making AYP, and some are not, a school team may elect to target "at risk" students. Although targeting allows schools to focus their limited resources on those most in need, targeting may also restrict opportunities to learn (e.g., targeted students may have less opportunity to learn social studies because their reading time is increased). More widespread failure argues in favor of more general, rather than targeted, school changes; conversely, meeting AYP targets tends to validate current practices and programs.

TABLE 1. Resources to Guide Selection and Implementation of Evidence-Based Practices to Improve Student Outcomes

Resource	URL
Assessing Opportunity to Learn in Schools (Stevens, 1999)	http://www.temple.edu/LSS/htmlpublications/spotlights/300/spot307.htm
Assessing Opportunity to Learn Survey (Stevens, 1999)	http://www.temple.edu/lss/pdf/publications/pubs1999-8appendix.pdf
Considerations when Selecting a Reading Program	http://www.k8accesscenter.org/training_resources/readprograms.asp
CRESST (Center for Research on Evaluation, Standards, & Student Testing)	www.cresst.org
Defining, Developing, and Using Curriculum Indicators (Porter & Smithson, 2001)	http://www.cpre.org/Publications/rr48.pdf
Educators' Guide to Schoolwide Reform (Am. Institutes for Research)	http://www.aasa.org/issues_and_insights/district_organization/Reform/
English Learners: Assessing Opportunity to Learn (OTL) in Grade 6 Language Arts (Boscardin, et al., 2004)	http://www.cse.ucla.edu/r/l.asp?r=728
ERIC Digest on Opportunity to Learn (Schwartz, 1995)	http://www.ericdigests.org/1996-3/urban.htm
Evidence-based interventions searchable data base (Campbell Collaborative)	http://www.campbellcollaboration.org/
Improving student performance in math (US Dept. of Ed.)	http://www.ed.gov/teachers/how/math/edpicks.jhtml?src=ln
Improving student performance in reading (US Dept. of Ed.)	http://www.ed.gov/teachers/how/read/edpicks.jhtml?src=ln
Issues in Assessing English Language Learners' Opportunity to Learn Mathematics (Herman & Abedi, 2004)	http://www.cse.ucla.edu/r/l.asp?r=726
Mathematics Instruction Resources (National Academy Press)	http://www.nap.edu/catalog/10434.html http://www.nap.edu/catalog/9822.html
National Institute of Child Health and Human Development (NICHD) Reading research & practice resources	http://www.nichd.nih.gov/crmc/cdb/reading.htm
National Institute for Literacy (research, interventions, publications preK-adult)	http://www.nifl.gov/
National Reading Panel	www.nationalreadingpanel.org
NCREL Opportunity to Learn site	http://www.ncrel.org/sdrs/areas/issues/methods/assment/as8lk18.htm
Oregon's Reading First Review of Curricula/Programs (Science/materials alignment)	http://reading.uoregon.edu/curricula/or_rfc_review_2.php

TABLE 1 (continued)

Resource	URL
Reading intervention/prevention resources (National Academy Press)	http://books.nap.edu/catalog/10130.html http://books.nap.edu/catalog/6023.html http://books.nap.edu/catalog/6014.html
Rigorous research policy statement by Robert Slavin	http://www.americanprogress.org/site/pp.asp?c=biJRJ8OVF&b=492641
Standards for interventions based on rigorous evidence (US Dept. of Ed.)	http://www.ed.gov/rschstat/research/pubs/rigorousevid/index.html
Survey of Enacted Curriculum	www.SECsurvey.org
Task Force for Evidence-Based Interventions (APA Div. 16, SSSP)	http://www.indiana.edu/~futures/kratochwill.pdf
Ten Myths of Reading Instruction, Southwest Educational Development Laboratory	http://www.sedl.org/pubs/sedl-letter/v14n03/2.html
What Works Clearinghouse	www.w-w-c.org
Writing Difficulties Prevention and Intervention for Students w/ LD (Graham, Harris, & Larsen, 2001)	http://www.ldonline.org/ld_indepth/writing/prevention_intervention.html
Writing interventions (meta analysis by Gersten, Baker, & Edwards)	http://www.ld.org/research/ncld_writing.cfm

FIGURE 2. A Decision Tree for Using High Stakes Test Data for Program Planning and Evaluation

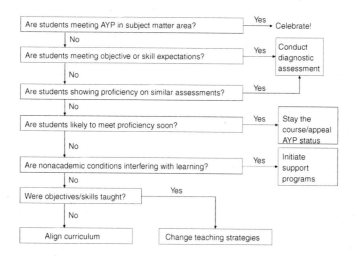

Are Students Meeting Objective or Skill Expectations?

AYP judgments are based on composite (i.e., broad) scores in reading, mathematics, and science. Many states also provide information on specific objectives or skills within an academic domain. Analysis of students' performance on objectives may help pinpoint causes of general academic deficits. Ideally, objective scores should be reported as a proportion of the student group meeting or exceeding proficiency, but some states report objective performance using means. If a school is working with means, it is useful to consider if the distribution of scores are approximately normal (indicating a uniform group of students). Non-normal distributions imply different responses. For example, positively skewed distributions (where most students do poorly, but the mean is inflated by some exceptionally high scorers) underestimates the magnitude of the problem, whereas negatively skewed distributions (i.e., most students do well, but the mean is deflated by some exceptionally low scorers) over-estimate the problem. Multimodal distributions imply two or more distinctly different groups. This pattern suggests targeting some students but not others.

The goal of this step is to develop hypotheses about instruction and programming that might account for failure to meet AYP. Generally, poor performance on one or more objective suggests deficits in how those objectives are taught. Additional diagnostic assessment of a small (ideally, randomly selected) group of students may help identify specific skill deficits within an academic domain. However, keep in mind that objective skill performances are estimated with a small number of items, and are therefore unreliable, which leads to the next step in the process.

Are Students Showing Proficiency on Similar Assessments?

The preceding step should generate hypotheses about problems with current instruction and curricula; this stage should test those hypotheses by obtaining additional data. There are two reasons why school psychologists must collect additional data to evaluate hypotheses generated from high stakes test data. The first is scientific integrity; the same data that lead to a hypothesis cannot be used to test the hypothesis. The second reason is to enhance stakeholder understanding of and commitment to the hypothesis. Many educators question the value of high stakes test data (Johnson, Arumi, & Ott, 2006), but if they reach the same conclusion about causes of poor student performance by data that they value, they will be more likely to accept the hypothesis as valid and useful for considering instructional, curricular, and programmatic changes.

Independent data may come from other tests (if available); analysis of student work samples, in-class quizzes, and exams; and teachers' observations of student performances. Teachers are generally good at predicting how students will do on specific tasks or test items (Demaray & Elliott, 1998), so it is important to provide teachers with clear examples of the kinds of tasks and the degree of proficiency demanded by high stakes tests. When provided with such structure, teachers are often quite accurate in estimating student skills, although they tend to underestimate skills for students with disabilities (Hurwitz, Elliott, & Braden, in press). If additional data are required, sampling methodology (e.g., groups of 20 students) and targeted assessments (e.g., criterion-referenced tasks that may be administered in a few minutes) can produce them quickly and relatively cheaply. Ideally, stakeholders should collect data, and may use nonrandom sampling (e.g., selecting 10 students who passed and 10 who failed a particular objective) to evaluate the veracity of high stakes test results.

Are Students Likely to Meet Proficiency Soon?

Schools and LEAs that have strong progress monitoring systems as part of the general education program will not only have extant data to help test hypotheses in the previous stage, but may also be able to predict rates of growth towards AYP proficiency goals. Progress demonstrated on curriculum-based measures and other progress monitoring tools such as DIBELS (Good, Gruba, & Kaminski, 2002) are good to excellent predictors of who will and will not meet proficiency on high stakes tests (Ax, 2004; Shapiro, Keller, Lutz, Santoro, & Hintze, 2006). If progress monitoring data, or longitudinal data on high stakes tests (i.e., growth models) indicate that low-scoring students are likely to acquire proficiency, it could lead the team to decide to "stay the course" with respect to current instruction, curricula, or programs. Note, however, that such judgments require strong progress monitoring systems (see the National Center on Student Progress Monitoring, n.d.) and strong measurement and technical capacities to reliably identify trends towards proficiency. Such predictions should not be based on teacher judgments.

Are Nonacademic Conditions Interfering with Learning?

Although AYP and high stakes tests focus on students' academic proficiency, nonacademic indicators such as student attendance, disciplinary events, psychosocial screenings, and teacher observations may indicate nonacademic causes for low academic proficiency. School psychologists should be skeptical about accepting nonacademic causes, because many off-task behaviors are motivated by students' seeking to escape inappropriate instructional demands (Hanley, Iwata, & McCord, 2003). Coordinating academic and nonacademic responses is usually better than exclusively focusing on nonacademic features to improve student learning. Resources to evaluate and intervene with nonacademic features of programming include the Research and Training Center for Children's Mental Health (see Kutash, Duchnowski, & Lynn, 2006), the UCLA Mental Health Project Center for Mental Health in Schools (e.g., Center for Mental Health in Schools, 2003), and the National Technical Assistance Center on Positive Behavioral Interventions and Supports (2004).

Were Objectives/Skills Taught?

The presumptive answer to this question is "Yes"; however, careful inspection of teaching behaviors and conditions may suggest students lacked sufficient opportunities to learn. There are many approaches to identifying opportunities to learn (Schwartz, 1995), including structured self-report surveys, direct observations, teacher journals, student surveys, and teacher interviews (see Porter, 2002). Surveys of the "enacted curriculum" (Council of Chief State School Officers, n. d.; Porter & Smithson, 2001) list state academic objectives and invite teachers to report the degree to which they offer frequency and depth on instruction for each objective. Teachers' instructional allocations strongly predict students' performance on high stakes tests (Herman & Abedi, 2004). Less formal approaches to evaluate students' opportunities to learn include analysis of lesson plans, examination of work assigned to students, and teacher absenteeism.

Deciding What to Do: Alignment vs. Change

NCLB presumes that schools afford students opportunities to learn the standards adopted by each state, and that those opportunities should be guided by scientific, research-based methods of instruction. The practice of ensuring that schools afford students opportunities to learn state standards is termed alignment, meaning the school aligns its instructional activities and materials to state standards. Determination that the curricula provided and the standards assessed in high stakes tests are not aligned suggests increasing alignment as a logical focus of program planning, whereas determining that curricula are aligned–but students have not acquired proficiency–suggests changes in the nature of learning opportunities, such as methods and materials used in instruction, should be the focus of program planning.

Alignment. When the decision process indicates that students have not had sufficient opportunities to learn standards, program stakeholders should align program activities to state standards. Although there are many approaches to increasing alignment, some of the most common are:

Vertical integration of curricula across grade levels. Often, what is taught at one grade is not well coordinated with what is taught at other grades. When curricula are not thoughtfully integrated between grades, some aspects of the curriculum may receive more attention than they need, whereas others get less.

Annual lesson planning within a grade. Although flexibility and adaptability are essential characteristics of any teacher, some standards may be neglected because teachers do not manage learning opportunities across the academic year. Careful consideration of what needs to be covered when (i.e., scope and sequence) must be balanced with non-academic aspects of the school year (e.g., the time between Thanksgiving and winter holiday breaks is better for review than introduction of new information).

Selection of teaching materials. The alignment between instructional materials (e.g., textbooks) and standards influences learning opportunities. Therefore, educators must consider using supplemental materials (or omitting portions of a text) when developing annual lesson plans.

In guiding this decision-making process, school psychologists should recognize that educators tend to assign meanings to state standards that match their current expectations and contexts, rather than appreciate the degree to which standards might diverge from their current expectations and contexts (Hill, 2001; Ogawa, Sandholtz, Martinez-Flores & Scribner, 2003).

Change programming. If the program evaluation process indicates that students have been afforded appropriate opportunities to learn, but still do not exhibit proficiency on high stakes tests, the school or program should consider whether current practices could be replaced by more effective and efficient (i.e., evidence-based) methods to support student learning. Adoption of evidence-based practices is particularly important for schools serving students who are at risk of or currently experiencing academic failure (Slavin, 2005). However, the ability of practitioners to reliably identify and implement evidence-based practices is constrained, in part because there is only limited availability of vetted sources, and in part because collecting, reading, rating, and categorizing the literature on a given practice is an extremely time-consuming process that invokes disagreements even among highly trained professionals. Until reputable sources (e.g., the What Works Clearinghouse) provide a list of vetted practices, practitioners may find it quite difficult to identify, much less implement, evidence-based practices at their schools.

The resources needed to implement and sustain changes in programs or instruction must be considered when replacing current practices with evidence-based practices. Underestimation of the resources needed to implement substantial change may undermine the sustainability of long-term improvements. School psychologists should also consider carefully the unintended consequences of test use, and take steps to minimize those consequences in planning their activities (see Jones, 2007; Kruger, Wandle, & Struzziero, 2007).

CONCLUDING COMMENTS

This article is intended to help school psychologists understand and use high stakes test data to evaluate and improve educational programs. The proposed decision-making process attempts to capitalize on assets unique to school psychologists, including knowledge of assessment, ability to understand test results, quantitative skills for analyzing and presenting test data, and strong grounding in evidence-based practices. However, school psychologists are unlikely to be in a position of administrative authority over educational stakeholders, and so the role herein described is one of data-based consultation. It must be acknowledged that, although such a role is consistent with professional practice guidelines (e.g., Ysseldyke, Burns, Dawson, Kelly, Morrison, Ortiz, Rosenfield, & Telzrow, 2006), it is not one that would meet the standards identified for evidence-based practice–that is, there is no rigorous experimental evidence to show that such a role reliably enhances student outcomes. Therefore, school psychologists are cautioned to be critical consumers of this (and other) recommendations for practice; and to consider carefully the consequences of inaction in response to the increasing pressures created by high stakes tests, and the consequences of choosing not to participate in the presentation, understanding, and use of high stakes test data for program planning and improvement.

REFERENCES

Armbruster, B. B., Lehr, F., & Osborn, J. (2001). *Put reading first: The research building blocks for teaching children to read*. Washington, DC: US Department of Education.

Ax, E. E. (2004). *Relationship between curriculum-based measurement reading and statewide achievement test mastery for third grade students*. Unpublished Masters thesis. University of South Florida, Tampa, FL. Retrieved July 6, 2006, from: http://purl.fcla.edu/fcla/etd/SFE0000568.

Braden, J. P. (2002). Educational accountability: High stakes testing and educational reform. In A. Thomas & J. Grimes. (Eds.): *Best practices in school psychology (4th ed.)*, pp. 301-319. Silver Spring, MD: National Association of School Psychologists.

Braden, J. P., & Tayrose, M. P. (in press). Best practices in educational accountability: High stakes testing and educational reform. In A. Thomas & J. Grimes (Eds.), *Best practices in school psychology (5th ed.)*. Silver Spring, MD: National Association of School Psychologists.

Center for Mental Health in Schools (2003). *An introductory packet on assessing to address barriers to learning*. Los Angeles, CA: Author. Retrieved 3 July, 2006, from http://smhp.psych.ucla.edu/pdfdocs/barriers/barriers.pdf.

Center on Positive Behavioral Interventions and Supports (2004). *School-wide positive behavior support: Implementers' blueprint and self-assessment*. Eugene, OR: Author. Retrieved June 13, 2006, from http://www.pbis.org/files/Blueprint%20draft%20v3%209-13-04.doc.

Council of Chief State School Officers (no date). *Surveys of enacted curriculum*. Washington, DC: Author. Retrieved 18 June, 2006, from www.SECsurvey.org.

Council of Chief State School Officers (2005, October). *Policymakers' guide to growth models for school accountability: How do accountability models differ?* Washington, DC: Author. Retrieved 18 June, 2006, from http://www.ccsso.org/content/pdfs/Growth%20Models%20Policymaker%20 Guide%202005.pdf.

Demaray, M., & Elliott, S. N. (1998). Teachers' judgments of students' academic functioning: A comparison of actual and predicted performances. *School Psychology Quarterly, 13*(1), 8-24.

Department of Public Instruction (2002, August). *Objectives performance summary* (data file). Available from Wisconsin Department of Instruction web site, http://dpi.wi.gov/oea/xls/opi99-02s.xls.

Education Week. (2006). Quality Counts at 10: A decade of standards-based education. *Education Week, 25*(17). (Retrieved June 18, 2006, from http://www.edweek.org/ew/toc/2006/01/05/).

Elliott. S. N., Braden, J. P., & White, J. L. (2001). *Assessing one and all: Educational accountability for students with disabilities*. Reston, VA: Council for Exceptional Children.

Ferrara, S., Johnson, E., & Chen, W. H. L. (2004, April). *Vertically moderated standards: Logic, procedures, and likely classification accuracy of judgmentally articulated performance standards*. Paper presented at the Annual Meeting of the National Council on Measurement in Education, San Diego.

Good, R. H., Gruba, J., & Kaminski, R. A. (2002). Best practices in using Dynamic Indicators of Basic Early Literacy Skills (DIBELS) in an outcomes-driven model. In A. Thomas & J. Grimes. (Eds.): *Best practices in school psychology (4th ed.)*, pp. 699-720. Silver Spring, MD: National Association of School Psychologists.

Haertel, E. H. (1999). Validity arguments for high stakes testing: In search of the evidence. *Educational Measurement Issues and Practice, 18*(4), 5-9.

Hanley, G., Iwata, B., & McCord, B. (2003). Functional analysis of problem behavior: A review. *Journal of Applied Behavior Analysis, 36*(2), 147-185.

Herman, J. L., & Abedi, J. (2004). *Issues in assessing English Language Learners' opportunity to learn mathematics* (Center for the Study of Evaluation Report No. 633). Los Angeles: National Center for Research on Evaluation, Standards, and Student Testing. Available: www.cresst.org

Heubert, J. P., & Hauser, R. M. (1999). *High stakes: Testing for tracking, promotion, and graduation*. Retrieved, January 4, 2006, from http://books.nap.edu/execsumm_pdf/6336.pdf.

Hill, H.C. (2001). Policy is not enough: Language and the interpretation of state standards. *American Educational Research Journal, 38*(2), 289-318.

Hurwitz, J. T., Elliott, S. N., & Braden, J. P. (in press). The influence of test familiarity and student disability status upon teachers' judgments of students' test performance. *School Psychology Quarterly*.

Johnson, J., Arumi, A. M., & Ott, A. (2006). *Is support for standards and tests fading?* (Reality Check Educational Insights Issue No. 3). Washington, DC: Public Agenda. Retrieved June 18, 2006, from (http://www.publicagenda.org/research/research_reports_details.cfm?list = 100).

Jones, B. (2007). The unintended outcomes of high stakes testing. *Journal of Applied School Psychology, 23* (2), 67-88.

Kruger, L. J., Wandle, C., & Struzziero, J. (2007). Coping with the stress of high stakes testing. *Journal of Applied School Psychology, 23* (2), 109-128.

Kutash, K., Duchnowski, A. J., & Lynn, N. (2006). *School-based mental health: An empirical guide for decision-makers*. Tampa, FL: The Research and Training Center for Children's Mental Health, Louis de la Parte, Florida Mental Health Institute, University of South Florida. Retrieved July 3, 2006, from: http://rtckids.fmhi.usf.edu/rtcpubs/study04/.

Linn, R. L. (2005). *Fixing the NCLB accountability system* (CRESST Policy Brief No. 8). Los Angeles, CA: National Center for Research on Evaluation, Standards, and Student Testing.

Lissitz, R. W. & Huynh, H. (2003). Vertical equating for state assessments: Issues and solutions in determination of adequate yearly progress and school accountability.

Practical Assessment, Research, & Evaluation, 8(10). Retrieved March 30, 2006 from http://PAREonline.net/getvn.asap?v = 88&n = 10.

McCall, M. S., Kingsbury, G. C., & Olson, A. (2004). *Individual growth and school success.* Lake Oswego, OR: Northwest Evaluation Association. Retrieved 24 June, 2006, from http://www.coloradoleague.org/New%2520Leadership%2520Wkshp%252004/NWEA%2520Growth.pdf.

McDonnell, L. M., McLaughlin, M. J., & Morison, P. (Eds) (1997). *Educating one & all: Students with disabilities and standards-based reform.* Washington, DC: National Academy Press.

Meyer, R. L. (1996). Value-added indicators of school performance. In E. A. Hanushek & D. W. Jorgenson (Eds.), *Improving America's schools: The role of incentives* (pp. 171-196). Washington, DC: National Academy Press.

National Center on Student Progress Monitoring (no date). *What is progress monitoring?* Washington, DC: Author. Retrieved 10 July, 2006, from http://www.studentprogress.org/.

National Council of Teachers of Mathematics (no date). *Standards for school mathematics.* Reston, VA: Author. Retrieved July 3, 2006, from http://www.nctm.org/standards/standards.htm.

National Reading Panel (2000). Report of the National Reading Panel: Teaching children to read–An evidence-based assessment of the scientific research literature on reading and its implications for reading instruction (Summary). Washington, DC: US Department of Health and Human Services.

Newmann, F. M. & Wehlage, G. G. (1995). *Successful school restructuring: A report to the public and educators.* Madison, WI: Center on Organization and Restructuring of Schools, Wisconsin Center for Education Research, University of Wisconsin-Madison.

Ogawa, R.T., Sandholtz, J. H., Martinez-Flores, M., & Scribner, S. P. (2003). The substantive and symbolic consequences of a district's standards-based curriculum. *American Educational Research Journal, 40*(1), 147-176.

Porter, A. C. (2002). Measuring the content of instruction: Uses in research and practice. *Educational Researcher, 31,* 3-14.

Porter, A. C., & Smithson, J. L. (2001). *Defining, developing, and using curriculum indicators* (Research Report Series RR-048). Philadelphia, PA: University of Pennsylvania, Consortium for Policy Research in Education. Retrieved June 18, 2006, from http://www.cpre.org/Publications/rr48.pdf.

Raudenbush, S. (2004). *Schooling, statistics, and poverty: Can we measure school improvement?* (Report PIC-ANG9). Princeton, NJ: Educational Testing Service. Retrieved June 18, 2006, from http://www.ets.org/portal/site/ets/menuitem.c988ba0e5dd572bada20bc47c3921509/?vgnextoid=4fffaf5e44df4010VgnVCM10000022f95190RCRD&vgnextchannel=e2a5be3a864f4010VgnVCM10000022f95190RCRD.

Reckase, M. D. & Marineau, J. (2004, Oct.). *The vertical scaling of science achievement tests.* National Academy of Sciences. Retrieved 12 June, 2006, from http://www7.nationalacademies.org/bota/Vertical%2520Scaling.pdf.

Schulte, A. C., & Villock, D. N. (2004). Using high-stakes tests to derive school-level measures of special education efficacy. *Exceptionality, 12*(2), 107-126.

Schwartz, W. (1995). *Opportunity to learn standards: Their impact on urban students.* (ERIC/CUE Digest No. 110; ERIC Document No. 389816).

Shapiro, E. S., Keller, M. A., Lutz, J. G., Santoro, L. E., & Hintze, J. M. (2006). Curriculum-based measures and performance on state assessment and standardized tests: Reading and math performance in Pennsylvania. *Journal of Psychoeducational Assessment, 24*(1), 19-35.

Shinn, M. R. (2002). Best practices in using curriculum-based measurement in a problem-solving model. In A. Thomas & J. Grimes. (Eds.). *Best practices in school psychology (4th ed.)*, pp. 671-698. Silver Spring, MD: National Association of School Psychologists.

Slavin, R. E. (2005). *Evidence-based reform: Advancing the education of students at risk.* Washington, DC: Center for American Progress. Retrieved 3 July, 2006, from http://www.americanprogress.org/atf/cf/{E9245FE4-9A2B-43C7-A521-5D6FF2E06E03}/Slavin%203%2017%20FINAL.pdf.

Swanson, C. (2006, January). *Making the connection: A decade of standards-based education reform and achievement* (Editorial Projects in Education Research Center). Washington, DC: Education Week. Retrieved June 18, 2006, from http://www.edweek.org/media/ew/qc/2006/MakingtheConnection.pdf.

U.S. Department of Education (2006, May). *Growth models: Ensuring grade-level proficiency for all students by 2014.* Retrieved June 18, 2006, from http://www.ed.gov/admins/lead/account/growthmodel/proficiency.html.

Ysseldyke, J., Burns, M., Dawson, P., Kelley, B., Morrison, D., Ortiz, S., Rosenfield, S., & Telzrow, C. (2006). *School psychology: A blueprint for training and practice III.* Bethesda, MD: National Association of School Psychologists.

doi:10.1300/J370v23n02_08

The School Psychologist as Leader and Change Agent in a High-Stakes Era

David Shriberg

Loyola University Chicago

SUMMARY. School psychologists are well prepared to provide leadership in an era when gathering and interpreting data is center-stage in education reform. The leadership literature is not well known in school psychology and a summary of major leadership theories pertinent to the practice of school psychology is provided. Strategies for leading change in a high stakes testing climate are provided through case studies of two school psychologists who have assumed leadership roles in advocating for fair, effective, and comprehensive uses of data with children. doi:10.1300/J370v23n02_09 *[Article copies available for a fee from The Haworth Document Delivery Service: 1-800-HAWORTH. E-mail address: <docdelivery@haworthpress.com> Website: <http://www.HaworthPress.com> © 2007 by The Haworth Press, Inc. All rights reserved.]*

KEYWORDS. High stakes tests, leadership, school psychologist, change agent

---

Address correspondence to: David Shriberg, PhD, School Psychology Program, 820 North Michigan Avenue, Lewis Towers #1147, Loyola University Chicago, Chicago, IL 60611 (Email: dshribe@luc.edu).

[Haworth co-indexing entry note]: "The School Psychologist as Leader and Change Agent in a High-Stakes Era." Shriberg, David. Co-published simultaneously in *Journal of Applied School Psychology* (The Haworth Press, Inc.) Vol. 23, No. 2, 2007, pp. 151-166; and: *High Stakes Testing: New Challenges and Opportunities for School Psychology* (ed: Louis J. Kruger, and David Shriberg) The Haworth Press, Inc., 2007, pp. 151-166. Single or multiple copies of this article are available for a fee from The Haworth Document Delivery Service [1-800-HAWORTH, 9:00 a.m. - 5:00 p.m. (EST). E-mail address: docdelivery@haworthpress.com].

Available online at http://japps.haworthpress.com
© 2007 by The Haworth Press, Inc. All rights reserved.
doi:10.1300/J370v23n02_09

This is an exciting time to be a school psychologist. As calls for "paradigm change" (Reschly & Ysseldyke, 2002) are increasingly being realized, school psychologists are poised to assume the expanded roles involving systems-level involvement across a variety of domains (e.g., academic, social-emotional, mental health) that have long been sought and promoted by many in the profession (Ysseldyke, Burns, Dawson, Kelley, Morrison, Ortiz, Rosenfield, & Telzrow, 2006) and that offer the most hope that students may ultimately benefit from the full repertoire of the talents that school psychologists have to offer.

This change is not occurring in a vacuum. Regardless of where one personally stands on the merits of high-stakes testing, there can be no disputing the centrality of assessment generally and of high-stakes exams specifically to current educational policy. These policies have a direct impact on children, families, and school personnel and thus, by extension, for school psychologists working in public schools. As the school-based professionals who often have the greatest expertise in assessment and as representatives of a profession that has long since sought to escape the perception that school psychologists can and should only give IQ tests, this current emphasis on assessment provides an opportunity for the field of school psychology both to redefine its role as relates to assessment and to promote best practices in achieving the best possible outcomes for students.

Surprisingly, there is relatively little research in school psychology that speaks directly to school psychology practice within the context of a high-stakes educational reality. This article seeks to contribute to this literature by describing a concept–leadership–that is often identified as an important component of being an effective school psychologist (e.g., Ysseldyke, Burns, Dawson, Kelley, Morrison, Ortiz, Rosenfield, & Telzrow, 2006) but yet also is a concept that at present is not well-defined for school psychologists.

It is the position of this author that all school psychologists have the ability to be leaders and that school psychologists who are able to successfully tap into their leadership skills have the best opportunity to serve students effectively. In order to view how leadership applies to the practice of school psychology in a high-stakes climate, one first needs a basic understanding of the major leadership models that are most pertinent to school psychology practice. As will be seen, these models are best understood within the context that they are employed, so the application of each of these models to a high-stakes climate will be highlighted. Finally, two case studies will be provided of school psychologists who have utilized their leadership skills to promote improved outcomes for students in a high-stakes climate. In these two case studies, key insights and strategies will be highlighted.

HOW MIGHT LEADERSHIP MANIFEST IN SCHOOL PSYCHOLOGY?

A cursory review of any major bookstore reveals that there is no shortage of books devoted to the topic of leadership and no shortage of models from which to choose from when formulating a leadership model specific to school psychology. In a comprehensive review of major leadership models, Shriberg, Shriberg, and Kumari (2005) identified twelve primary models of leadership that characterize the present leadership literature. In the following sections, leadership models or ideas which have the most direct bearing on the practice of school psychology are presented, with application to high-stakes testing highlighted.

Situational Leadership

The central premise of situational leadership, a model that dates back to the late 1960s (Hersey & Blanchard, 1969), is that there is no one best style of leadership that can be applied equally effectively across situations. Rather, proponents of a situational leadership approach (e.g., Blanchard & Zigarmi, 1999; Hersey, 2006) describe effective leadership practice as based on the interplay of the following three dimensions: (a) the amount of guidance and direction a leader gives (task behavior), (b) the amount of social/emotional support a leader provides (relationship behavior), and (c) the readiness level that followers exhibit related to the particular leadership task at hand (Hersey, 2006). Depending on the followers' need for direction and support (which in combination determines readiness) the leader may respond in one of four ways–directing, coaching, supporting, and delegating (Blanchard, Zigarmi, & Zigarmi, 1985). For example, in a situation where the follower has minimal competence and minimal commitment to the leadership task, a "coaching" approach where the leader both defines the roles and provides both direct training of skills and personal social/emotional support is likely to be the most effective leadership method. By contrast, in a situation where the follower has a high degree of competence and a high degree of commitment, the most effective leadership practice would be to take on more of a "delegating" role where control is with the follower in terms of when and how the leader (e.g., the school psychologist) is involved.

While the empirical rigor of this model has not been well substantiated (Graeff, 1997; Fernandez & Vecchio, 1997), the model continues to have widespread popularity in the business sector (its authors claim that it is the most widely used leadership model in the world) in large part because of its intuitive appeal. Viewed from a high-stakes lens, school psychologists working from this perspective would be advised to adjust their leadership style based on the knowledge base and motivation of those that they are interacting with. For example, a teacher may be very motivated to engage in activities that might have the effect of increasing student test scores, but may lack the knowledge required to, for example, evaluate whether or not their teaching practices are aligned with test content. A school psychologist working with such a teacher would be advised to assume a "directing" approach that emphasizes skills training and places less emphasis on providing personal support since this teacher is already highly motivated to learn and grow. By contrast, another teacher who has a high degree of competence but variable commitment to the desired task would in this model merit more of a "supporting" style of leadership from the school psychologist where skills training would be less prominent and providing personal social/ emotional support would be given greater emphasis.

In the course of working with others to address the same problem or related set of problems, followers may move back and forth along the situational leadership continuum. The essential point of a situational leadership model remains that effective leadership involves assessing the competence and motivation of others and then adjusting one's behavior accordingly. If you are working with someone who is highly competent and highly motivated to succeed, a micro-managing style is likely to be ineffective. Similarly, if you are working with someone who is not that competent or motivated, this person may require more of a "coaching" approach emphasizing both skills development and emotional support until their competence reaches a certain level where a "supporting" style that is less directive is more appropriate.

Transformational Leadership

Transformational leadership is an approach that presently enjoys wide popularity and is most strongly associated with the work of Bernard Bass (e.g., Bass & Riggio, 2006) and James McGregor Burns (e.g., Burns, 1979). This approach is often presented in contrast with transactional leadership. Transactional leadership occurs when the leader adjusts his or her behavior based on the adequacy of the follower's performance (Bass, 1998). If the follower performs his or her responsibilities effectively, the leader responds positively and if the follower does not perform effectively, the leader responds with punishment or inattention.

While a transactional approach is characterized by a barter without any accompanying obligation or desire for improvement by either party, transformational leadership implies a much stronger commitment between the parties involved and a shared desire for improvement (Burns, 1979). Placed into a school psychology context, the idea of transformational leadership implies that the practice of school psychology involves both a commitment to work with others in need regardless of their past history of success (e.g., we do not stop working with a teacher simply because he or she does not achieve a desired goal) and also that the purpose of our work is to produce better outcomes for children, not to enhance our own status or pocketbooks. That is, transformational leadership is relational and intends to produce meaningful change in others (Rogers & Shriberg, 2005). As such, a school psychologist operating from a transformational leadership approach would be actively involved in working to improve academic performance not simply because schools will be penalized if student scores on high stakes exams do not continuously increase (although this reality is acknowledged), but because the school psychologist is committed to supporting innovations and changes that support success in all students, families, and educators regardless of their ability and previous performance.

Social Power and Influence

Schools often are intensely political places and, regardless of the specific leadership model one embraces, obtaining social power and influence within the school setting is an important mechanism for achieving real change. Much of what is known about social power in organizations is based on a typology first developed by French and Raven in 1959 (Raven, Schwartzwald, & Koslowsky, 1998). This model of social power and influence was based on five dimensions–expert power (based on knowledge and competence), referent power (based on relationships and personal drawing power), legitimate power (bestowed by formal organization), reward power (the ability to offer and withhold types of incentives), and coercive power (the ability to force someone to comply through threat of punishment) (French & Raven, 1959). In 1965, informational power (based on presentation of persuasive material or logic) was added as a sixth dimension (Raven, 1965). Informational power is related to expert power but is also distinct from it. In expert power, the person being influenced may not necessarily understand why a particular suggestion offered by the school psychologist is a good idea but may choose to follow the school psychologists' advice anyway because he/she sees the school psychologist as an expert. In informational power, the person being influenced has been persuaded by the logic provided by the school psychologist.

Since 1965, each of these dimensions have been further elaborated, with the most recent model containing 14 distinct power sources derived from these six dimensions (Erchul & Raven, 1997). In 2001, Koslowsky, Schwarzwald, and Ashuri found evidence for a two-factor model of social power and influence where French and Raven's dimensions were divided into "soft power" and "hard power" dimensions. "Hard" power refers to influence techniques that rely on a combination of coercion, overt, and heavy-handed methods (such as punishing those who do not comply) whereas "soft" power derives from more subtle influence processes such as providing others with information without any accompanying pressure or threats (Koslowsky, Schwarzwald, & Ashuri, 2001). Erchul, Raven, and Ray (2001) report that this hard/soft dichotomy has been replicated in several recent studies. Building on this framework, Erchul et al. (2001) found that a sample of school psychologists believed that the use of soft power tactics would result in greater teacher compliance than use of hard power tactics. In a larger sample involving both teachers and school psychologists, both groups agreed that informational and expert power are the most effective power bases in the school psychologist/teacher consultation process and teachers considered informational, expert, legitimate, and referent power as the most influential power bases (Erchul, Raven, & Whichard, 2001). Most recently, Erchul, Raven, and Wilson (2004) examined the use of power bases in consultation through the filter of consultant gender with the expectation that female school psychologists would view the employment of soft power bases as more effective. They found support for this hypothesis. Both male and female school psychologists viewed soft power bases as more effective than hard power bases.

From a social power and influence perspective, school psychologists seeking to influence others to use best practices in interpreting and using high stakes test data would be well advised to consider using the wide range of soft power tactics (e.g., referent, expert, and informational) commonly available to them. It is likely that being seen as high in all three of these forms of power will lead to greater influence than being high in one form and low on another. For example, if one has a lot of knowledge about how best to interpret high stakes testing data (informational power) but presents this knowledge in an arrogant, off-putting way, this knowledge is less likely to lead to real change than if that person also has strong personal drawing power (referent power). Similarly, if a school psychologist has strong drawing power but either lacks expertise in high-stakes testing or has expertise but this expertise is not seen as credible because it falls outside of the expected knowledge base of the school psychologist, it will be more challenging to produce real change.

Organizational Development/Systems Change

School psychologists typically operate within the confines of a larger organizational structure (e.g., the school and school district where they are employed) and thus it is not surprising that "organizational development/systems change" is the leadership model with the greatest representation in the school psychology literature. A recurrent theme in this literature involves the challenges associated with bringing good ideas into practice in an applied setting. For example, the Evidence-Based Intervention Work Group at the University of Wisconsin-Milwaukee (2005) reviewed eight different change models–social influence theory (see previous section), the concerns-based adoption model, the theory of reasoned action, Rogers' innovation-diffusion theory, generalization theory, the transtheoretical model of change, functional assessment, and the organizational analytic model–for their usefulness in helping to facilitate adoption of evidence-based interventions in practice settings. These authors noted that each model emphasized the importance of communication and collaboration between researchers and practitioners and that these groups often had different frameworks for evaluating the effectiveness and usefulness of interventions. These differences could either be barriers or opportunities depending on the openness to change and ability to listen on either side. Thus, a school psychologist who seeks to lead on a systems level should not be dismissive of any ideas that do not immediately fit into the original plan of action. Particularly as relates to a topic that can be as personally and politically charged as high-stakes testing, this model places a premium on openness and flexibility in order to meet the needs and concerns of pertinent stakeholders.

Calling on school psychologists to embrace an organizational development and strategic planning perspective, to view themselves as systems change agents who are part of the school system, and to position themselves as individuals who are seen by others as experts who can lead systems change efforts, Knoff (2000, pp. 18-19) offers the following action steps for school psychologists seeking to lead systems change efforts, using his experiences with the Project ACHIEVE program as a blueprint: (a) understand the full practical and empirical breadth of the problem you are seeking to address; (b) conduct a comprehensive needs assessment,; (c) explore the possibility of creating a coalition of resource people who will initiate discussions at the district level; (d) write a briefing paper that summarizes all of the above and that describes the goals and objectives of the proposed initiative, a possible sequence of events and activities, the people and other resources needed to accomplish the objectives described, and specific outcomes that will define and demonstrate success; and (e) outline and begin the administrative process.

Knoff (2000) notes that this entire process likely will take a year or more and this is a second recurring theme in the organizational/systems change literature. In this vein, Bonner, Koch, and Langmeyer (2004) describe their efforts in a six year project working towards a full inclusion model in an elementary school in the Midwest through the lens of organizational theory principles. When reflecting on their experience with systems change as part of this long-term process, Bonner et al. (2004) note how often patience was required along the way and comment that while the goal of many organizational interventions is to minimize and/or eliminate conflict, they believe this to be both an impossible and an undesirable goal, recommending instead that change agents seek to make the organizational conflict inherent in any kind of change effort "manageable, but not managed" (Bonner et al., 2004, p. 468). For example, in describing their long-term involvement working with students and staff of an alternative day school for students with emotional and behavioral disorders towards bringing research to practice, Miller, George, and Fogt (2005) report that many school personnel were at first highly resistant to their suggestion that the use of physical restraints be eliminated. After the change was implemented (reluctantly by some) and the use of restraints, which previously had been quite common, was virtually eliminated, these researchers questioned the initially reluctant teachers. These teachers identified three factors that led to them overcoming their initial resistance–early, small-scale success of the change, the use of data, and the practical, positive impact on working conditions

(Miller et al., 2005, p. 561). The authors conclude by stating that the most important role for school psychologists in systems change efforts is in the area of organizational consultation. They state that school psychologists should be encouraged to work smarter rather than harder and to start small but think big, and that the pathway to systemic change involves agreement amongst key stakeholders as to the presence of a problem and shared commitment to find solutions for the problem (Miller et al., 2005).

CASE STUDIES

The previous sections describe four significant and related models of/approaches to leadership and their potential relevance to the practice of school psychology in a high-stakes testing world. While models such as these provide an important conceptual structure for understanding how leadership may best be applied by school psychologists, real-life contexts rarely follow a prescribed format. In this section, the experiences of two school psychologists, David Lillenstein of the Derry (PA) Township School District and recently retired James G. Somers of the Lansing (MI) School District are described. Each of these leaders has stories to tell and their experiences inform the practice of school psychologists seeking to be effective leaders and change agents in a high-stakes world.

Case Study #1–David Lillenstein, Derry (PA) Township School District

David Lillenstein, NCSP, Ed.D., never was your typical school psychologist. He notes that when he began his first position, the assumption was that he would assume a "traditional" school psychology role in that he was expected to provide a series of IQ and achievement tests and do little else. He states that when he arrived at this position, he inherited a form for documenting his activities and this form included boxes for only a very narrow range of activities. So, rather than conform to preset expectations, he decided that his best course was to proceed in a manner that he felt would be more effective for students (e.g., greater emphasis on consultation, centering his practice not on what you call a problem but what you do about the problem). As such, he began to practice in a more comprehensive fashion than was indicated in the checkboxes that he inherited and he began to keep dueling activity forms. That is, he continued to complete the form that his supervisor had provided to him at the outset, but also created his own form (based on NASP standards) in which he documented the range of functions that he was actually doing.

Lillenstein states that at first he was met with some resistance by his supervisor and by some of his fellow school psychologists, but as he continued to document the wide range of tasks he was performing and, critically, the positive outcomes of his work, eventually his supervisor and many of his peers began to appreciate his efforts and to view his work as an opportunity for role expansion. He also notes that not everyone, including his fellow school psychologists, was thrilled with what he was trying to accomplish.

When he decided to move to a different part of the state a few years later, at his first job interview Lillenstein received the standard questions about his proficiency with IQ tests specifically and with the test and place model more generally. He responded by asking his own questions about why the school felt that this was important and offered an alternative vision of the role of the school psychologist that centered on ideas such as consultation, prevention, and effective intervention. He states that this school district was "looking to do something different" and, as such, was open to the ideas and challenges that he presented in his job interview. Once hired, he went on to radically transform his school psychology position from a "test and place" model to one that emphasized the skills that he had promoted in his initial job interview, building critical alliances with teachers, parents, and administrators along the way.

After six years, a new superintendent was installed and, according to Lillenstein, he was told to stop doing what he was hired to do and to return to a more "traditional" role. Thus, in 2002 he began his present position as Director of Psychological Services (a position created for him) in the Derry (PA) Township School District. In this position, he has supervisory responsibility over one school psychologist and two school psychology interns and also is the school psychologist for grades 3-5 and 9-12 in this district. He states that when he was hired in Derry, people at first "were a bit offended" when they did not see him carrying a WISC kit everywhere, so he spent much of his first few months educating others about his role and about the various competencies that school psychologists possess. Lillenstein states that the best opportunity to make inroads towards role expansion was in the area of assessment. This was because, as he challenged others' assumptions that he should spend most of his time giving IQ tests, doubters invariably asked, "If IQ tests are not effective, what's a better method?" These types of questions and the recognition that children were not being well-served by the preexisting model provided him with the opportunity to introduce DIBELS and the concept of linking assessment to instruction to his district.

As with his previous setting, while Lillenstein assumed a leadership role at the outset, the path towards major systems change involved collaboration with many others, including parents, teachers, and administrators. In particular, Lillenstein notes that during the past several years he and the district's curriculum coordinator both have been visible leaders and have spent considerable time working behind the scenes to support their principals' roles as the instructional leaders in their schools. Lillenstein states, "We feed information to the principals and they are the visible leaders. As principals began to deliver the message, teachers saw what we were doing as not just a special education initiative, but as a schoolwide initiative."

Lillenstein states that crucial to successes he has achieved has been his ability to collect pertinent data and then use these data to measure effectiveness. He notes that at first many of his colleagues in education provided considerable resistance to his efforts and that he still encounters much resistance but, "now that I have data showing effectiveness, I am not getting questioned or challenged as much." Initially, he held back on sharing data with parents until he was sure that the changes he was promoting were achieving positive outcomes, but after he began sharing these data with parents, "they were absolutely thrilled" and became vocal supporters.

As part of his role, Lillenstein has been actively involved in his schools' efforts as relates to his state's high stakes exam. He states, "Whether we like it or not, these tests are what is being used to measure our effectiveness as educators, so we might as well take a look and see what we can do instructionally that translates to improved scores on this measure. More importantly, we can take formative data to enhance instructional effectiveness, which will have the effect of improving scores on high stakes exams." He notes that, while he is far from a statistician, he now devotes much of his time towards educating others on how to apply statistics, how to critically analyze literature, and how to select the most appropriate assessment tools to enhance teaching effectiveness. In July 2006, his role shifted somewhat and he became what he calls his district's "data guru." In this role, he is looking at the high stakes testing data trends for his school district during the last several years with an eye towards asking questions that will lead to goal setting related to this data.

Case Study #2: James G. Somers, Lansing (MI) Public Schools

James G. Somers, NCSP, a recently retired school psychologist in the Lansing (MI) school system, is the first to admit that he hates public speaking and has little use for politics. Yet, there he was in May 2004 providing testimony to the Michigan Senate Education Committee on the topic of high-stakes assessment in Michigan. A practicing school psychologist for 31 years in urban Lansing, Somers states that his interest in high stakes arose out of a sense of equity and fairness. Specifically, Somers describes himself as a "data-driven practitioner" and felt that the students in his district were being shortchanged by the assessment and accountability measures in place in Michigan.

As part of a graduate course he was taking at Michigan State University, Somers teamed with graduate students in mathematics and educational psychology to track changes in reading achievement scores between urban and suburban students in Michigan. Somers describes this project as "a life-changing event for me." According to Somers, what they found was that, compared to students in suburban districts, students in urban schools typically started school behind their suburban peers, that this gap in reading achievement continued through the second grade, and then after the second grade both suburban and urban students progressed at similar rates, but by this point the urban students typically were well behind their suburban peers.

When the state of Michigan was considering making changes to their high-stakes exam and invited testimony on this topic, Somers was approached by his state school psychology association (Michigan Association of School Psychologists (MASP)) to speak on their behalf. In providing testimony to the Michigan state house, Somers argued in favor of a growth (or value-added) standard for evaluating students rather than the fixed standard which was in place. In his testimony, he stated,

> Assume that your daughter has decided to join the track team and enter the high jump. As you work with her in your back yard, where do you set the bar? Even if you know that five feet is a respectable height for high school, do you set it at five feet? Or do you determine how high she is jumping now, and set the bar a little higher than that level, moving it upward as she improves? Now, assume that you want to know how the high jumpers are progress-

ing across the country, on each team. Do you measure that by seeing how many can clear five feet? Or would you rather know how much improvement each athlete has made during the season? Which of these would tell you who has been coached the best, the team that has the most athletes clearing five feet, or the team that has made the most improvement? This is the difference between a fixed standard and a growth standard. The MEAP (Michigan Educational Assessment Program, Michigan's high stakes exam) cutoff for many students is at five feet. For those far below, it is pretty discouraging. And for those easily above, it provides no incentive to do better. But if we used a rate of growth criterion, all could be credited for their progress, at whatever level that may be. And if we use an individualized rate of growth criterion, we would no longer have the confounding effect of the child's background, because we are comparing each child to themselves (longitudinally comparing their previous score to current score). Under this model, a child's rate of growth in an urban school can be compared to another child's rate of growth in a suburban school, giving us a better measure of instructional effectiveness in each setting.

Noting that MASP was one of the few sources to provide research-driven testimony to the state, Somers' remarks were based on a position statement developed by himself, Matthew Burns (then of Central Michigan University) and Susan M. Petterson of Oakland (MI) Schools which was adopted by MASP in 2004. In this position statement and in Somers testimony, the following recommendations were offered: (a) use the MEAP for group, not individual progress, (b) add vertical scaling, yearly testing, and use rate of growth as a measure of progress, (c) do not use single scores for student sanctions or rewards, (d) do not use scores for school sanctions or rewards, (e) give and score the test in the Fall so instruction can be adjusted, (f) report mobility rates, (g) add a veracity scale to the MEAP, and (h) the Michigan Department of Education should regularly caution about the misuse of test results.

Stating that "leadership is not something you seek, it is something that is thrust upon you," Somers indicated that his leadership as relates to high-stakes testing was a result of his personal passions around the topics of data, fairness, and equity, and of timing in terms of these passions being relevant to current debate and discourse. He notes that it is very important for school psychologists to join their state association and to stay current through taking classes and working with interns in order to develop and sustain a knowledge base that others will want to tap.

Somers suggests that school psychologists who seek to assume leadership as relates to high-stakes testing practices in their school or district should first find out what department and/or individuals in their school district deal with testing. He then suggests that school psychologists get to know the individuals involved with the district's assessment procedures and their background and expertise. Somers states that often school psychologists will bring important areas of expertise that may not be present amongst the individuals who handle testing in a particular district. He also states that it is important to become very knowledgeable about the high-stakes tests in your state and how they are being used both at the state level and in your district. For example, do the individuals who are handling the high-stakes data for your school district know how to interpret test data and how to link these data to instruction? Based on how data is being used (or perhaps misused or misunderstood) by those in your district, Somers suggests providing information and leadership to those involved in this process and using the tools of the school psychologist to advocate for a more "humanistic" approach to how high-stakes tests are typically used and interpreted.

Somers states that his vision for the future involves school psychologists increasingly being active participants and leaders of district-wide assessment teams that go beyond special education. In his vision, school psychologists would have involvement in all district assessment procedures (not unlike David Lillenstein's "data guru" position), high stakes or otherwise, and their role would be to provide assistance and intervention to any students, regular or special education, who are not progressing well. In this way, school psychologists position themselves as data-driven interventionists whose primary functions include promoting enhanced academic outcomes for all students.

CONCLUSION

The real-life examples of David Lillenstein and James G. Somers highlight the leadership opportunities available to school psychologists and also reflect many of the core ideas central to the leadership models described in this article. For example, both school psychologists described assuming a transformative role where the school psychologist is involved not only in working with high stakes data, but in analyzing school assessment procedures more broadly and working towards processes that have the potential to impact all students. Both school psychologists also stressed the importance of developing relationships with others and working to create change within a complex broader system in which obstacles abound and resistance is likely. Finally, both school psychologists stressed the importance of being data-driven and using data as one's ally in assuming leadership roles.

These individuals grasped the practical reality that high stakes testing provides new opportunities for school psychologists. To date, the field of school psychology suffers from a lack of knowledge about major leadership theories and also from a lack of research highlighting the real-life work of school psychologists who have assumed a leadership role as relates to high stakes testing. While individual situations vary, school psychologists who can combine their vision for role expansion and positive change with a commitment to data, advocacy, and interpersonal savvy within a complex educational structure have the opportunity to assume leadership in this current educational climate where test scores have been given tremendous prominence and importance.

REFERENCES

Bass, B.M., & Riggio, R.E. (2006). *Transformational leadership* (2nd ed.). Mahwah, NJ: Lawrence Erlbaum Associates.

Bass, B.M. (1998). *Transformational leadership: Industrial, military, and educational impact.* Mahwah, NJ: Lawrence Erlbaum & Associates.

Blanchard, K.H., Zigarmi, P., & Zigarmi, D. (1985). *Leadership and the one minute manager.* New York: William Morrow.

Blanchard, K. & Zigarmi, P. (1999). *Leadership and the one minute manager: Increasing effectiveness through situational leadership.* New York: William Morrow.

Bonner, M., Koch, T., & Langmeyer, D. (2004). Organizational theory applied to school reform: A critical analysis. *School Psychology International, 25,* 455-471.

Burns, J.M. (1979). *Leadership.* New York: Harper & Row.

Erchul, W.P., & Raven, B.H. (1997). Social power in school consultation: A contemporary view of French and Raven's bases of power model. *Journal of School Psychology, 35,* 137-171.

Erchul, W.P., Raven, B.H., & Wilson, K.E. (2004). The relationship between gender of consultant and social power perceptions within school consultation. *School Psychology Review, 33,* 582-590.

Erchul, W.P., Raven, B.H., & Ray, A.G. (2001). School psychologists' perceptions of social power bases in teacher consultation. *Journal of Educational and Psychological Consultation, 12,* 1-23.

Erchul, W.P., Raven, B.H., & Whichard, S.M. (2001). School psychologist and teacher perceptions of social power bases in school consultation. *Journal of School Psychology, 39,* 483-497.

Fernandez, C.F. & Vecchio, R.P. (1997). Situational leadership revisited: A test of an across-jobs perspective. *Leadership Quarterly, 8,* 67-84.
French, J.R.P., Jr., & Raven, B.H. (1959). The bases of social power. In D. Cartwright (Ed.), *Studies in social power* (pp. 150-167). Ann Arbor, MI: Institute for Social Research.
Graeff, C.L. (1997). Evaluation of situational leadership theory: A critical review. *Leadership Quarterly, 8,* 153-170.
Hersey, P. & Blanchard, K.H. (1969). Life cycle theory of leadership. *Training and Development Journal, 23,* 26-34.
Hersey, P. (2006). Situational leadership. In J.L. Pierce & J.W. Newstrom (Eds.), *Leadership and the leadership process: Readings, self-assessments, and applications,* pp. 210-211. Boston: McGraw-Hill Irwin.
Knoff, H.M. (2000). Organizational development and strategic planning for the millennium: A blueprint toward effective school discipline, safety, and crisis prevention. *Psychology in the Schools, 37,* 17-32.
Koslowski, M., Schwarzwald, J., & Ashuri, S. (2001). On the relationship between subordinates' compliance to power sources and organisational attitudes. *Applied Psychology: An International Review, 50,* 455-476.
Miller, D.N., George, M.P., & Fogt, J.B. (2005). Establishing and sustaining research-based practices at Centennial School: A descriptive case study of systemic change. *Psychology in the Schools, 42,* 553-567.
Raven, B.H. (1965). Social influence and power. In I.D. Steiner & M. Fishbein (Eds.), *Current studies in social psychology* (pp. 371-381). New York: Holt, Rinehart, & Winston.
Raven, B.H., Schwarzwald, J. & Koslowsky, M. (1998). Conceptualizing and measuring a power/interaction model of interpersonal influence. *Journal of Applied Social Psychology, 28,* 307-332.
Reschly, D.J. & Ysseldyke, J.E. (2002). Paradigm shift: The past is not the future. In A. Thomas & J. Grimes (Eds.), *Best Practices in School Psychology IV, Vol. 1,* pp. 3-20. Bethesda, MD: National Association of School Psychologists.
Rogers, J.L. & Shriberg, A. (2005). Leadership theories and approaches for today and tomorrow. In A. Shriberg, D. Shriberg, & R. Kumari (Eds.). *Practicing leadership: Principles and applications* (3rd ed.), pp. 202-224. New York: Wiley.
Shriberg, A., Shriberg, D. & Kumari, R. (2005). *Practicing leadership: Principles and applications (3rd Ed.).* New York: Wiley.
The Evidence-Based Intervention Work Group (2005). Theories of change and adoption of innovations: The evolving evidence-based intervention and practice movement in school psychology. *Psychology in the Schools, 42,* 475-494.
Ysseldyke, J., Burns, M., Dawson, P., Kelley, B., Morrison, D., Ortiz, S., Rosenfield, S., & Telzrow, K. (2006). *School psychology: A blueprint for training and practice III.* Bethesda, MD: National Association of School Psychologists.

doi:10.1300/J370v23n02_09

Index

Academic achievement
  impact of high-stakes testing on, 47-64
    research studies about, 49-53
    relationship to social and economic development, 22-23
Academic support, for teachers and students, 87-107
Accountability
  criticisms of, 67
  effect on mathematics performance, 55
  growth models of, 133-134
  improvement models of, 132-133
  measurement of variation in, 58-59
  "new," 8-9
  regression analysis of, 55-56
  status models of, 131-132
    versus growth models, 134-136
  as stress source, 110
  support for, 66-67
  of teachers, 49
  test-based, 66-69
  in Texas, 51-52
Accountability index, of high-stakes testing, 55
"Achievement gap," 79
Achievement testing. *See also* High-stakes testing
  widespread use of, 2
Adolescents, test anxiety in, 117
Aerobic activities, for stress management, 120
African-American students, 79-80, 116
Alaska, 39

Alignment, between instruction and assessment, 17-18, 135-136, 144-145
American Educational Research Association (AERA), 67-68
American Psychological Association, 67-68
Anxiety, high-stakes testing-related, 59, 60, 116-117
  cognitive-behavioral approach to, 122, 123-124
  in learning-disabled student, 76-77
  parents' role in, 122
  relaxation training for, 122
Assessment Pressure Rating (APR), 56-57
Autonomy, of teachers, 112, 119
Avoidance, as coping style, 115
Awareness training, about stress, 120

Basic interpersonal communication skills (BICS), 92
Bass, Bernard, 154
Bias, in testing, 36-37, 42
Biofeedback, 120
Boston Globe, 111
Breathing techniques, for stress management, 120
Bureaucracy, 9
Burnout, in teachers, 119-120
Burns, James McGregor, 154-155
Bush, George W., 11, 28
Bush, Jeb, 68

California
    curriculum changes in, 81
    SAT-9 scores in, 81
California High School Exit Exam
        (CAHSEE), 91
Center on Education Policy, 59
Change agents, school psychologists
        as, 151-166
Charter schools, 18-19
Chicago Public School district
    high-stakes testing in, 52-53
    social promotion termination in, 52
Coercive power, 155,156
Cognitions, self-defeating, 120
Cognitive academic language
        proficiency (CALP) in, 92-93
Cognitive-behavioral approach, in
        stress management,
        122,123-124
Cognitive skills, development of, 69
Colorado, high-stakes testing in, 42
Community, collaboration schools, 118
Competition, academic, 122-123
Concerns-based adoption model, of
        leadership, 157
Confirmatory factor analysis, 31,36
Connecticut, high-stakes testing in., 42
Connecticut State Department of
        Education, 74-75
Consultation, systems-level, 118-119
Coping, with testing-related stress,
        114-115
    definition of, 114
    strategies for, 120-124
        avoidant, 115
        cognitive-behavioral, 122
        physiological, 120
        problem-focused, 115,124
        voluntary disengagement-type,
            114-115
        voluntary engagement-type, 114,
            115
Coping Cat program, 122,123-124
Coping with Stress program, 123

CTB McGraw-Hill, 39
Cubberly, Ellwood, 10
Curriculum
    alignment of, 17-18,135-136,
        144-145
    effect of high-stakes testing on,
        69-70,76,81
    "enacted," 144
Curriculum-based measurement, 21

Data Recognition Corporation, 39
Derry (Pennsylvania) Township
        School District, 159-162
Desensitization training, parental, 122
Differential item function (DIF),
        37,39,42
Drills, as preparation for high-stakes
        testing, 59,70-71
Dyslexia, 76

Early Reading First program, 16
Economically-disadvantaged students,
        77-79
    "teaching to the test" with, 41
    testing accommodations for, 42
Education, goals of, 69-70
Educational systems
    moral purpose of, 22-23
    scientific management of, 10
Educational Testing Service, 39
Education Summit (1989), 13
Elementary and Secondary Education
        Act (ESEA), 11,12
Emotionality, as test anxiety
        component, 117
English language learners (ELLs),
        77,80-81,116
    basic interpersonal communication
        skills (BICS) of, 92
    cognitive academic language
        proficiency (CALP) of, 92-93
    with disabilities, 92

exclusion from assessment testing, 13
high-stakes testing-related stress in, 121
testing accommodations for, 22,37, 42,93,94
school psychologists' role in, 92-96
English-language proficiency, students' lack of. *See* English language learners (ELLs)
Ethnic groups, NAEP scores in, 55-57
Expert power, 155,156-157

Fairness, in testing, 36-37
504 plans, 92,93-94,95-96
Florida, high-stakes testing in, 114
as basis for school ratings, 68-69
economic cost of, 74
effect on school curriculum, 69
invalid methodology in, 40
"pacing calendars" for, 71
in poor school districts, 78
Sunshine State Standards for, 66-67
as teacher attrition cause, 74
"three-point-five essay" approach in, 71
Ford, Henry, 8
Friends for Life, 122
Functional assessment model, of leadership, 157

GED tests, 40
Generalization theory model, of leadership, 157
Grade promotion, 28,110,130
Grade retention, as stress cause, 113

Harcourt Assessment, 39
"Hard power," 156

Headaches, high-stakes testing-related, 73
High schools
dropping out of, 73
graduation examinations, 2,28,53, 73,110,116,130
High-stakes testing
administration during February and March, 70
alignment approach in, 17-18, 135-136,144-145
as basis for teacher evaluation, 69
continuing assessment and improvement of, 42-43
cost-effectiveness of, 12-13
cut-off scores in, 43
definition of, 130
deleterious and unintended effects of. *See* Unintended outcomes, of high-stakes testing
economic cost of, 74-75
factors affecting performance on, 102
during "gateway" school years, 52-53
inflated test scores in, 49-50
"low stakes" consequences of, 130
mandated proficiency levels in, 131
measurement issues in, 27-46
publications about, 3
rationale for, 49
relation to school psychology practice, 3-4
research studies of, 47-64
implications of, 58-60
standards for application of, 37-43
reliability and validity in, 38,39-40
single verus multiple tests in, 37, 38-39
standards for reliability and validity of, 37-44
public information about, 38,40-42
test-curriculum alignment, 38,41
"teaching to the test" in, 59

testing accommodations in, 76
Hispanic students, 79
Home-school collaboration, 118
Houston, Texas, 69

Individual Education Plans (IEPs), 92,93-94,95-96
Individuals with Disabilities Act (IDEA), 88,89,90
Individuals with Disabilities Education Improvement Act of 2004 (IDEIA), 89
Informational power, 155-157
Innovations-diffusion theory model, of leadership, 157
Instructional planning, 21
Instructional planning pyramid, 98-101
Intelligence (IQ) tests, 152
Iowa Test of Basic Skills (ITBS), 49-51,52,52-53
Irritability, high-stakes testing-related, 73
Item response testing (IRT), 31-36,39,44
    differential item function (DIF) in, 37
    individual variability in, 43
    item characteristic curves (ICC) in, 33,35
    reliability in, 34-36
    standard error in, 41-42
    validity in, 36

Job demands-resources theory, 112
Job enrichment strategies, for teachers, 119

Keillor, Garrison, 50
Kentucky, high-stakes testing in
    invalid methodology in, 40
    score variability in, 67

"Lake Wobegon effect," 49-51,52
Language arts, 100 % proficiency in, 2-3
Lansing (Michigan) Public School system, 162-164
Large-scale assessment systems. *See also* High-stakes testing; No Child Left Behind
    characteristics of, 9
    theoretical basis for, 8-9
Latent trait theory, 28
Latino students, 116
Leadership, school psychologists' role in, 103-105,151-166
    case studies of, 159-165
        David Lillenstein, 159-162,164-165
        James Somers G., 162-165
    organizational development/systems change context of, 157-159
    situational leadership, 153-154
    social power and influence perspective on, 155-157
    transformational leadership, 154-155
Learning
    cooperative, 122-123
    effect of high-stakes testing on, 52,57-58,70-71,72-73
    love of, 72-73
    with understanding, 70
Learning-disabled students
    avoidant coping in, 115
    high school exit test failure in, 116
    high-stakes testing of
        intended outcomes in, 75
        as stress and anxiety cause, 76-77,121
        underperformance in, 75-76
        unintended outcomes in, 75-77,121
    remedial courses for, 76
    testing accommodations for, 37,42
Lillenstein, David, 159-162,164-165

Literacy assessment, 20
Literacy instruction, 81
Little Grunt and the Big Egg, 71
Lyon, Reid, 89

Massachusetts
  English Language Arts test in, 70
  high-stakes test scores in, 116
Massachusetts Comprehensive Assessment System (MCAS), 39, 77
Mass media, ranking of schools' performances by, 111
Mathematics performance
  Assessment Pressure Rating (APR) of, 56-57
  computation skills in, 52
  effect of accountability policy on, 55
  higher-level thinking skills in, 52
  Iowa Test of Basic Skills scores in, 50
  mandated proficiency levels in, 131
  No Child Left Behind requirements for, 12
  number concept skills in, 52
  100% proficiency in, 2-3
  trend analysis of, 54-55
Mathematics proficiency, variability in, 14
"McDonaldization," 10, 11-19, 23
Meditation, 120
Michigan Association of School Psychologists (MASP), 162-163
Minnesota, 114
Minority-group students, 79-80
Motivation, academic, 76-77, 115-116, 123
  extrinsic, 71-72
  intrinsic, 71-73, 115-116
Multiple-choice tests, 12-13, 76
Muscle relaxation training, 120

National Assessment of Educational Progress (NAEP) scores
  Assessment Pressure Rating (APR) of, 56-57
  comparison with
    high-stakes test scores, 40
    Iowa Test of Basic Skills scores, 51
    Texas Assessment of Academic Skills (TAAS) scores, 51-52
  ethnic factors in, 55-57
  trend analysis of, 54-55
National Association of School Psychologists, 67-68
National Center for Research on Evaluation, Standards, and Student Testing (CRESST), 19, 20
National Educational Longitudinal Survey (NELS), 53
National Institute of Child Health and Human Development, Child Development and Behavior Branch, 89
New Jersey, "teaching to the test" in, 78
No Child Left Behind, 48. *See also* High-stakes testing
  Adequate Yearly Performance (AYP) requirement of, 3
  composite scores as basis for, 142
  definition of, 12
  for economically-disadvantaged students, 12, 77
  for English language learners, 12, 80
  growth model-based assessment of, 133-134
  improvement model-based assessment of, 132-134
  schools' failure to achieve, 12, 18-19, 110-111, 130
  states' additional requirements for, 130

status models of, 131
for students with disabilities,
  12, 89-90
basis for, 11
goals of, 2-3, 11, 22
implementation issues pertaining to,
  88-89
"McDonaldization"-based analysis
  of, 10, 11-19
  calculability, 10, 11-15
  control, 10, 18-19
  efficiency, 10, 15-16
  predictability, 10, 17-18
responses to, 19-23
"safe haven" provision of, 132
sanctions imposed by, 110-111
Title I, 3
  Part A, 19
  Statement of Purpose, 66
Title IX, Section, 9101 (34), 20
No Child Left Behind Act of 2001, 2
  impact on school psychologists, 2
No Child Left Behind website, 41
North Carolina, high-stakes testing in,
  71
  Adequate Yearly Performance
    determinants in, 134
  as basis for teachers' bonuses,
    130-131
  mandated proficiency levels in, 131

Ohio, high-stakes testing in
  effect on school curriculum, 69
  effect on student motivation, 72
Organizational analytic model, of
  leadership, 157
Organizations
  bureaucratic, 9
  "McDonaldized," 10

Paige, Rod, 8
Parents
  collaboration with schools, 118

educational level of, 67
  role in test anxiety management,
    122, 123
Personalized education plans, 118
Physical restraints, 158-159
Poverty. *See also* Economically-
  disadvantaged students
  effect on academic achievement,
    77-78
Power, centralized, 23
Problem solving
  as coping style, 115
  as response to stress, 121-122
  schools' capacity for, 118-119
Problem-solving teams, 119
Program planning and evaluation,
    high-stakes test data use in,
    129-150
  implementation of, 138-146
    decision tree for, 139, 141
    resources for, 140-141
  improvement models of, 132-133
  status models of, 131-132
  status *versus* growth models of,
    134-136
  value of, 136-138
Project ACHIEVE, 158
Public education, negative image of,
  75

Quality circle teams, 119
Queensland Early Intervention and
    Prevention of Anxiety Project
    (QEIPAP), 124

Rationality, formal, 9, 19, 23
Reading First program, 16
Reading performance
  Assessment Pressure Rating (APR)
    of, 56-57
  effect of high-stakes testing on
    trend analysis of, 54-55

effect of high-stakes testing on, 52-53
Iowa Test of Basic Skills scores in, 50
mandated proficiency levels in, 131
No Child Left Behind requirements for, 12
Reasoned action model, of leadership, 157
Referent power, 155,156-157
Relaxation training, 122,124
Reliability, in testing, 27-46
  in classical test theory, 29-30
  definition of, 29
  effect of non-random human errors on, 39-40
  in item response testing (IRT), 34-36
Research, in high-scores testing, 42-43
  scientifically-based, 15-16
Response to Intervention (RtI), 93,100-101
Reward power, 155
Rewards, for high test scores, 72
Rote memorization, 70-71

SAT-9,81
SAT scores, 53
School psychologists, roles in high-stakes testing, 3-4
  as academic support source, 59-60,87-107
  as leaders and change agents, 151-166
  stress management, 117-125
  test preparation, 102,103
Schools
  Average Yearly Performance failures of, 12,130
  effect of high-stakes test-related stress on, 110-111
  enrichment activities offered by, 78
  high-stakes testing-based ratings of, 68-69,75

No Child Left Behind sanctions imposed on, 110-111
  rural, 78
  social power and influence within, 155-157
Science testing, No Child Left Behind requirements for, 12
Scientific management, 9-10,19
Self-efficacy, academic, 115-116,123
Self-esteem, effect of high-stakes testing on, 76-77
"Skunk works," 22
Sleep disturbances, high-stakes testing-related, 73
Social power, 155-157
Social promotion, 52-53
Social support, 115,116
"Soft power," 156-157
Somers, James G., 162-165
Spearman-Brown formula, 35
Special education students. *See also* Learning-disabled students
  effective instructional practices for, 96-103
  exclusion from assessment and accountability systems, 89
Standardized tests
  cost-effectiveness of, 12-13
  as indices of educational quality, 15
Standards for Educational and Psychological Testing, 29
"Stereotype threat," 79-80
Stress, high-stakes testing-related, 59,109-128
  prevention and interventions for, 117-124
    at school level, 117-119
    school psychologists' role in, 117-125
    at student level, 120-124
    at teacher level, 119-120
  protective factors against, 114-115
  at school level, 110-112,117-119
  at student level, 73,113-117, 120-124

at teacher level, 73-74,112-113
Stress Inoculation Training, 123
Structural equation modeling, 36
Students
    with disabilities
        exclusion from assessment testing, 13
        high-scores testing accommodations for, 90
        high-stakes testing-related stress in, 113-117
        anxiety as risk factor for, 116-117
        effect of coping style on, 114-115
        effect of motivation on, 115-116
        effect of social support on, 115,116
        in high-risk students, 121
        positive behavioral support model for, 120-121
        prevention and intervention efforts with, 120-124
    impact of high-stakes testing on, 49
    with learning disabilities
        alternative assessment systems for, 22
    low socioeconomic. *See* Economically-disadvantaged students
Sunshine State Standards in, 66-67
Systems theory, 111

Taylor, Frederick Winslow, 9-10
Teachers
    accountability of, 49,66-67,77-78
    assessment of, 19,69
    autonomy of, 112,119
    burnout in, 119-120
    effects of high-stakes testing on, 2,49
        attrition, 73-74
        job loss, 130-131
        salary raises and bonuses, 28,113,130-131
        sanctions, 130-131
        stress, 73-74,112-113,119-120
    highly qualified status of, 19
    high-stakes testing practices of, 59
    high-stakes testing-related dilemmas of, 59-60
    job enrichment strategies for, 119
    less qualified status of, 78
    role in stress management, 122-123
    support for, 119-120
Teaching
    complexity of, 98-101
    effective, 96-103
    effect of high-stakes testing on, 70-71
    instructional planning pyramid for, 98-101
    as stressful occupation, 112
"Teaching to the test," 18,41,50-51,70,78
Tennessee, Adequate Yearly Performance determinants in, 134
Test performance, norm-referenced, 50
Tests
    length of, 35
    traditional, internal consistency in, 30
Test taking, as percentage of students' time, 13
Test-taking strategies, 102
Test theory, classical, 29
    bias detection methods of, 36
    reliability and validity, 29-31
Texas
    high-stakes testing in, 51-52
        invalid methodology in, 40
    SAT-9 scores in, 81
Texas Association of Academic Skills (TAAS), 51-52
"Texas Miracle," 40
Theory of reasoned action model, of leadership, 157

Thinking skills, 69
Thorndike, Ellwood, 10
"Three-point-five essay," 71
Time-and-motion studies, 9
Transtheoretical model, of leadership, 157

Unintended outcomes, of high-stakes testing, 48,65-86
   effects on at-risk students, 74-82
      on economically-disadvantaged students, 77-79
      on English language learners, 80-81
      on minority group students, 79-80
      on students with behavior problems, 75-77
      on students with learning disabilities, 75-77
   effects on instruction, 69-71
   public awareness of, 38,41-42
   related to accountability, 66-69
United Kingdom, 113,114,123
United States Department of Education, No Child Left Behind website, 41

University of Wisconsin-Milwaukee, Evidence-Based Intervention Work Group, 157

Validity, 27-46,52,58
   in classical test theory, 30-31
   concurrent, 30
   construct, 31,36
   content, 30-31
   criterion-related, 30
   definition of, 30
   in item response testing (IRT), 36
   predictive, 30
Virginia, high-stakes testing passing rates in, 67
Vomiting, high-stakes testing-related, 73

Weber, Max, 9,10
Worry, as test anxiety component, 73, 117
Writing, "three-point-five essay" approach in, 71